'Inspirational.'
Matthew d'Ancona *Sunday Telegraph*

'Eloquent and honest.'
New York Times

'Compelling.'
Time

'A remarkable personal history... unconventional and interesting.'
Washington Post

'McCain's character has withstood tests the average politician can only imagine... He may be the last of his kind.'
Newsweek

'A good read... engaging sometimes funny, and often profoundly moving... The family stories, the naval history, the fighter-jock anecdotes, and the stoic bravery of the POWs make for a large, almost unwieldy, and sublimely American story...'
National Review

'A fascinating history of a remarkable military family... He gets to the core of those ineffable qualities of wartime brotherhood and self-sacrifice that are so far beyond common notions of patriotism. *Faith of My Fathers* does this better than any other book b
Christia

Faith of My Fathers

Faith of My Fathers

A Family Memoir

John McCain

with Mark Salter

GIBSON SQUARE
London

First published in 2008 in Britain by

    Gibson Square
    47 Lonsdale Square
    London N1 1EW
    UK

UK Tel: +44 (0)20 7096 1100
  Fax: +44 (0)20 7993 2214

US Tel: +1 646 216 9813
  Fax: +1 646 216 9488

Eire Tel: +353 (0)1 657 1057

    info@gibsonsquare.com
    www.gibsonsquare.com

    ISBN — 9 7 8-1 9 0 6 1 4 2 2 7 8

Printed by Clays Ltd.

Index

Preface

A survivor of Auschwitz, Viktor Frankl wrote movingly of how man controls his own destiny when captive to a great evil. "Everything can be taken from man but one thing: the last of human freedoms—to choose one's own attitude in any given set of circumstances, to choose one's own way."

I have spent much of my life choosing my own attitude, often carelessly, often for no better reason than to indulge a conceit. In those instances, my acts of self-determination were mistakes, some of which did no lasting harm, and serve now only to embarrass, and occasionally amuse, the old man who recalls them. Others I deeply regret.

At other times, I chose my own way with good cause and to good effect. I did not do so to apologize for my mistakes. My contrition is a separate matter. When I chose well I did so to keep a balance in my life—a balance between pride and regret, between liberty and honor.

My grandfather was a naval aviator, my father a submariner. They were my first heroes, and earning their respect has been the most lasting ambition of my life. They have been dead many years now, yet I still aspire to live my life according to the terms of their approval. They were not men of spotless virtue, but they were honest, brave, and loyal all their lives.

For two centuries, the men of my family were raised to go to war as officers in America's armed services. It is a family history that, as a boy, often intimidated me, and, for a time, I struggled halfheartedly against its expectations. But when my own time at war arrived, I realized how fortunate I was to have been raised in such a family.

From both my parents, I learned to persevere. But my mother's extraordinary resilience made her the stronger of the two. I acquired some of her resilience and her felicity, and that inheritance made an enormous difference in my life. Our family lived on the move, rooted not in a location, but in the culture of the Navy. I learned from my mother not just to take the constant disruptions in stride, but to welcome them as elements of an interesting life.

The United States Naval Academy, an institution I both resented and admired, tried to bend my resilience to a cause greater than self-interest. I resisted its exertions, fearing its effect on my individuality. But as a prisoner of war, I learned that a shared purpose did not claim my identity. On the contrary, it enlarged my sense of myself. I have the example of many brave men to thank for that discovery, all of them proud of their singularity, but faithful to the same cause.

First made a migrant by the demands of my father's career, in time I became self-moving, a rover by choice. In such a life, some fine things are left behind, and missed. But bad times are left behind as well. You move on, remembering the good, while the bad grows obscure in the distance.

I left war behind me, and never let the worst of it encumber my progress.

This book recounts some of my experiences, and commemorates the people who most influenced my choices. What balance I have achieved is a gift from them.

Acknowledgements

I could not have written this book without the encouragement and assistance of many people to whom I am greatly indebted. My mother, a natural storyteller if ever there was one, reminded me of a great many family stories I had either forgotten or had never heard before. She was quite generous with her time despite her initial suspicion that I was "just trying to show off." My brother, Joe McCain, keeper of family papers and legends, was an invaluable help in organizing and fact checking.

My father's dear friend Rear Admiral Joe Vasey (ret.), who time and again interrupted his busy schedule to answer at length my many queries, gave me the best sense of my father as a submarine skipper and a senior commander. Moreover, he directed me to a wonderful website, hometown.aol.com/jmlavelle2, the work of Admiral Vasey and Jim Lavelle, which is a fountain of information about the experiences of the officers and crew of the USS *Gunnel*, one of the submarines my father commanded during World War II. I cannot praise or thank them enough for keeping the memory of their service alive and on-line.

Many thanks are due as well to Admiral Eugene Ferrell, my old skipper, who reminded me of how proud I was, so many years ago, to have learned from a master ship handler how to be a sailor. Veteran war correspondent Dick O'Malley, a friend and keen observer of my grandfather during the war, told me many good tales about the old man in his last days at sea.

My old friend and comrade Orson Swindle reviewed the manuscript and kindly marked for excision anything that smacked of self-aggrandizement. Keeping me honest is a role he has often played in my life and will, I hope, continue to play for a good while longer. My Academy roommate Frank Gamboa resurrected a few stories from our misspent youth that I had managed to bury years ago. Lorne Craner, son of my dear friend Bob Craner, shared many of his father's memories of our time in prison, and was a great help in sorting out times and places that I had gotten thoroughly confused.

Dr. Paul Stillwell, director of the Oral History Project at the Naval Institute, kindly allowed me to read the interviews of my father and many of my father's and grandfather's contemporaries, a wonderful resource for anyone interested in learning about the men who made the modern U.S. Navy. I am grateful for the assistance of Chris Paul, who spent a part of his vacation sorting through volumes of my father's papers. Thanks also to Joe Donoghue for successfully tracking down information and photographs that had eluded me.

Three others deserve special recognition and gratitude. Academy graduate, Vietnam veteran, and gifted reporter Bob Timberg, who often gives me the unsettling feeling that he knows more about me than I do, was a great source of encouragement and guidance. Just as important, Bob suggested that I meet with his agent, and now mine, Philippa (Flip) Brophy, who succeeded where others had failed by convincing me that Mark Salter and I could write a good story. She was a patient, steady influence throughout the drafting of the manuscript, as was my editor, Jonathan Karp. Although Jon is the only editor I have ever worked with, I cannot imagine how anyone could have done a better job. He and Flip kept us on track and calm, a tough assignment when working with a couple of amateur writers.

Finally, both Mark and I would like to thank our wives, Cindy McCain and Diane Salter, and our children for tolerating yet another demand on our time that kept us from our more important, and better loved responsibilities. Any merit in this book is due in large part to the help of the kind souls named above.

John McCain
Phoenix, Arizona

I

Faith of our fathers, living still,
In spite of dungeon, fire and sword;
O how our hearts beat high with joy
Whenever we hear that glorious word!

Faith of our fathers, holy faith!
We will be true to thee till death.

—Frederick William Faber,
"Faith of Our Fathers"

CHAPTER ONE

In War and Victory

I have a picture I prize of my grandfather and father, John Sidney McCain Senior and Junior, taken on the bridge of a submarine tender, the USS *Proteus*, in Tokyo Bay a few hours after the Second World War had ended. They had just finished meeting privately in one of the ship's small staterooms and were about to depart for separate destinations. They would never see each other again.

Despite the weariness that lined their faces, you can see they were relieved to be in each other's company again. My grandfather loved his children. And my father admired my grandfather above all others. My mother, to whom my father was devoted, had once asked him if he loved his father more than he loved her. He replied simply, "Yes, I do."

On the day of their reunion, my father, a thirty-four-year-old submarine commander, and his crew had just brought a surrendered Japanese submarine into Tokyo Bay. My grandfather, whom Admiral Halsey once referred to as "not much more than my right arm," had just relinquished command of Halsey's renowned fast carrier task force, and had attended the signing of the surrender aboard the USS *Missouri* that morning. He can be seen in a famous photograph of the occasion standing with his head bowed in the first rank of officers observing the ceremony.

My grandfather had not wanted to attend, and had requested permission to leave for home immediately upon learning of Japan's intention to capitulate.

"I don't give a damn about seeing the surrender," my grandfather told Halsey. "I want to get the hell out of here." To which Halsey replied, "Maybe you do, but you're not going. You were commanding this task force when the war ended, and I'm making sure that history gets it straight." In his memoir, Halsey described my grandfather "cursing and sputtering" as he returned to his flagship.

To most observers, my grandfather had been as elated to hear of Japan's decision to surrender as had the next man. Upon hearing the announcement, he ordered the doctor on his flagship to break out the medicinal brandy and passed cups around to all takers. He was a jocular man, and his humor could at times be wicked. He told a friend, as they prepared for the surrender ceremony, "If you see MacArthur's hands shaking as he reads the surrender documents it won't be emotion. It will be from too many of those mestiza girls in the Philippines."

In the days immediately following the announcement that Emperor Hirohito had agreed to surrender, a few of the emperor's pilots had either not received or not believed the message. Occasionally, a few Japanese planes would mount attacks on the ships of my grandfather's task force. He directed his fighter pilots to shoot down any approaching enemy planes. "But do it in a friendly sort of way," he added.

Some of his closest aides sensed that there was something wrong with the old man. His operations officer, Commander John Thach, a very talented officer whom my grandfather relied on to an extraordinary extent, was concerned about his health. Thach went to my grandfather's cabin and asked him if he was ill. In an account of the exchange he gave many years later, Thach recalled my grandfather's answer: "Well, this surrender has come as kind of a shock to all of us. I feel lost. I don't know what to do. I know how to fight, but now I don't know whether I know how to relax or not. I'm in an awful letdown."

Once on board the *Missouri*, however, he was entirely at ease. Rushing about the deck of the battleship, hailing his friends and reveling in the moment, he was the most animated figure at the ceremony. He announced to Admiral Nimitz, Commander in Chief, Pacific, that he had invented three new cocktails, the July, the Gill, and the Zeke, each one named for a type of Japanese plane his task force had fought during the war's last hard months. "Each time you drink one you can say 'Splash one July' or 'Splash one Zeke,'" he explained.

After the surrender, Halsey reports, my grandfather was grateful for having been ordered to join the others on the *Missouri.* "Thank God you made me stay, Bill. You had better sense than I did."

Immediately after father and son parted company that day, my grandfather left for his home in Coronado, California. Before he left, he issued his last dispatch to the men under his command.

I am glad and proud to have fought through my last year of active service with the renowned fast carriers. War and victory have forged a lasting bond among us. If you are as fortunate in peace as you have been victorious in war, I am now talking to 110,000 prospective millionaires. Goodbye, good luck, and may God be with you.

McCain

He arrived home four days later. My grandmother, Katherine Vaulx McCain, arranged for a homecoming party the next day attended by neighbors and the families of Navy friends who had yet to return from the war. Standing in his crowded living room, my grandfather was pressed for details of the surrender ceremony, and some of the wives present whose husbands were POWs begged him for information about when they could expect their husbands' return. He responded to their inquiries courteously, seemingly content, as always, to be the center of attention.

Some of the guests remembered having observed that my grandfather seemed something less than his normally ebullient self; a little tired from his journey, they had thought, and worn out from the rigors of the war.

In the middle of the celebration my grandfather turned to my grandmother, announced that he felt ill, and then collapsed. A physician attending the party knelt down to feel for the admiral's pulse. Finding none, he looked up at my grandmother and said, "Kate, he's dead."

He was sixty-one years old. He had fought his war and died. His Navy physician attributed his fatal heart attack to "complete fatigue resulting from the strain of the last months of combat." Halsey's chief of staff, Admiral Robert Carney, believed he had suffered an earlier heart attack at sea and had managed to keep it hidden. According to Carney, the admiral "knew his number was up, but he wouldn't lie down and die until he got home."

My grandfather had made his way to the *Proteus* to join my father immediately after the surrender ceremony. During a luncheon aboard ship hosted by the commander of U.S. submarines in the Pacific, father and son retreated to a small stateroom for a private conversation. In an interview my father gave thirty years later for the Naval Institute's Oral History Project, he briefly described their last moment together. Nothing in my grandfather's manner gave my father reason to worry about the old man's health. "I knew him as well as anybody in the world, with the possible exception of my mother. He looked in fine health to me," my father recalled. "And God knows his conversation was anything but indicative of a man who was sick. And two days later he died of a heart attack."

Little else is known about their last conversation. To the best of my knowledge, my father never talked about it to anyone except the Naval Institute interviewer. And the only detail he offered him, besides the description of my grandfather's apparent well-being, was a remark my grandfather had made about how dying for your principles and country was a privilege.

His obituary ran on the front page of the *New York Times* as it did in many major metropolitan papers. My grandmother received condolences from the nation's most senior military and civilian commanders, including President Truman, General MacArthur, and Admirals Nimitz and Halsey. Navy Secretary *Forrestal* wrote her that "the entire Navy mourned."

In the Naval Academy yearbook for 1906, the year my grandfather graduated, the editors chose quotations from the classics to describe each member of the class. For my grandfather, the choice was prophetic, a line from Milton: "That power which erring men call chance."

He was laid to rest in Arlington National Cemetery following a Washington funeral attended by *Forrestal* and the Chief of Naval Operations, Fleet Admiral Ernie King. Among his pallbearers was General Alexander Vandergrift, who had commanded the Marines on Guadalcanal, and Vice Admiral Aubrey Fitch, the Superintendent of the United States Naval Academy. He was awarded a fourth star posthumously.

My father, who had left for the States immediately upon receiving word of the admiral's death, arrived too late to pay his respects. My mother found him standing on the tarmac at San Diego when she returned from Washington. He was in the throes of deep grief, a grief that took years to subside. He told my mother he was relieved to have missed the funeral. "It would have killed me," he explained.

There was, however, an event near the end of my grandfather's life that no one discussed. In none of the published accounts of my grandfather's death nor in any of the many tributes offered by his contemporaries was mention made of the incident that had cost my grandfather his command just one day before the war's end.

Less than three months earlier, he had been ordered by Nimitz to resume command of Task Force 38, which at that time constituted almost the entire Third Fleet as it provided air support to the American invasion of Okinawa. One week after he resumed command, my grandfather and Halsey received the first reports from search planes of a tropical storm south of Okinawa that was fast becoming a typhoon.

When the first reports of the June typhoon were received, the fleet meteorologists advised Halsey not to move the fleet. But Halsey, fearing that the typhoon would drive him westward and in range of Japanese planes based in China, ordered his task groups to sail southeast in an attempt to get around the storm. My grandfather was aboard his flagship, the *Shangri-La*. Puzzled by his instructions, he turned to his friend, a war correspondent for the Associated Press, Dick O'Malley, and said, "What the hell is Halsey doing, trying to intercept another typhoon?" His observation was a reference to Halsey's actions during a typhoon that had struck the fleet in December 1944, sinking two destroyers. According to John Thach, my grandfather had recommended a heading for the fleet that would have avoided the earlier storm, as had Admiral Nimitz. But Halsey had insisted on another course, a course that tragically failed to take his ships out of harm's way.

A little less than six months later, at one o'clock on the morning of June 5, Halsey received a late report from an amphibious command ship that this latest storm was too far to the south for the fleet to get safely around it. Halsey attempted to get out of its way by reversing course from southeast to northwest, greatly surprising the commanders of his task groups, who were now in imminent peril.

At four o'clock, one of those commanders, Admiral J. J. Clark, signaled my grandfather (to whom Halsey had given tactical command of the fleet's race to safer waters) that their present course would bring his task group directly into the storm. A few minutes later he signaled, "I can get clear of the center of the storm quickly by steering 120. Please advise."

My grandfather consulted Halsey, who advised against a course change. He then signaled Clark for an updated report of the position and bearing of the storm's eye before ordering Clark to use his best judgment. After communicating with Halsey and Clark, my grandfather could have spent only a few minutes considering the matter before deciding to reject Halsey's advice. But it was a few minutes too long. His order came twenty minutes after Clark signaled for advice and too late for his task group to escape the worst of the storm.

Although none of Clark's ships sank, many of them were damaged, including four carriers. One hundred and forty-two aircraft were lost. Six men from Clark's task group and a nearby fueling group were swept overboard by the storm-tossed seas and drowned. Four others were seriously injured.

A few days after Task Force 38 resumed operations off Okinawa, my grandfather and Halsey were ordered to appear before a court of inquiry on June 15. In the court's opinion, the fleet's encounter with the typhoon was directly attributable to Halsey's order to change course and my grandfather's failure to instruct Clark for twenty minutes.

Upon receiving the court's report, Secretary *Forrestal* was prepared to relieve both Halsey and my grandfather. But Admiral King persuaded *Forrestal* that Halsey's relief would be too great a blow to the Navy's and the country's morale.

Two months later, my grandfather was ordered to relinquish his command.

Professional naval officers constitute a small community today. It was a much smaller one in the years when my father and grandfather made their living at sea. Yet I only learned of the episode that closed my grandfather's career when, many years later, I read an account of the typhoon in E. B. Potter's biography of Admiral Halsey.

My father never mentioned it to me.

CHAPTER TWO

Slew

In his memoirs, Admiral Halsey makes brief mention of the typhoon, blaming his task group's encounter with it on late warnings and erroneous predictions of the storm's course, but he offers no description of my grandfather's role in the disaster.

My grandfather's request to return home rather than witness the drama of Japan's surrender was a measure of his despair over losing his command. Halsey did write of his subordinate's outrage at being relieved of his command, describing him as "thoroughly sore."

I once suspected, as my father probably had, that the court's findings had hastened my grandfather's death. But as I grew older, it became easier to dismiss my suspicion as the dramatization of the end of a life that needed no embellishment from a sentimental namesake. My grandfather had not been banished into retirement after losing his command. President Truman had ordered him to Washington to serve under General Omar Bradley as the deputy director of the new Veterans Administration to help integrate back into civilian society the millions of returning American veterans, a prestigious and important appointment.

I doubt any assignment would have eased immediately the indignation he must have felt over losing his last wartime command. But by all accounts, my grandfather was a tough, willful, resilient man who, had he lived, would have resolved to serve with distinction in his new post as the surest way to put a great distance between himself and that fateful storm.

I was a few days shy of my ninth birthday when my grandfather died. I had seen very little of him during the war, and most of those occasions were hurried affairs. I remember being awakened in the dead of night on several occasions when he dropped in unannounced on his way from one assignment to another. My mother would assemble us on the parlor couch and then search the house for her camera, to record another brief reunion between her children and their famous grandfather. Even before the war, my father's career often kept a continent or more between my grandparents and me. And the recollections I have of him have dimmed over the half century that has elapsed since I saw him last.

The image that remains is that of a rail-thin, gaunt, hawk-faced man whose slight build was disguised by a low-timbered voice and a lively, antic presence. It was fun to be in his company, and particularly so if you were the primary object of his attention, as I remember being when we were together.

He rolled his own cigarettes, which he smoked constantly, and his one-handed technique fascinated me. While the skill was anything but neat (Admiral Halsey once ordered a Navy steward to follow him around with a dustpan and broom whenever he was aboard the admiral's flagship), that it could be accomplished at all struck me as praiseworthy. He would give me his empty bags of Bull Durham tobacco, which I valued highly, and which deepened my appreciation of the performance.

In today's slang, he lived large. He was called Sid by his family and Slew by his fellow officers, for reasons I never learned. He liked to take his shoes off when he worked and walk around the office in his stocking feet. He smoked, swore, drank, and gambled at every opportunity he had. His profile in the 1943 Current Biography described him as "one of the Navy's best plain and fancy cussers."

Rear Admiral Howard Kuehl served on my grandfather's staff as a young lieutenant during the campaign for the Solomon Islands, when my grandfather commanded all land-based aircraft in the South Pacific. In an article he wrote about his wartime experiences, he affectionately recounted an example of his boss's colorful idiosyncrasies.

In addition to his other duties, Kuehl served as the wine mess treasurer, an assignment that obliged him to maintain a meager inventory of liquor for the officers' recreational use and to obtain from my grandfather and his staff officers adequate funds for that purpose. When an officer received transfer orders, he was entitled to a refund of his wine mess share. In September 1942, after my grandfather had received orders reassigning him to Washington, Kuehl visited him on the afternoon before his scheduled departure. Dutifully attempting to return my grandfather's share of the kitty, he was momentarily taken aback when my grandfather ordered that it be returned "in kind." Summoning considerable courage, Kuehl informed his boss that because liquid spirits were a precious commodity aboard ship it was an unofficial but scrupulously observed custom that an officer returning to the States would not take any with him. Assuming no further admonishment was necessary, Kuehl then handed over to my disgruntled grandfather the money owed to him.

The next morning, my grandfather's staff lined up at the gangway to shake his hand and bid him an affectionate farewell. When he reached his intrepid wine mess treasurer, he shot him a look of affected displeasure and said, "Kuehl, goddammit, you're a crook."

My mother often recounts the occasions when her father-in-law would order her to accompany him on a long night of carousing in his favorite gambling den of the moment. He seemed to have one in every place he was stationed. He also managed to spend considerable time at horse tracks, where his enthusiasm for the sport was evident in the sums of money he spent to make it interesting. As commanding officer of the aircraft carrier USS *Ranger*, he would order his yeoman into the first boat headed ashore whenever the *Ranger* came into home port, tasking him with the urgent business of placing his bets with the local bookie.

A young ensign, William Smedberg, fresh from the Naval Academy, reported for duty to the USS New Mexico, where my grandfather was serving as executive officer. An hour after he arrived he was summoned to my grandfather's cabin. Apparently, the ship's home port hosted a rowing regatta among the officers and enlisted men of the various ships stationed there, and my grandfather, being a sporting man who enjoyed a good wager, had taken a keen interest in the event. He had examined Ensign Smedberg's record at the Academy and discovered he had been coxswain on an Academy crew. Smedberg recounted their exchange:

"Young man, I understand that you were a coxswain at the Naval Academy?"

"Yes, sir, I was coxswain of the hundred-and-fifty-pound crew."

"Well, that's good, because you're going to be coxswain now of the officers' crew and the enlisted crew. You're to take them both out every morning we're in port at five o'clock. And you're to win both those races."

They won both races, making my grandfather a happy and somewhat more prosperous man. (Ensign Smedberg would eventually reach flag rank, serve as Superintendent of the Naval Academy when I was a midshipman there, and retire a vice admiral.)

My grandmother once informed my grandfather of a new treatment for ulcers she had just read about in a magazine. Pounding his fist on a table, he shouted, "Not one penny of my money for doctors. I'm spending it all on riotous living." My grandmother was reported to have given him an adequate allowance for that purpose while retaining unchallenged control over the rest of the family's finances.

While serving as a pallbearer for one of his Naval Academy classmates on a cold, rainy day at Arlington National Cemetery, my grandfather listened to a young officer suggest that he button up his raincoat to protect himself from the elements. The old man, raincoat flapping in the wind, looked at his solicitous subordinate and said, "You don't think I got where I am by taking care of my health, do you?"

My mother, who was enchanted by him, keeps in her living room a large oil portrait of the admiral, distinguished and starched in his navy whites. In reality he was a disheveled-looking man with a set of false teeth so ill-fitting that they made a constant clicking noise when he moved his jaw and caused him to whistle when he spoke.

Admiral Halsey and he were such good friends that even in the strain of war, when my grandfather was Halsey's subordinate, theirs was a relaxed and open relationship marked by mutual respect and candor. They delighted in ribbing each other mercilessly and playing practical jokes on each other. On the evening before a trip to Guadalcanal together, my grandfather had spent the night in Halsey's quarters. He had absentmindedly left his teeth sitting on a bureau in Halsey's bathroom. Halsey saw the teeth sitting there and, delighted by an opportunity to discomfit his old friend, slipped them into his shirt pocket. One of my grandfather's aides recalled the scene that followed as the party was departing for Guadalcanal, my grandfather frantically searching for his missing teeth while Halsey badgered him to hurry up.

"Can't go, I can't go. I've lost my teeth," he implored. To which the much-amused Halsey responded, "How do you expect to run naval aviation if you can't take care of your own teeth?"

After another fruitless search, and a few more minutes of Halsey poking fun at him, and my grandfather hurling insults right back, my grandfather resigned himself to going to Guadalcanal toothless. At the plane, a grinning Halsey handed the teeth back to him, and caught, I am sure, a torrent of abuse from my grandfather.

When in combat, he dispensed with all Navy regulations governing the attire of a flag officer. Disheveled, stooped, weighing only 140 pounds, and looking many years older than his age, he was, nevertheless, unmistakably Navy. Sailors who served under him called him, behind his back but affectionately, "Popeye the sailor man." He wore a ratty, crushed green cap with its frame removed from the crown and an officer's insignia sewn onto the visor. Halsey once described it as "unique in naval costume." Like most sailors, my grandfather was a superstitious man, and he treasured his "combat cap" as a good luck talisman. So did everyone else on his flagship, fearing that any misfortune that befell the old man's hat was a sign of approaching calamity. Whenever the wind blew the hat from its perch, men would dive to the deck and frantically scramble for it lest it be blown overboard. My grandfather, who was aware of the crew's shared regard for the supernatural powers of his unorthodox headgear, watched in amused silence and grinned broadly when a relieved sailor handed it back to him.

The cap was a gift from the wife of a naval aviator. My grandfather was much admired by the aviators under his command and by their families, who knew how deeply he grieved over the loss of his pilots. I have heard from colleagues of my grandfather that he would cry routinely when he received casualty reports. "Whenever a pilot was lost," John Thach said of him, "it was not just a sad thing, but it seemed like a personal loss to him and it took a lot out of him." He loved life, and lived his as fully as anyone could. It is easy to understand how greatly it must have pained him to see any man, especially someone under his command, lose his life prematurely.

Commander Thach recalled how my grandfather liked to talk to the pilots just after they returned from a strike. Thach would select those pilots whose experiences he knew would most interest the old man and bring them immediately to the admiral's cabin. My grandfather would give them a cup of coffee and listen intently as his young flyers described the details of their mission, always asking them at the end of the interview, "Do you think we're doing the right thing?"

The pilots loved these exchanges, recognizing in my grandfather's genuine interest in their views a regard for them that was not always apparent in the busy, distracted mien of other senior commanders. My grandfather valued the interviews as well. He believed an able commander profited from the insights of the men under his command and should always take care to see that his own decisions were informed by the assessments of those who were charged with executing them. "He never quit learning," Thach observed. "He didn't have complete and abiding faith in his own judgment, and I don't think anyone should."

Cecil King, a retired chief warrant officer, had served under my grandfather's command at the naval air station in Panama in 1936. My grandfather had ferociously chewed him out once for writing false dispatches as a practical joke, one of which reported a Japanese attack on an American embassy. Although he gave the young sailor the tongue-lashing of his life, he didn't have him court-martialed or even seriously discipline him. Eight years later, when my grandfather was commanding the fast carriers in the Pacific in the last year of the war, King happened to be standing in a crowd of sailors in New Guinea when my grandfather and several of his aides walked by. A few paces after he passed King and his buddies, my grandfather stopped and turned around. Pointing his finger at King, he said, "You're the son of a bitch who almost started World War Two by yourself," and laughed.

That he would remember so many years later, with his mind preoccupied with the demands of a wartime command, one of the tens of thousands of sailors he had commanded over his career is a remarkable testament not only to his memory, but to his devotion to his men. Certainly King thought so. "Every skipper's a legend to his people. And he was a legend to us. The fact that he smoked Bull Durham cigarettes, rolled them himself; the fact that he didn't wear shoes; the fact that he was just a giant of a guy. Everything he did was first-class."

An aviator under my grandfather's command was believed to have been drunk when he crashed his airplane and died. According to King, for the benefit of the dead man's family, my grandfather kept the suspected cause of the accident from coming to light in an official inquiry. "I was so struck by his compassion and understanding," King remarked. "The common conception was that he would go the last mile and some more too [for his men]."

James Michener knew my grandfather, and wrote briefly about him in the preface to his famous work Tales of the South

Pacific: "I also knew Admiral McCain in a very minor way. He was an ugly old aviator. One day he flew over Santo and pointed down at the island wilderness and said, 'That's where we'll build our base.' And the base was built there, and millions of dollars were spent there, and everyone agrees that Santo was the best base the Navy ever built in the region. I was always mighty proud of McCain, for he was in aviation, too."

My father believed him to be the most exemplary leader in the United States Navy. "My father," he said, "was a very great leader, and people loved him.... My mother used to say about him that the blood of life flowed through his veins, he was so keenly interested in people.... He was a man of great moral and physical courage."

In pictures of him from the war you sense his irreverent, eccentric individualism. He looked like a cartoonist's rendering of an old salt. As a boy and a young man, I found the attitude his image conveyed irresistible. Perhaps not consciously, I spent much of my youth—and beyond—exaggerating that attitude, too much for my own good, and my family's peace of mind.

Of more lasting duration, and of far greater consequence, was the military tradition he bequeathed to my father and me; the tradition he was born to, the latest in a long line of my ancestors who had worn the country's uniform.

He was the first McCain to choose the Navy. Until he entered the Academy in 1902, the men of his family had served in the Army; his brother, William Alexander, a cavalry officer who was known in the Army as "Wild Bill," was the last. Bill McCain had chased Pancho Villa with Pershing, served as an artillery officer in World War I, and later been a brigadier general in the Quartermaster Corps. He was the last McCain to graduate from West Point.

No one in my family is certain if we are descended from an unbroken line of military officers. But you can trace that heritage through many generations of our family, finding our ancestors in every American war, in the War for Independence, on the side of the Confederacy in the Civil War. One distinguished ancestor served on General Washington's staff. Camp McCain in Grenada, Mississippi, is named for my grandfather's uncle Major General Henry Pinckney McCain, a West Pointer, and reputedly a stern autocrat who was known as the father of the Selective Service for organizing the draft in World War I.

We trace our martial lineage through two families, the McCains and the Youngs. My great-grandfather, yet another John Sidney McCain, married Elizabeth Young in 1877. Both were descendants of Scots Presbyterians who, in the aftermath of Queen Mary's death at the hands of her royal English cousin, suffered the privations that were the fate of those who had remained loyal to the Scottish crown.

The McCains, bred to fight as Highland Scots of the Clan McDonald, arrived in the New World shortly after America gained her independence, when Hugh McCain settled his wife and six children in Caswell County, North Carolina, and built his estate, Lenox Castle.

Hugh's grandson, William Alexander McCain, died while serving in the Mississippi cavalry during the Civil War. William's oldest son, Joseph Watt McCain, also fought for the Confederacy. In his first battle he passed out at the sight of blood and was mistakenly left for dead by his comrades. William's third son, the aforementioned father of the Selective Service, Henry Pinckney McCain, was the first to serve the flag of the restored Union.

William McCain's second son, my great-grandfather, barely fourteen years old at the end of the Civil War, offered to enlist as well, giving his age as eighteen. He was rejected, but later in his life would express his patriotism by serving as sheriff of Carroll County, Mississippi, and inspiring his sons, my grandfather and great uncle, to pursue careers as professional officers. His wife's family, however, claimed a more distinguished and ancient military history.

The Youngs, of the Clan Lamont from the Firth Cumbrae Islands, arrived in America earlier than the McCains, having first fled to Ireland during England's "Great Rebellion." In 1646, Mary Young Lamont and her four sons crossed the Irish Sea in open boats after her husband and chief of the clan, Sir James Lamont, and his clansmen were defeated in battle by the forces of Archibald Campbell, the eighth Duke of Argyle.

The long-feuding clans had fought on different sides in the civil war, the Campbells for Cromwell, and the Lamonts loyal to Charles I. After surrendering to the Campbells, two hundred Lamont men, women, and children had their throats cut by the villainous duke, and Sir James and his brothers spent five years in a dungeon.

Fearing further reprisals, Sir James's wife and sons wisely fled their hostile native land, adopted Mary's maiden name, Young, and settled quietly in County Antrim, Ireland. Two generations later, the family immigrated in the person of Hugh Young to Augusta County, Virginia.

In 1764, Hugh's sons, John, a captain in the Augusta County militia, and Thomas, fought a brief skirmish with Indians in the Battle of Back Creek. Thomas was killed and scalped. Like his descendants, Captain Young was not one to suffer such an insult quietly. He tracked the killers for three days, fought them again, killed a number of them, and recovered his brother's scalp, burying it with Thomas's body.

It was John Young who, as a militia captain during the Revolutionary War, caught the attention of George Washington, joined the infantry, and was welcomed to the general's staff. Valorous and exceedingly diligent about safeguarding his family's honor, John Young set an example emulated by generations of Youngs and McCains who eagerly reinforced the family reputation for quick tempers, adventurous spirits, and love for the country's uniform.

John Young's three elder sons all died in childhood. His fourth son, David Young, held the rank of captain in the United States Army and fought in the War of 1812. David's son, Samuel Hart Young, moved the family to Mississippi, where Samuel's eldest son, Dr. John William Young, fought for the Confederacy.

The fifth of Samuel Young's eight children, Elizabeth Ann, united the McCain and Young families by her marriage to my great-grandfather, and their union gave life to two renowned fighters, my great-uncle Wild Bill and my grandfather Sid McCain.

Wild Bill joined the McCain name to an even more distinguished warrior family. His wife, Mary Louise Earle, was descended from royalty. She claimed as ancestors Scottish kings back to Robert the Bruce. But her family took their greatest pride in their direct descent from Emperor Charlemagne.

Although it was his brother's children who extended the Charlemagne line, I suspect my grandfather felt justified in borrowing the distinction for the rest of the family. He took considerable pride in the McCains' association with the distinguished conqueror, thinking it only fitting that his descendants share in the reflected glory.

As a boy and young man, I may have pretended not to be affected by the family history, but my studied indifference was a transparent mask to those who knew me well. As it was for my forebears, my family's history was my pride. When I heard my father or one of my uncles refer to an honored ancestor or a notable event from our family's past, my boy's imagination would conjure up some future day of glory when I would add my own paragraph to the family's legend. My father was a member of the Society of the Cincinnati, an association of direct descendants of General Washington's officers. His evident pride in claiming such distinguished ancestry gave me the sense not only that I had a claim on my country's history, but that it would fall to me to represent the family when the history of my generation was recorded. As a teenager, I would occasionally show my closest friends the picture of the surrender ceremony aboard the USS *Missouri* and point with pride to the McCain who stood among the conquerors.

At a point early in my own naval career, I was stationed as a flight instructor at McCain Field, an air station in Meridian, Mississippi, named for my grandfather. One day, as I made my approach to land, I was waved off. Radioing the tower, I demanded, "Let me land, or I'll take my field and go home," earning a rebuke from the commanding officer for disrespectfully invoking the family history.

It is a formidable history, not easily escaped even today by descendants who might wish to pursue some interest outside the family business.

My grandfather was born and raised on his father's plantation in Carroll County, Mississippi. The property had been in our family since 1848, when William Alexander McCain moved there from the family estate in North Carolina. My great-grandmother had named the place Waverly, after Walter Scott's Waverly novels, but it was always called Teoc, after a Choctaw Indian name for the surrounding area that meant "Tall Pines."

I spent some time there as a boy and loved the place. The house, which had once belonged to a former slave, became the family's home after their first manor burned down, and was a more modest structure than the white-columned antebellum mansions of popular imagination. But I spent many happy summer days in outdoor recreation on the property in the congenial company of my grandfather's younger brother, Joe, who ran the plantation. The house still stands, I have been told, uninhabited and dilapidated, with no McCain in residence since my Uncle Joe died in 1952.

I have been told that the McCains of Teoc were clannish, devoted to one another and to their traditions. They never lamented the South's fall, although they had been loyal to its flag, nor did they discuss the war much, even among themselves. Neither did they curse the decline in the family's fortunes, the lot they shared with many plantation families in the defeated South. By all accounts, they were lively, proud, and happy in their world on the Mississippi Delta. Yet my uncle and grandfather left the comfort of the only world they knew, never to be rooted to one location again.

I am second cousin to the gifted writer Elizabeth Spencer. She is the daughter of my grandfather's sister and was raised in Carrollton, Mississippi, near the family estate. In her graceful memoir, Landscapes of the Heart, she wrote affectionately of her two uncles and the first stirring of their lifelong romance with military adventures.

What could they do around farms and small towns in an impoverished area, not yet healed from a civil war? The law? The church? Nothing there seemed to challenge them.

I wonder if their dreams were fed by their reading. They favored bold adventure stories and poems—Kipling, Scott, Stevenson, Henty, Macaulay, Browning. Stuck away in trunks in the attic in Carrollton, school notebooks I came across when exploring were full not only of class notes but also of original verses that spoke of heroism and daring deeds. Their Latin texts with Caesar's Gallic Wars were in our bookshelves. They were cavalier....

I thought of my uncles years later, when I read in Henry James' The Bostonians how Basil Ransom of Mississippi had gone to Boston in the post–Civil War years because he was bored sitting around a plantation.

After two years at "Ole Miss," my grandfather decided to follow his older brother to West Point. At his brother's urging, my grandfather prepared for the exacting entrance exams by taking for practice the Naval Academy exams that were given some weeks earlier at the post office in the state capital. His scores were high enough to earn him an appointment to Annapolis, which, with little reflection, he accepted.

He was a popular midshipman but a less than serious student, graduating in the bottom quarter of his class. That rank, however, exceeded the grasp of his son and grandson, who graduated well beneath it and were lucky to receive their commissions at all.

In his third year at Annapolis, he failed his annual physical. In a report to the Academy Superintendent, the examining medical officer rejected him for further service "on account of defective hearing." The superintendent responded by noting the "great need of officers at the present time, and the fact that this Midshipman has nearly completed his course at the Naval Academy at great expense to the Government," and recommended to the Surgeon General that "this physical disability be waived until the physical examination, prior to graduation, next year." The Surgeon General approved the waiver.

Whether or not his hearing recovered by the time he graduated is unknown. I can find no record of his last physical examination at the Academy. I can only assume that if the hearing defect persisted the following year, the examining physician overlooked it. In his quarterly fitness report of June 30, 1906, all that is noted on the single line describing the midshipman's health is "very good."

My grandfather's undistinguished record at the Academy did not affect his subsequent career in the Navy. In those days, an Academy graduate was not immediately commissioned an ensign, but was required to serve for two years as a "passed midshipman." Following graduation, he saw action on the Asiatic Station in the Philippines, serving first on the battleship *Ohio* and then on the cruiser *Baltimore*.

He caught the approving eye of his first commanding officer, Captain L. G. Logan, skipper of the *Ohio*, who filed laudatory quarterly fitness reports, remarking that "Midshipman McCain is a promising officer, and I commend him for favorable consideration of the Academic Board." Six months later, a more skeptical CO, Commander J. M. Helms, skipper of the *Baltimore*, reserved judgment about the young officer, noting, "I have not been acquainted with this officer long enough to know much about him."

By his next fitness report, my grandfather had apparently run afoul of his new skipper, who had by that time become acquainted enough with him to fault him as "not up to the average standard of midshipmen" and to advise that he "not be ordered to any ship as a regular watch officer until qualified."

While giving him mostly good marks for handling the various duties of a junior officer, Commander Helms apparently found my grandfather's discipline wanting. He noted that he had suspended him "from duty for three days for neglect of duty." While standing as the officer of the watch, he had allowed officers who had attended a party in the navy yard to return to ship and continue to "get drunk." The next quarter, Commander Helms again reported that my grandfather was "not up to the average standard of midshipmen."

Shortly thereafter, my grandfather was spared further reproaches from the disapproving Commander Helms. He was ordered to serve on the destroyer *Chauncey*, where he was highly regarded by his new commanding officer. Six months later, he reported for duty as executive officer to the great Chester Nimitz, then a young ensign, on a gunboat captured from the Spanish, the USS Panay, and had, by all accounts, the time of his life sailing around the southern islands of the Philippine archipelago.

Their mission allowed them to sail virtually wherever they pleased, call on whatever ports they chose, showing the flag, in essence, to the Filipinos at a time when the United States feared a Japanese challenge for control of the Philippines. The Panay was less than a hundred feet long and had a crew of thirty, handpicked by Nimitz. They cruised an immense expanse of the archipelago, putting in for fresh water and supplies at various ports, arbitrating minor disputes among the locals, and generally enjoying the exotic adventure that had come their way so early in life. Both Nimitz and my grandfather remembered the experience fondly for the rest of their lives. Nimitz once said of it, "Those were great days. We had no radio, no mail, no fresh food. We did a lot of hunting. One of the seamen said one day he 'couldn't look a duck in the beak again.'"

His tour in Asia ended in late 1908, when, after being commissioned an ensign, he sailed for home on the battleship USS Connecticut, the flagship of Teddy Roosevelt's Great White Fleet, then en route home from its famous world cruise.

In the First World War my grandfather served as an engineering officer on the armored cruiser *San Diego*, escorting wartime convoys across the Atlantic through schools of German U-boats and learning how to keep his composure in moments of great peril and stress.

In 1935, Captain McCain enrolled in flight training, complying with a new Navy regulation that required carrier skippers to learn to fly. Unlike many of his contemporaries, whose flight training was more verbal than practical, my grandfather genuinely believed that flight instruction would be indispensable to him if he was to command a carrier competently. Recognizing its potential importance, he had begun to study naval aviation as early as 1926. "I was stubborn about it," he said. But that did not mean he felt it necessary to become a skilled pilot. Cecil King remarked that in Panama, "the base prayed for his safe return each time he flew."

He would never enjoy the reputation of an accomplished pilot. According to the superintendent of training at the naval flight school in Pensacola, Florida (where I would learn to fly twenty-three years later), in the last two weeks of his training, my grandfather "cracked up five airplanes." Reportedly, before he soloed for the first time, he told his instructor, "Son, the Bureau of Navigation sent me down here to learn to fly. Now, you do it." Nevertheless, he did solo, and he completed a full course at the naval flight school. He was fifty-two years old when he earned his wings, among the oldest men ever to become Navy pilots.

If he never felt obliged to learn how to fly well, he did love the sensation of flying. He had interrupted his training to spend time on the carrier *Ranger*, to observe how the ships he longed to command worked. He told the skipper that he wanted to spend all his time flying in the backseat of the carrier's planes. The pilot designated to fly him on these excursions recounted the experience many years later, admitting the *Ranger*'s skipper had mischievously told him to give the old man "the works."

At fifteen thousand feet, the pilot began a simulated dive-bombing run on the *Ranger*. He threw the plane into a vertical dive, straight down and at full throttle, toward the pitching carrier. By the time the pilot pulled out of the dive they had approached the carrier so closely and at such a high speed that they "blew the hats off the people on the *Ranger* bridge."

As they began their ascent, the pilot turned around to see how his passenger was doing. Instead of finding a frightened old man in his backseat, the pilot was pleased to see my grandfather with

"a grin up around both ears and shaking his hands like a boxer."
Taking this as an indication that my grandfather wouldn't object
to a repeat performance, the pilot dove on the carrier again. This
time, however, my grandfather's ears failed to pop during their
steep descent, and when the pilot turned to check on him after
pulling out of the second dive he saw that my grandfather was suffering considerable pain from the pressure in his head. The pilot
signaled that he wanted to come in, and landed the plane safely on
the carrier deck. The ship's doctor rushed to attend my grandfather and in short order managed to equalize the pressure in my
grandfather's ears.

The pilot didn't know what kind of reception he would get
from my grandfather after the doctor had finished treating him.
He worried that the pleasure my grandfather had expressed in the
thrill of their first dive might have been replaced by annoyance at
having been put through the rigors of a second dive without giving his express consent. The concern was unnecessary. My grandfather simply thanked him "for a very swell ride."

"I liked the old boy from then on. So did most of the rest of
the gang. They weren't worried about him. He could take it."

CHAPTER THREE

Gallant Command

For five months, early in the Second World War, my grandfather commanded all land-based aircraft operations in the South Pacific, and he was serving in that capacity during the first two months, August through September 1942, of the battle for Guadalcanal in the Solomon Islands.

Lasting from August 1942 to February 1943, the Guadalcanal campaign, in the words of historian Samuel Eliot Morison, was "the most bitterly contested in American history since the Campaign for Northern Virginia in the Civil War," comprising "seven major naval engagements, at least ten pitched battles, and innumerable forays, bombardments and skirmishes."

On August 7, in the first amphibious operation conducted by American forces since the Spanish-American War, the 1st Marine Division landed on Guadalcanal to prevent the Japanese from using a nearly completed airfield for their land-based bombers. Simultaneously, three thousand Marines landed on nearby Tulagi Island to seize its harbor and the Japanese seaplane base there. Despite being harried by Japanese bombers, the landings were astonishingly successful. The Marines, encountering ineffective opposition on the ground, had secured all beachheads on the two islands as well as the air base on Guadalcanal by the evening of August 8. They renamed the captured base Henderson Field.

Whatever relief American commanders may have felt over the initial success of the operation was soon forgotten in the disaster that occurred forty hours after the first Marines had waded

ashore. Shortly after midnight on August 9, a task group from the
Japanese Eighth Fleet surprised the divided Allied naval force pro-
tecting the landings. The ensuing Battle of Savo Island, named for
a small volcanic island several miles off Guadalcanal, ended in
what Morison accurately termed "the worst defeat ever inflicted
on the United States Navy in a fair fight." By the time the
Japanese admiral in command of the enemy force called off the
attack for fear of being counterattacked by American carrier
planes, his ships had sunk four heavy cruisers and one destroyer,
killing 1,270 men.

Fortunately, the Japanese, having gained by their victory command of the sea, failed to land adequate reinforcements on the
islands. Thus the Allied defeat was not a decisive event in the battle for the Solomon Islands. It was, however, a bloody defeat, giving a name to the water between Savo and Guadalcanal islands—
Ironbottom Sound. Worse, the surviving Allied ships that had
been forced from the area had not completed off-loading the landing force's food and arms. Sixteen thousand Marines were left
stranded with only half their weapons and supplies on the densely forested, mountainous island. They were forced to live on
reduced rations and whatever rice they could scrounge.
Consideration was given to withdrawing them, but the value of
the easily taken Henderson Field, with sufficient space and level
ground for large bombers and poorly defended by a small
Japanese garrison, motivated Allied commanders to continue the
campaign.

On August 15, my grandfather ordered the first Marine Corps
planes to land at Henderson. Supplies and reinforcements arrived
the same day by sea. On August 18, the Japanese landed a small,
inadequate force of a thousand men. The Marines destroyed them
two days later. More Japanese reinforcements were under way,
arriving almost nightly. By mid-September, six thousand Japanese
were ashore, still not a sufficient number to dislodge the Marines,
but battles raged daily throughout most of the month. In the
Battle of Bloody Ridge a thousand Japanese were killed at a cost
of forty Marines. Nevertheless, the Japanese managed to continue

reinforcing their garrison, and the most serious land battles for Guadalcanal would not begin until October, after my grandfather had been ordered to Washington by President Roosevelt to serve as Chief of the Bureau of Naval Aeronautics and Deputy Chief of Naval Operations.

In the early weeks of the campaign, Japanese planes and ships made up for lack of progress on the ground by pounding Guadalcanal daily with shells and bombs. My grandfather rushed planes, fuel, and ammunition to the island and organized air strikes against the enemy. Gasoline was in terribly short supply on the island, and extraordinary heroics were performed by the skippers and crews of seaplane tenders, their ships overloaded with drums of fuel, who sailed through exceedingly dangerous waters and under skies thick with enemy planes to carry gasoline to Guadalcanal. He spoke often and gratefully of the courage of the crews that brought gasoline to his dry planes at Henderson.

He also became emotional, often crying, when he recalled the faces and spirit of the Marines and pilots defending the airfield in those exhausting, dangerous early weeks of the campaign. He spoke of his young pilots who "took a beating unequaled in the annals of war. Without relief, they fought day after day, night after night, for weeks."

In September he twice flew to Guadalcanal in a B-17, leading large contingents of fighter planes to Henderson, "slipping them in at dusk when the Japs couldn't see us." He stayed ashore, under fierce bombing from Japanese aircraft.

He later told one of his air commanders that the pilots he met there had resigned themselves to die for their country and had shaken his hand with the attitude of men "taking a last farewell." For the rest of the war, the loss of a single pilot would distress him terribly. I suspect every casualty report he read must have summoned up the faces of those fatalistic pilots on Guadalcanal who were ready to die at his command.

There was one story from his experiences on Guadalcanal that he always delighted to tell. One night after he had gone to sleep, a wave of Zeros attacked, and a Marine lieutenant escorted him to a trench, where he took cover with a crowd of tired Marines. One sergeant, particularly weary of this nightly ritual, expressed his displeasure by shouting a string of profanities over the noise of the attacking planes. The lieutenant yelled at him, "Pipe down! We've got an admiral in here." The offending Marine paused for a moment and then loudly sighed, "I'll be good and almighty damned," causing the admiral in question to laugh heartily, grateful to be so amused at a moment of peril.

My grandfather was awarded the Distinguished Service Medal for his leadership during the early days of the Solomon Islands campaign. The citation commended his "courageous initiative," "judicious foresight," and "inspiring devotion to duty."

As Chief of the Bureau of Naval Aeronautics, he made one last visit to Guadalcanal in January 1943. Halsey, Nimitz, and my grandfather flew to Guadalcanal together to inspect the airfield and the condition of the men still fighting what remained of the enemy garrison.

Bull Halsey had assumed command of the South Pacific fleet in October. After a series of legendary sea battles during which Halsey had secured his reputation as a daring and determined commander, culminating in the Battle of Guadalcanal from November 12 to the 15th, Japanese hopes of retaking the island became futile. Over a period of six days beginning on October 20, significantly reinforced Japanese troops were defeated in fierce jungle fighting by the now battle-hardened Marine defenders. Their grim, bloody battles ensured Guadalcanal's vaunted place in American military lore. By the middle of November, Japan's defeats on land and sea had guaranteed that the island would remain in American hands. Yet they fought on for nearly three more months.

My grandfather, returning to the island in the last days of the campaign, was impressed by what he found, relieved to see fit, vigorous, well-supplied, and confident Marines mopping up the last of the enemy. The valiant 1st Marine Division had by this time been relieved by fresh reinforcements. And he went to sleep that night in a small hut near the airfield, happy and confident that the long, difficult struggle was nearly won.

Halsey's biographer, E. B. Potter, wrote: "There were few wiser or more competent officers in the navy than Slew McCain, but whenever his name came up, somebody had a ridiculous story to tell about him—and many of the stories were true." Potter was right. Even today, I receive letters from men who served with my grandfather and want to share an anecdote about him. Among my favorites is the story of his last night on Guadalcanal.

After he, Halsey, and Nimitz had retired for the night, at about ten-thirty, Japanese bombers attacked. The admirals had just survived an attack the day before, while they were conferring at the naval base on Espíritu Santo. With the evening attack at Henderson, it was clear that Japanese intelligence had learned of the presence of three admirals in the field, and that they were the target of the attack. Halsey and my grandfather left their huts as the first bombs struck, each diving for cover into a different trench. As legend has it, my grandfather's trench was a latrine ditch—the latrine had been moved that morning, but the trench had not yet been filled in with dirt. My grandfather is said to have spent the rest of the raid there shivering in foul conditions and the mosquito-infested night air.

As the Chief of the Bureau of Naval Aeronautics, he coordinated the design, procurement, and maintenance of naval aircraft. Coming late to naval aviation made him suspect in the eyes of career aviators, who would have preferred one of their own in command. But his success at Guadalcanal convinced Roosevelt and *Forrestal* that he was the right man for the job. He would rather have stayed in the Pacific. Administrative work did not suit his restless nature. A subordinate remarked that he was "an excellent fighter, but a poor planner and administrator." Whenever he could, he avoided the interminable meetings of the various production boards he served on, Allied conferences, and other planning discussions, designating a subordinate to attend in his place. He was, it was said, a frequent figure at the Army-Navy Club, where he indulged his love of pinochle. But if deskwork and its attendant bureaucracies bored him, he was, nevertheless, a man who took pride in accomplishing the objective of his mission. He showed, if not great attention to detail, his usual abundant energy in pursuit of his chief objective, to procure the world's greatest naval air force.

His experiences at Guadalcanal had taught him what the Navy needed in the Pacific. Too few planes and too few men to fly them had forced the pilots under his command to fly constantly, and they had been reduced to a state of near lifelessness by the strain. When he arrived in Washington, he declared, "I want enough planes for the United States Navy and enough pilots to fly them." He wanted two crews for every plane in the Navy. And he charged ahead procuring aircraft and personnel at a lightning pace. One observer likened him to a "little fighter plane trying to get at the enemy, darting and sweeping through the rambling Navy building."

He ordered the production of Wildcats and Avengers accelerated, confident of the planes' value as indispensable new instruments of war. "[They] prevented the invasion of Australia. They stopped the enemy at Guadalcanal and destroyed his airplanes at a ratio of several to one. They helped to drive him off at Midway and thus prevented the invasion of the Hawaiian Islands." My grandfather knew how to fight the Japanese, and he outfitted the Navy for the task.

An approving Roosevelt appointed him to a newly created post, Deputy Chief of Naval Operations for Air. He was the Navy's air boss, responsible for every aspect, human and material, of naval aviation (often catching hell from a quarrelsome Halsey for his personnel decisions). He served in that command until the pace of war in the Pacific accelerated as the war in Europe approached its end.

In August 1944, he returned to the Pacific to temporarily command Task Group 38.1, one of the fast carrier groups in the Third Fleet's powerful Task Force 38, in preparation for assuming command of the entire task force a few months later. This was the command my grandfather had aspired to above all others; the moment, I suspect, he had waited for all his life. An obituary writer for the *New York Herald Tribune* wrote of my grandfather's return to the Pacific, "In September, 1944, a minor newspaper item revealed that Admiral McCain was off to sea again. The assignment was undisclosed, but the Japanese, and then America, had not long to wait before they knew."

He was a born leader, fit for command not because of an imposing physical presence, but because he possessed an easy, natural authority with his men, whom he seemed to understand as if he had known them all their lives. Dick O'Malley, a veteran war correspondent, considered him one of the finest, most effective leaders in the Pacific Theater. With his reporter's practiced eye for character details, Dick was struck by the unaffected qualities that made my grandfather such a gifted commander. "Admiral John S. McCain was a very quiet-spoken man but when he gave an order in his soft, clear voice, there was never any doubt there was command in it. I always remember that Admiral McCain seemed to get his orders carried out more promptly than others and there was a puzzling feeling that those doing his bidding didn't feel pushed by authority so much as persuaded by reason.... I remember a day when we had a hell of a time with both kamikazes and land-based fighter planes. We were on the bridge after it was over and he smiled at a young lieutenant. 'Well done,' he said. 'I'm putting you in for a citation. It was a very busy day.' That was his style: relaxed, muted and soft-voiced, but when you heard it, it made your heart beat a little faster."

He had been in command of the task group for barely two months when the long-awaited campaign to liberate the Philippine Islands began, leading to the largest naval battle of World War II, the Battle of Leyte Gulf. A week before the campaign began, my grandfather would prove himself as brave and resolute a fighter as any of his illustrious forebears had been. And although circumstances kept him away from most of the action during the Battle of Leyte Gulf, before the guns were silent he would demonstrate again that like his old friend Halsey, he was a daring and resourceful commander, and perhaps the better tactician of the two.

In preparation for the assault, my grandfather's fast carriers launched strikes against Japanese airfields on Formosa on October 12. Their mission was to destroy the enemy's airpower available to defend against an attack on the Philippines. This they accomplished quite successfully, although they met with stiff resistance. Over the next two days, 520 Japanese planes were destroyed and considerable damage was inflicted on Japanese installations ashore.

The Japanese did manage a counterstrike, fiercely attacking the ships of Task Group 38.1. On October 13, an enemy torpedo plane penetrated the task group's defense screen of fighter planes and hit the cruiser *Canberra*. The torpedo hit flooded the *Canberra*'s engine rooms, rendering her dead in the water. Rather than sink the wounded cruiser, my grandfather ordered another cruiser, the *Wichita*, to take her in tow while two destroyers circled them. He then assembled a covering force composed of destroyers and cruisers from three task groups to protect the *Canberra* as she was towed to port.

The next day and night, Japanese planes attacked in large numbers. The cruiser *Houston* was torpedoed. Badly damaged, without power, and listing seven degrees to starboard, the cruiser was in dire straits. The *Houston*'s skipper believed she was breaking up, and many of her crew jumped overboard. My grandfather told him to abandon ship, and ordered several destroyers to help rescue her crew. He gave orders to sink the cruiser once her crew was safe, but when he received word that her skipper thought she could be salvaged he ordered the cruiser Boston to tow the crippled *Houston* to safety.

Admiral Mitscher commanded the task force at the time. He had ordered my grandfather to save the cruisers if he could. In Commander Thach's words, "Mitscher took the other task groups and got the hell out of there, leaving McCain with Task Group 38.1 alone to do the job."

Using most of the entire task group as a protective screen, my grandfather had his ships steam ahead of the "crippled division," which included the two damaged cruisers and their cruiser and destroyer escorts. They endured repeated fierce attack from enemy sorties, but ships' guns and fighters from two of the task group's light carriers managed to destroy most of the attackers. My grandfather wrote in his battle action report that until seven o'clock that evening "there were almost always bandits overhead." All the while, planes from his heavy carriers continued to strike their targets on Formosa.

On the 15th, enemy planes again attacked, and one managed to hit the *Houston* with another torpedo. My grandfather had risked much to salvage the cruisers. It had taken almost eight hours to get the two ships under tow, and once that was accomplished the task group had been able to make a top speed of only two or three knots as it ran a gauntlet of Japanese air attacks. Wave after wave of Japanese planes were determined to make my grandfather's decision to save the ships cost him dearly. Had they succeeded in finishing off either of the two cruisers, or worse, had they sunk any of his other ships, the decision to save the ships would have been regarded as a terribly costly mistake.

Battle action reports, with their dry, matter-of-fact recitation of successive events, portray little of the intense anxiety my grandfather must have felt during those five October days. An action of this complexity requires the commander to make hundreds of instant decisions, anticipating the extent and location of enemy assaults, positioning his ships accordingly, evaluating reports from anxious subordinates, and answering their urgent requests for instructions. Whatever strain he felt throughout this arduous battle was not apparent in my grandfather's report.

In one sentence he notes a second hit on the *Houston* and the damage it inflicted. In the sentence below he reports "little activity on 17 October, routine Combat Air and anti-submarine patrols being maintained." In the next sentence he signals the success of his venture and the relief he must have experienced by reporting simply, "At the end of the day, Task Group 38.1 turned to course 250, and headed back toward the Philippines on a high speed run at 25 knots."

The author of a book on the fast carrier battles in the Pacific disparaged my grandfather, dismissing him as nothing more than a deputy to Halsey who was never given tactical command of his task force. Furthermore, the author alleged that my grandfather had relied completely on John Thach for tactical innovations. My grandfather did give enormous responsibilities to his operations officer and had always taken care to credit Thach with many of the task force's innovations. When he hired Thach for the job, having never met him prior to that, Thach had asked him why he had selected him. "I've heard you're not a yes man," my grandfather answered, "and I don't want any yes man on my staff."

Thach, who admired my grandfather greatly, strongly disputed the author's harsh criticism and insisted that "he had command all the time."

He was a brave man, and he commanded with courage. Dick O'Malley, who observed him closely in the last, strenuous days of his command, said, "There wasn't anything that could put the wind up in him." In a letter Dick wrote to me, he recalled my grandfather's courage under fire. "One day a kamikaze came out of the sun heading either for us or the *Essex*, which was close behind. [McCain] just stood leaning on the rail, watching. 'They'll get him with those five-inchers,' he said calmly. They did."

A little over three months after my grandfather brought the crippled cruisers safely to port, Admiral Halsey decorated him with the Navy Cross. Had the enterprise turned out differently, my grandfather might have been relieved of his command.

* * *

The Battle of Leyte Gulf began on October 23, 1944, when two U.S. submarines patrolling waters off Palawan Island in the southeastern tip of the Philippine archipelago encountered elements of an enormous Japanese battleship force under the command of Vice Admiral Takeo Kurita. Over the next three days, four separate battles would be fought pitting a Japanese carrier fleet and two battleship forces against elements of the U.S. Third and

Seventh fleets. When the last battle ended, the Japanese Navy was finished as an effective fighting force for the remainder of the war, but not before the United States Navy had nearly suffered a defeat of catastrophic dimensions.

On October 20, under the overall command of General Douglas MacArthur, the Sixth Army, commanded by Lieutenant General Walter Krueger, had staged amphibious landings on the beaches of Leyte Island in the middle of the archipelago, escorted and protected by the Seventh Fleet, commanded by Vice Admiral Thomas Kinkaid. The operation was hugely successful. By the end of the day, seventy to eighty thousand troops were ashore.

Halsey's Third Fleet, under the overall command of Admiral Nimitz, was ordered to cover and support the Seventh Fleet. Nimitz had added a clause to Halsey's orders instructing his subordinate to seize an opportunity to destroy a major portion of the Japanese fleet if one arose in the course of the battle, giving Halsey, who had dreamed all his life of commanding an epic battle at sea, leave to fulfill his lifelong ambition. Nimitz's failure to place both U.S. fleets under one naval command inevitably led to poor communications between the two fleets. When Halsey perceived an opportunity to take offensive action against the enemy and seized it, the dual command structure nearly resulted in strategic disaster.

On October 22, Halsey ordered my grandfather's task group, the strongest carrier force in his fleet, to detach from the fleet and sail 660 miles to Ulithi Island to refuel. Even after the two American submarines discovered Kurita's force in the Palawan Passage and destroyed three of its heavy cruisers, Halsey still saw no reason to order my grandfather to return. It was a decision that both Halsey and my grandfather would soon regret.

The Japanese knew that the loss of the Philippines would destroy any hope that Japan could yet prevail against its vastly superior enemy. They devised a desperate gamble to destroy the invading American force, risking virtually all that remained of the Japanese Navy in the attempt. A Northern Force with four carriers serving as a decoy was ordered to entice the offensive-minded

Halsey into giving chase, leaving the Seventh Fleet exposed in Leyte Gulf.

Meanwhile, two Japanese battleship forces, Kurita's powerful Center Force and a Southern Force, sailed for the central Philippines. The Southern Force would enter south of Leyte through the Surigao Strait. If Halsey fell for the decoy and left his station off the San Bernardino Strait, Kurita's Center Force would force the unprotected strait from the north, sail down the coast of Samar Island, converge with the Southern Force, and destroy the unsupported American invasion fleet.

On the 23rd, Third Fleet aircraft located the Center Force, and Halsey prepared to do battle. The next day, he recalled my grandfather, but it was too late for him to get within range of the enemy, and Halsey was deprived of 40 percent of his air strength as he fought what is known as the Battle of the Sibuyan Sea.

In Leyte Gulf, Admiral Kinkaid was readying his Seventh Fleet to do battle with the small Japanese Southern Force. Lacking the big carriers of the Third Fleet, the Seventh Fleet had only eighteen small, unarmored escort carriers to provide airpower with lightly armed planes and poorly trained pilots. Nevertheless, Kinkaid knew his fleet, 738 ships in all, was more than a match for the enemy force approaching from the south.

The Japanese Northern Force had gone undetected until seventy-six of its aircraft attacked one of Halsey's carrier groups late in the Battle of the Sibuyan Sea. Now aware that Japanese carriers were in the area, Halsey's blood was up; he believed that "an opportunity to destroy a major portion of the enemy fleet" was at hand. He broke off the attack on Kurita's force and ordered all of his carrier groups north to seek and annihilate Ozawa's carriers. The decoy had succeeded. Halsey left the Seventh Fleet unguarded, vulnerable to and unaware of the threat approaching from the north.

Halsey had not even bothered to inform Kinkaid that he had left the strait. Before he ordered his forces north, he had signaled Nimitz that he intended to form three groups of his fast battleships into a new, powerful surface task force, Task Force 34.

Kinkaid had intercepted the signal and assumed that the "three groups" were carrier groups that would be left behind to guard the strait. In fact, Halsey's decision to attack the decoy force had preempted the formation of Task Force 34, and all the ships that would have constituted it were now steaming away from the strait.

As Kinkaid had expected, the Seventh Fleet's cruisers, destroyers, and battleships quickly and effectively destroyed the Japanese Southern Force. But a few minutes after the last shots were fired, at dawn on October 25, Kurita's ships began shelling one of the Seventh Fleet's three escort carrier groups operating just north of the entrance to Leyte Gulf. This group, known by its radio call sign, "Taffy Three," was seriously overmatched by the powerful enemy force now descending upon it. Nevertheless, the unit fought valiantly, losing one carrier, two destroyers, and one destroyer escort in the ensuing Battle of Samar Island.

As he raced toward the Northern Force, Halsey finally formed Task Force 34, and ordered the battleships to steam ahead of the carriers. Third Fleet aircraft began attacking the Japanese carriers at eight o'clock on the morning of the 25th, and continued until evening.

When the second strike of the day was under way, Halsey received an urgent message from Kinkaid informing him that the Seventh Fleet's small carriers were under attack off Samar Island by a superior enemy force and pleading for assistance from Halsey's carriers. Halsey ignored the message and continued north. He received several successive messages from Kinkaid, the last warning that Kinkaid's battleships were running out of ammunition. At nine-thirty, Halsey signaled back, informing Kinkaid that my grandfather's task group was on the way.

At ten o'clock, Halsey received a message from Admiral Nimitz: where is, repeat, where is task force thirty four? the world wonders. The message infuriated Halsey, who interpreted the sentence "The world wonders" as an insulting rebuke. He threw his cap to the deck after reading it.

Clearly, Nimitz was alarmed about the Seventh Fleet's precar-

ious situation and wanted Halsey's battleships to defend the battered escort carrier units off Samar Island and prevent the enemy
from entering Leyte Gulf. The success of the invasion hung in the
balance. But the message to Halsey had been a mistake. The last
three words had been included as padding to confuse enemy
decoders. The signal clerk who received the message before it was
handed to Halsey should have deleted them. The irate Halsey considered his response for an hour before signaling Nimitz, i have
sent mccain.

My grandfather was already on the way before Halsey recalled
him to the battle. He had intercepted Kinkaid's messages to
Halsey and had made the decision to render whatever assistance
he could to the outgunned escort carriers without waiting for
orders from the fleet commander. He turned his task group
around and raced downwind at a speed of thirty knots toward the
battle.

At the time, he had two squadrons of dive-bombers in the air
that had not returned from scouting patrols. Carriers have to turn
into the wind before aircraft can land on them. In order not to
slow down the entire task group while the returning scouts landed, he ordered his carriers to race ahead of the rest of the task
group at a top speed of thirty-three knots. When six or more of
their planes returned they approached upwind to begin their landing patterns. The carriers whipped around into the wind and took
them aboard. Once the planes landed, the carriers turned sharply
downwind again and resumed their thirty-three knots until the
next planes returned, and the maneuver was repeated. Thus, the
carriers were able to take on their planes without impeding the
forward movement of the entire task group, which maintained an
overall speed of thirty knots. It was a very difficult maneuver that
had never been attempted before, nor since to the best of my
knowledge. It required split-second timing on the part of the carrier skippers and the returning pilots, and steel nerves on the part
of the commander who ordered its execution.

Halsey had also dispatched his battleships and one of his carrier groups to join the fight. But Halsey's response had come too

late to inflict much additional damage on the main Japanese force.

My grandfather was now steaming toward the battle, but he was still nearly 350 miles to the east. He went to his cabin for a few minutes to consider the situation and decide what to do. A short time later, at ten-thirty, he emerged from his cabin, gave the order for his carriers to "turn into the wind," and launched his aircraft. He knew that at such a distance from their targets, they would burn all their fuel reaching the battle and would have to land on other carriers or in the Philippines if they didn't run out of fuel while striking the enemy force. It was a daring move, and one of the longest-range carrier strikes of the Pacific war.

By the time Task Force 34 and the accompanying carriers arrived off Samar Island, Kurita had broken off his attack and turned north, fearing that he faced a much larger fleet than the greatly outnumbered Taffy Three. At the time of his withdrawal, his ships were within forty miles of the invasion force. He initially intended to reassemble his disorganized force and resume the attack on Leyte Gulf. But the Japanese commander suddenly lost his nerve and made for the San Bernardino Strait. The commander of Taffy Three, Vice Admiral Clifton Sprague, who had commanded his ships with courage and resourcefulness during the fierce attack, credited the battle's abrupt end to divine intervention.

John Thach credited Kurita's unexpected retreat to intelligence the Japanese commander had received that warned him of the approaching strike from my grandfather's planes. Thach had read an interview Kurita had given after the war. The old admiral explained his decision to withdraw from the battle by recalling information he had received of a large air strike coming from an unknown location. Kurita's chief of staff gave the same explanation for the force's withdrawal.

According to Thach, until Kurita received the intelligence that precipitated his decision to run, he "thought the whole task force was up there, and he didn't know about McCain. As a matter of fact, neither did Halsey and Mitscher know what McCain was doing at the time."

Kurita's forces escaped through the strait, despite being harried by my grandfather's planes. In several accounts of the Battle of Leyte Gulf, historians praised my grandfather for understanding the predicament confronting Kinkaid's carriers and the stakes at risk in the battle better than had the other commanders of Task Force 38. They also judged him a much better tactician than his old friend and commander, Halsey.

Halsey had glimpsed the prospect of a moment of glory and hurried recklessly toward it. He had not fought at the battles of Midway and the Coral Sea, and he was hell-bent to seize this opportunity to destroy the last of the enemy's once mighty carrier force. In fact, he managed to sink four carriers and one destroyer. But his disregard for the Seventh Fleet's situation had jeopardized the entire invasion and had allowed the main Japanese battleship force to escape.

My grandfather, grasping the size of the threat that Halsey had so badly underestimated, had risked his planes in a desperate attempt to fill the gap left by Halsey's run for glory.

A few days after the Battle of Leyte Gulf, my grandfather relieved Admiral Mitscher and assumed command of the entire Task Force 38. He directed its operations until the Philippine Islands were retaken, and then, after a four-month interval, until the warend. In that command he directed assaults against Japanese strongholds in Indochina, Formosa, China, and the Japanese home islands. By the war's end, his ships were "steaming boldly within sight of the Japanese mainland."

At his death, he was a leading figure in naval aviation, credited with devising some of the most successful innovations in the use of attack carriers. "Give me enough fast carriers," he said, "and let me run them, and you can have your atom bomb."

Near the end of the Battle of Leyte Gulf, the Japanese introduced their last desperate offensive measure to prevent the inexorable Allied advance to the Japanese homeland—the kamikaze attack. Throughout the rest of the Philippines campaign, kamikaze assaults wreaked horrible damage on the Third and Seventh Fleets.

In December, my grandfather and John Thach devised an innovation to keep Japanese planes based on Luzon from attacking the invasion convoy or joining the terrifying suicide missions. He called it the "Big Blue Blanket." He had his planes form an umbrella that flew over Luzon's airfields twenty-four hours a day, destroying over two hundred Japanese planes in a few days. In a series of Japanese raids on ships participating in the invasion of Mindoro, not one plane had flown from Luzon. My grandfather's pilots had kept them all grounded.

He increased the striking power of his carriers by reducing the number of dive-bombers by half and doubling the number of fighters, fitting them with bombs so that they could serve, as circumstances warranted, as both fighter and bomber.

He also concentrated his antiaircraft fire by reducing his four task groups to three. He dispatched "picket" destroyers to patrol waters sixty miles from the flanks of his force to warn him of an approaching strike. He assigned his pickets their own patrol aircraft. When his planes returned from a strike they were ordered to circle designated pickets so that the patrol aircraft could identify them as friendly and pick out any kamikazes that had attempted to slip past the force's defenses in company with the returning planes.

In a strike on Saigon, his pilots attacked four Japanese convoys and destroyed or damaged sixty-nine enemy ships in a single day, a record that endures to this day. During a three-month period, in preparation for the invasion of the Japanese home islands, my grandfather's task force sank or damaged 101 cruisers, destroyers, and destroyer escorts and 298 merchant ships. During that same period they destroyed or damaged 2,962 enemy planes. Japanese ships were no longer safe even in the waters off the Japanese mainland. Throughout this last campaign, which ended when atomic bombs dropped on Hiroshima and Nagasaki, my grandfather lost only one destroyer.

He was awarded his second Distinguished Service Medal for his "gallant command" of fast carriers from October 1944 through January 1945. The citation praised his "indomitable courage" as he "led his units aggressively and with brilliant tactical control in extremely hazardous attacks." He received a third DSM, posthumously, for his service in the last three months of the war, when he "hurled the might of his aircraft against the remnants of the once vaunted Japanese Navy to destroy or cripple every remaining major hostile ship by July 28."

Under my grandfather's command, TF 38 was considered the most powerful naval task force ever assembled for combat. Following his death, Secretary *Forrestal* stated: "His conception of the aggressive use of fast carriers as the principle instrument for bringing about the quick reduction of Japanese defensive capabilities was one of the basic forces in the evolution of naval strategy in the Pacific War."

An officer who served with him said it more succinctly: "When there isn't anything to be done, he's the kind of fellow who does it."

The night after my grandfather died, Paul Shubert, a radio network commentator, talked about the controversial wartime decision allowing men of advanced years like Halsey and my grandfather to hold strenuous combat commands, while younger, fitter officers remained in subordinate roles. Shubert took no side in the dispute, but he spoke of my grandfather, of his age and "frail physique." Despite his condition, my grandfather "had his will," Shubert allowed. Whether younger officers could have accomplished what he had or not, "John Sidney McCain did what his country called on him to do—one of those intrepid seafarers who refused to accept the traditional devotion to the past ... who learned to fly when he was past fifty, and went on to high rank in the Navy skies—one of the world's greatest carrier task force commanders, an outstanding example of American manhood at sea."

Eight years after my grandfather's death, I watched Admiral Halsey deliver the main address at the commissioning of the Navy's newest destroyer, the USS *John S. McCain*, in Bath, Maine. Halsey was an old man then. I remember he wore thick glasses and appeared very frail as he stood to make his remarks. As he began to talk about his friend of so many years, his eyes welled up with tears, and he began to sob. Barely a half minute had passed before he announced he was unable to talk anymore, and sat down.

Plainly, Halsey deeply mourned my grandfather's loss. But the audience sensed that the old admiral was overcome that day by more than sadness at his friend's passing. Many years had passed since my grandfather's death, and surely Halsey had gotten over his grief by then. I suspect that the commissioning had prompted a great tide of memories that overwhelmed the admiral. As old men do, Halsey could not think of a departed friend without evoking the memory of all they had gone through together. For Halsey, the memory of my grandfather's friendship conjured up all the grim trials and awful strain of combat, the losses they had endured, and the triumphs they had celebrated together as leading figures in a great war that had changed the world forever. The recollection had stunned the old man and left him mute.

I met Halsey that evening, at a reception after the ceremony. He asked me, "Do you drink, boy?"

I was seventeen years old, and had certainly experienced my share of teenage drinking by then. But my mother was standing next to me when the admiral made his inquiry, and I could do nothing but nervously stammer, "Well, no, I don't."

Halsey looked at me for a long moment before remarking, "Well, your grandfather drank bourbon and water." Then he told a waiter, "Bring the boy a bourbon and water."

I had a bourbon and water, and with his old commander watching, silently toasted the memory of my grandfather.

CHAPTER FOUR

An Exclusive Tradition

In 1936, while commanding the naval air station in Panama, my grandfather was introduced to me, his first grandson and namesake. My father was stationed in Panama at the same time, serving aboard a submarine as executive officer. He had brought his young, pregnant wife with him. I was born in the Canal Zone at the Coco Solo air base hospital shortly after my grandfather arrived there. My father was transferred to New London, Connecticut, less than three months later, so I have no memory of our time in Panama.

My mother has fond memories of the place despite the rough living conditions that junior officers and their families suffered in prewar Panama. Among those memories is an occasion when my parents left me in my grandfather's care while they attended a dinner party. My mother, mindful of my father's concerns about coddling infants, instructed my grandfather to put me to bed in my crib, and not to mind any protest I might make. When they returned they found me sleeping comfortably with my grandfather in his bed. Admonished by my mother for pampering me, he gamely insisted that the privilege was only fitting. "Dammit, Roberta, that boy has the stamp of nobility on his brow." Had he lived longer, he might have puzzled over my adolescent misbehavior, lamenting the decline of his once noble grandson.

My parents were married in 1933 at Caesar's Bar in Tijuana, Mexico. They had eloped. My mother's parents, Archibald and Myrtle Wright, objected to the match. For months prior to their elopement, my grandmother had forbidden my father to call on my mother, believing him to be associated with a class of men—sailors—whose lifestyles were often an affront to decent people and whose wandering ways denied their wives the comforts of home and family.

My mother, Roberta Wright McCain, and her identical twin, Rowena, were the daughters of a successful oil wildcatter who had moved the family from Oklahoma to Los Angeles. Wealthy and a loving father, Archie Wright retired at the age of forty to devote his life to the raising of his children. The Wrights were very attentive parents. They provided their children a happy and comfortable childhood, but they took care not to spoil them. And in their care, my mother grew to be an extroverted and irrepressible woman.

My parents met when my father, a young ensign, served on the battleship USS *Oklahoma*, which was homeported at the time in Long Beach, California. Ensign Stewart McAvee, the brother of one of my Aunt Rowena's boyfriends and an Academy classmate of my father's, also served on the *Oklahoma*. At his brother's urging, he had called on Rowena, and soon became a frequent visitor at the Wright home.

Eventually, Ensign McAvee developed a crush on my mother. He took her out on several occasions and often invited her to visit the *Oklahoma*. On one of those visits she met my father, who was dressed in his bathrobe when McAvee introduced them. My mother only remembers thinking how young my father looked, and small, with cheeks, she said, like two small apples. My father, however, was infatuated at once.

Until my parents' courtship, my mother had, in her words, "never teamed up with any man." She was, she confesses, immature and unsophisticated, possessing no serious aspirations, but cheerfully open to life's varied experiences. Her mother frequently complained to her, "If a Japanese gardener crossed the street and asked you to go to Chinatown, you would go." To which my mother always responded, "Why, sure I would." When she met my father, she was a beautiful nineteen-year-old student at the

University of Southern California. But unlike her twin sister, she had never fallen in love nor shown more than a casual interest in dating.

As my mother describes it, she would typically go out in large groups where the boys always outnumbered the girls. When a young man asked her for a date, she would reply by inquiring what he had in mind. If he proposed to escort her to the Friday-night dance at the Biltmore Hotel, or the Saturday-afternoon tea dance at the Ambassador Hotel, or the Saturday-evening dance at the Roosevelt Hotel, she consented, believing any other assignation to be a poor use of her time. But even obliging dates were rewarded with nothing more than my mother's charming company and had to content themselves with membership in her wide circle of frustrated suitors.

A short time after being introduced to my mother, my father appeared on her doorstep and asked her to accompany him the following Saturday to the Roosevelt Hotel. She agreed, assuming he was acting on behalf of Ensign McAvee. But McAvee would not be among the young naval officers consorting with my mother's crowd that evening. Instead, my mother found herself having "more fun than I had ever had in my life" with the diminutive, youthful Jack McCain.

Their romance progressed for over a year, despite my grandmother's growing anxiety and the aggrieved McAvee's angry reproaches. When my grandmother finally ordered an end to the relationship and banished my father from the Wright home, my mother prevailed on former suitors to call on her and take her surreptitiously to meet my father.

Until confronted with maternal opposition, my mother "had never planned on marrying anyone." By her own admission, she was a willful, rebellious girl. Her attraction to my father was only strengthened by her mother's disapproval, and when my father proposed marriage she consented. They eloped on a weekend when my grandmother was in San Francisco. Just before they departed for Tijuana, my mother informed her softhearted father of her intention. Despite his misgivings, he did not stand in her way.

My father had asked one of his shipmates to explain to the executive officer on the *Oklahoma* that he had gone off to get married, but the friend had thought my father was joking. That Saturday, during the ship's inspection, the captain asked, "Where's McCain?" My father's friend responded, "He said he was going to get married or something." When my father returned to the *Oklahoma* that Sunday, having dropped his new bride at home, he was confined to the ship for ten days with a stern censure from the captain for failing to ask leave to get married.

The bond between my mother and her parents was a strong one, and my grandparents' alarm at losing their daughter to the itinerant life of a professional sailor was understandable. It took several years for them to grow accustomed to the idea. But, in due course, they accepted the marriage and shared with my father the deep affection that distinguished their family.

Captain John S. McCain, Sr., thought the match to be an excellent one from the start. He was as charmed and amused by his new daughter-in-law as she was by him. Six months after my parents married, my father was suspected by the ship's physician of having contracted tuberculosis, and was admitted to a Navy hospital because he had suddenly lost a great deal of weight. When the doctors there asked if my father could explain his dramatic weight loss, he attributed it to his recent marriage.

Sometime later, my grandfather was in Washington, where he went to Navy Records and asked to see his son's latest fitness report. There he read of my father's condition and his response to the doctor's inquiries: "My wife doesn't know how to cook, and my meals are very irregular." Much amused, my grandfather kept a copy of the report, and delighted in showing his friends how his "son couldn't wait to get married, and within six months the girl had nearly killed him."

Stationed in San Diego at the time of my parents' elopement, my grandfather had traveled to Tijuana with them to attend the ceremony and stand at his son's side. Theirs was also an exceptionally close relationship.

The relationship of a sailor and his children is, in large part, a metaphysical one. We see much less of our fathers than do other children. Our fathers are often at sea, in peace and war. Our mothers run our households, pay the bills, and manage most of our upbringing. For long stretches of time they are required to be both mother and father. They move us from base to base. They see to our religious, educational, and emotional needs. They arbitrate our quarrels, discipline us, and keep us safe. It is no surprise then that the personalities of children who have grown up in the Navy often resemble those of their mothers more than those of their fathers.

But our fathers, perhaps because of and not in spite of their long absences, can be a huge presence in our lives. You are taught to consider their absence not as a deprivation, but as an honor. By your father's calling, you are born into an exclusive, noble tradition. Its standards require your father to dutifully serve a cause greater than his self-interest, and everyone around you, your mother, other relatives, and the whole Navy world, drafts you to the cause as well. Your father's life is marked by brave and uncomplaining sacrifice. You are asked only to bear the inconveniences caused by his absence with a little of the same stoic acceptance. When your father is away, the tradition remains, and embellishes a paternal image that is powerfully attractive to a small boy, even long after the boy becomes a man.

This is the life to which my older sister, Sandy, my younger brother, Joe, and I were born. It was the life my father was born to as well. And it was the life that adopted my mother, substituting its care for that of a loving and protective family.

CHAPTER FIVE

Small Man with the Big Heart

cMy father was born in Council Bluffs, Iowa. In several profiles and obituaries, he is described as a native of that Midwestern town, but he was no more a native of Council Bluffs than I am a native of Panama. My grandmother had gone into labor when visiting family in Council Bluffs while my grandfather was at sea.

His boyhood withstood the strain of the frequent interruptions, upheavals, travel, and separation that the Navy imposed on the lives of its officers' families. He would never know any other life. From early childhood, he understood he would share his father's vocation.

People who grow up without such expectations might think that anticipating so young the general course of your life would make a child self-assured. That may be the case for some. But I think for most of us our strong sense of predestination made us prematurely fatalistic. And while that condition gave us a kind of confidence, it was often a reckless confidence. We started with small rebellions against the conventions of our heritage. And as we grew older and coarser, our transgressions became more serious.

We often exceeded the limits of our parents' patience and earned the displeasure of educators. There were times in my youth when I harbored a secret resentment that my life's course seemed so preordained. I often wondered if my father had ever felt the same way. Neither of us ever misbehaved by design, or purposely threw some insurmountable obstacle in the path of our expected naval careers. Our antics were much more spontaneous than that. But did he, like me, occasionally speculate that his troublemaking might disrupt his family's plans for him, and was he as surprised as I was to discover that the thought did not fill him with dread? I don't know. But I do know that when both of us reached the end of our naval careers, we could not imagine finding a greater measure of satisfaction than we had found in a life at sea in our country's service. Neither of us ever sinned so grievously that we altered our fate. The Navy did not banish us. And years later, we realized we had mistaken our reaction to the Navy's forbearance for disappointment. In memory, it appears as relief.

My father was a slight boy, even smaller than his father. He never grew taller than five feet six, and near the end of his life he weighed no more than when he left the Naval Academy, 133 pounds. His irregular childhood, the constant disruptions occasioned by his father's transfers, were a challenge to him, as, I suspect, was his small stature. It intensified an adolescent compulsion to prove his courage and daring to his peers in whatever new social circumstances he found himself in. The quickest way to do so was to exhibit a studied indifference to the established order, devise imaginative circumventions of the rules, take your punishment, show no remorse, and fight at the drop of a hat.

He was only sixteen years old when his father delivered him to the United States Naval Academy for his plebe summer in June 1927; by his own admission, he was too young for the challenges of such a rigid institution and the highly competitive nature of the place. He had been included on President Coolidge's list of appointees that year, passed his preliminary physical in March, and completed the entrance exams in April.

His nervous father was at sea at the time, serving as executive officer aboard the USS *New Mexico*. When the ship made port in Panama on April 26, a fellow officer on the *New Mexico* sent a letter to a friend who was associated with the Naval Academy in some capacity and asked if he could find out if my father had passed the exams. "Our exec ... is very anxious to know if the boy made it." One month later, my grandfather's helpful friend received a brief telegram from an officer on the Academy Academic Board: john s mccain junior passed april examination standing seventh on presidential list.

Shortly before my father entered the Academy, my grandfather, whose ship was being overhauled in the navy yard in Bremerton, Washington, invited him to spend two weeks aboard ship. They were two weeks my father treasured all his life. He referred to them as a "final and farewell gesture before I went into the Naval Academy" and began his own life at sea.

It is difficult to imagine my grandfather being too concerned with my father's performance at the Academy, considering his own less than commendable record there. He was, however, a watchful father.

In April 1928 he was detailed as an instructor to the Naval War College in Newport, Rhode Island, and upon arrival he cabled a request to the Academy Superintendent that all reports on Midshipman McCain be sent to him there. Those reports, sent at the end of every term, were not encouraging. Had the old man been more of a spit-and-polish type, he might have reconsidered the career choice he had made for his son. As it was, while he might have been uneasy about the difficulty his son had staying out of trouble at the Academy, he would have become really alarmed only if it appeared that my father's shortcomings might result in his dismissal.

My father was constantly in trouble at the Academy. His grades were poor, his discipline worse. By the end of his first term his grades hovered barely above the lowest acceptable marks, where they would remain for four years. His class standing in his first term was 557 out of 601 midshipmen. That was his high-water mark for his first two troubled years at Annapolis. The next term, he stood 537 out of 549. The following year, he had dropped to 498 out of 504.

Unimpressive as they were, his grades seldom slipped below the minimum satisfactory level. The ever shrinking aggregate number of his classmates indicates the number of midshipmen whose performance was considered so deficient that they were expelled.

My father approached catastrophe on three occasions, in his first, third, and fourth years. On all three occasions he was warned that "the Superintendent notes with concern that you are unsatisfactory in your Academic work ... and he wishes to take this opportunity to point out that unless you devote your entire effort to improve your scholastic work you are in grave danger of being found deficient at the end of the year." "Copy to Parent" was written on the bottom left-hand corner of each notice.

The only consistently good marks my father received were for Seamanship and Flight Tactics, and Ordnance and Gunnery. These courses were taught only in the last three terms, and my father earned the equivalent of a B in both courses every term. In the first term of a midshipman's last year, his personal hygiene is graded. Here again my father, whom my mother once called "the cleanest man I've ever known," received an above-average mark. These were the only bright spots in an otherwise dismal academic performance.

My father was an intelligent man, and quite well read as a boy. His low grades as a student cannot be credited to a poor intellect. Rather, I assume they were attributable to his poor discipline, a failing that was almost certainly a result of his immaturity and the insecurity he must have felt as an undersized youth in a rough-and-tumble world that had humbled many older, bigger men.

"I went in there at the age of sixteen," he once told an interviewer, "and I weighed one hundred and five pounds. I could barely carry a Springfield rifle."

Even as an upperclassman, my father struggled to meet the robust physical standards imposed on midshipmen, who were expected to take athletics as seriously as their scholastic endeavors. In my father's third year, the superintendent informed him that he was "deficient in physical training for the term thus far completed." Consequently, my father's Christmas leave was canceled that year, and he was "required to remain at the Naval Academy for extra instruction during that period."

My father's roommates, two of whom were linemen on the varsity football team, treated him like a little brother and went to great lengths to protect him. They helped him through the relentless hazing of his plebe year, took the blame when they could for his infractions of Academy regulations, and made it clear that they would deal with any midshipman who thought to abuse him. However, when they were plebes, despite their formidable size, they could not prevent upperclassmen from physically disciplining my father. My father hated the hazing he was subjected to—some of it quite severe, even by the standards of his day—and forever after questioned the custom's usefulness to the task of making officers.

Even after my father graduated, he inspired almost paternal affection in many of his peers. A shipmate who occupied the bunk below my father on the *Oklahoma*, a huge man who had also played varsity football at Annapolis, would routinely wake up in the middle of the night to replace the blanket my father had kicked off in his sleep.

As hard as they tried, my father's friends could not spare him the consequences of his own natural rebelliousness. His report cards for every term, save one, list a staggering number of demerits for bad conduct—114 in his first term, an astonishing 219 his second. Except for the first term of his last year, my father never accumulated fewer than a hundred demerits a term, and usually he was closer to two hundred.

I, too, was a notoriously undisciplined midshipman, and the demerits I received were almost enough to warrant my expulsion. But I never racked them up as prodigiously as my father had. And when I read the accounts of his "unmilitary conduct" today, and the scores of demerits it earned him, I am little short of astonished by the old man's reckless disregard for rules. His offenses were various: talking in ranks; using obscenity; absent without leave; fighting; disrespect shown to an upperclassman. They ran the entire gamut of what the Academy considered serious offenses, and the punishments he received were onerous.

Typically, he found some value in his troublemaking and in

the punishment he earned for it. "You get to know people that you don't ordinarily know if you're one of the good boys. And sometimes the world's not always made up of all the good boys, either, not by a long shot," he said.

"I was known as a 'ratey' plebe, and that's the plebe who does not conform always to the specific rules and regulations of the upperclassmen," my father explained in his interview for the Naval Institute. "Some of these upperclassmen would come up and make some of these statements to you, and required you to do such things which only incited rebellion and mutiny in me. And although I did them, the attitude was there, and they didn't like that. But it was a fine institution."

In his last year, my father was removed from the watchful care of his concerned roommates. He was expelled from the dormitory, where his rebelliousness might have infected good order and discipline in the ranks, and exiled to quarters and a hammock for a bed aboard the Reina Mercedes, a ship seized from the Spanish during the Spanish-American War and kept moored at the Academy.

First classmen in my father's time were not allowed to exceed 150 demerits. During his final term, my father came perilously close to exceeding the number, and was informed by his battalion commander that his graduation from the Academy was anything but certain. "If we get one more demerit on you, McCain," he warned, "we're either going to turn you back into the next class, or you'll be dropped from the muster roll. I can't tell you which will happen. But you can rest assured one of the two will."

From that moment on, my father remembered, "I shined my shoes and everything else and did everything right. When it came time for me to graduate, I took my diploma, and I went. I think that was the closest call I had."

My father was reported to have suffered his punishments without complaint. He would have disgraced himself had he done otherwise. He was a principled young man. Strict obedience to institutional rules was not among his principles, but manfully accepting the consequences of his actions was.

Neither would my father have considered for a moment committing a violation of the Academy's honor code. Honor codes were something he had been raised from birth to respect, and I truly believe he would have preferred any misfortune to having his honor called into question for an offense he committed. He was a small man with a big heart, and the affection in which he was held by his peers was attributable in part to his unquestioning allegiance to the principles of honorable conduct. His profile in the Class of 1931 yearbook commended his character with the following inscription: "Sooner could Gibraltar be loosed from its base than could Mac be loosed from the principles which he has adopted to govern his actions."

The memory of his frequent clashes with its regulations and authorities never diminished my father's abiding reverence for the Academy's traditions and purpose, although he also never lost his realistic appreciation of a typical midshipman's many shortcomings. He once served for two years as an instructor at the Academy, and he boasted that "the lads learned soon enough never to try to hoodwink an old hoodwinker." And he looked back on his Academy days, as he looked back at most of his life, with a satisfaction that was remarkably free of nostalgia.

He remained until the end of his life one of the Academy's most steadfast defenders. In 1964, when my father had attained the rank of vice admiral, he got in a public dispute with one of the Navy's most prominent leaders, Hyman Rickover, the father of the nuclear submarine. In testimony before Congress reported in the Annapolis newspaper, Rickover had "blasted the Academy for everything from the quality of its teaching to the hazing of plebes and the relative competence of ROTC and Academy officers."

Rickover, an Academy graduate himself, had long complained to the Navy hierarchy that the Naval Academy was not turning out qualified officers for his nuclear submarines. This he attributed to the Academy's antiquated curriculum and traditions, which he derided as nothing more than quaint and anachronistic customs of an institution focused on the past. He believed it neither grasped nor concerned itself with the imperatives of leadership in the modern, nuclear Navy that he had, with peerless tenacity, set about creating.

My father understood that technological advances and the nature of Cold War rivalry necessitated innovations and profound changes in his beloved submarine service. Although he and Rickover were not friends and Rickover's cold, imperious personality made him difficult to like, my father admired Rickover's ability, intelligence, and vision, and he supported Rickover's efforts to revolutionize seapower.

Nevertheless, he strongly objected to Rickover's assault on the Naval Academy and to his call for systemic change in the way the Navy trained its future leaders. He felt that Rickover's remedies abandoned proven leadership principles. The primary mission of the Academy was to strengthen the character of its officers. Without good character, my father believed, all the advanced instruction in the world wouldn't make an officer fit for service.

As long as human nature remained what it was, the Academy's traditions were, by my father's lights, more effective at imparting the cardinal virtues of leaders than the methods devised by any other human institution. Rickover, he argued, was more interested in turning out technicians than officers whose worth would ultimately be measured by how well they inspired their subordinates to risk everything for their country.

My father called a press conference aboard his flagship the day after Rickover's testimony to rebuke his fellow admiral and reject the argument that naval officers were better trained in private institutions. "The Naval Academy is designed to make sure an officer is well founded in the sciences and liberal arts. But there's something else," he said. "In leadership there's no such thing as a master's degree. We've got to develop that type of officer who has the tools to develop his own leadership capabilities. I won't talk about Rickover except to say he may have overlooked this aspect."

This was not my father's first dispute with the irascible and solitary genius. Rickover had made admiral before my father, but not before being passed over for promotion on several occasions.

Rickover was Jewish, and some felt that he was the victim of the anti-Semitism harbored by many among the Navy's leadership. Others believed that Rickover, who professed no concern for the affection of his brother officers, was repaid for his indifference with the active dislike of a good many admirals. Whatever the reason, the Navy Selection Board had for several years unfairly left him off its list of flag rank recommendations to the Secretary of the Navy, which, for all practical purposes, determined who would and would not wear an admiral's star.

Rickover did have a number of supporters in the Navy, my father among them, who may have been as put off by Rickover's personality as was the Selection Board, but who recognized his genius and devotion to the Navy. He also had considerable political support in both the legislative and executive branches of government.

After several flag lists failed to reward Rickover's indisputable accomplishments, the Secretary of the Navy passed word to the Selection Board that he would refuse to accept any flag list that didn't include Rickover's name. Thus admonished, the Selection Board finally recommended that Rickover be made a rear admiral.

Shortly after Rickover's promotion, my father, still a captain, called to congratulate his new superior. An embittered Rickover responded to my father's courtesy by declaring curtly that he had made admiral without "the help of any damn officer in uniform."

"That's a damn lie, Admiral," my offended father replied before hanging up on the surprised Rickover. My father could never tolerate officers whose resentment over personal disappointments made them contemptuous of the service. Rickover, he felt, had earned his promotion, had deserved his stars earlier than he received him. But that didn't mean he had accomplished the feat entirely on his own. My father believed that the Navy, for all its faults, took care of its own, sometimes acting later than it should have, but eventually according all their due.

Their relationship didn't improve much after that angry exchange, and their dispute over the Academy only exacerbated the tension between them. Yet, near the end of their lives, they had a reconciliation of sorts, although neither of them would have characterized it as such because neither was the type who would have accorded incidental professional rancor the status of a personal animosity.

After my father had retired, and very late in Rickover's unusually long career, both men became quite ill and were admitted to the Naval Medical Center in Bethesda, Maryland. They were given rooms on the same floor. Both were expected to remain hospitalized for some time, and as there were no other Navy legends in residence at the time, they began spending a good part of every day together.

Perhaps they saw in each other qualities they had overlooked earlier. Perhaps they talked about the only thing they had in common, the Navy, the only thing either of them ever talked about. They may have simply enjoyed reminiscing, as old sailors are apt to reminisce, about their experiences and the vicissitudes of long Navy careers. Or perhaps, as old men, they recognized that they had each devoted every particle of their being to their shared cause, and were, for their devotion, more alike than not.

They left the hospital as friends, and remained so for the little time that remained to them.

My father suffered a serious disappointment his last year at Annapolis. In the same year that my grandfather was earning his naval aviator wings, my father was judged "not physically qualified" for aviation school. I suspect this was a hard blow to my father. His lifelong ambition was to emulate the man he most admired, and being deprived of this opportunity to follow in the old man's footsteps must have shaken his resolve considerably.

After graduating, barely, standing eighteenth from the bottom, my father was assigned to the *Oklahoma*. Before he left, he requested permission to attend the naval optical school in Washington, D.C. Dejected after being denied pilot training, he temporarily wavered in his desire to immediately commence building a successful naval career, preferring to spend a pleasant year enjoying the attractions of the nation's capital (where he had attended high school).

The request was routed through the Academy Superintendent, who offered his opinion that "young officers just graduated from the Naval Academy should join the ships of the Fleet as soon as possible." Two weeks later my father received his answer from the Bureau of Navigation. He was ordered to consider himself released from his current occupation or any other duty that he may have received earlier orders for and report without further delay to the commanding officer of the USS *Oklahoma*.

As he would throughout his career, he made the most of his opportunity. His father's career guidance to him had been limited to impressing on his son the importance of command. "It doesn't make any difference where you go," his father often said, "you've got to command." With that in mind, my father entered the submarine service after his tour on the *Oklahoma*. His father approved of the decision and told him "to make a good job of it," which my father did in his relentless pursuit of a command.

CHAPTER SIX

Mr Seapower

I hesitate to write that my father was insecure, but he was thrust into difficult circumstances at such a young age that it would have been very hard to resist some self-doubt. He was an aspiring man whose ambition to meet the standard of his famous father might have collided with his appreciation for the implausibility of the accomplishment. Nevertheless, he would succeed, and become the Navy's first son of a four-star admiral to reach the same rank as his father.

The Navy consumed nearly his every thought. He had few aspirations for success outside its narrow confines. Whatever other interests engaged his mind were in some way associated with the Navy, including his preferences in literature, history, philosophy, and the study of military tactics and strategy. He attended every Army-Navy football game he could, not because he loved football, but because it involved the Navy. It could have been the Army-Navy tiddlywinks championship and he still would have wanted to attend it.

He did not fish or hunt or share his father's fondness for gambling or my enthusiasm for sports. He played tennis often, and kept to a daily regimen of rope-jumping and sit-ups, not because he particularly enjoyed exercise, but because he intended to keep himself fit for combat command. During one of his tours in Washington, D.C., a local paper observed that he was "a familiar sight to Washington commuters who frequently see him stride across the 14th Street Bridge, walking the four miles between his

Capitol Hill home and the Pentagon."

He worked ceaselessly. Lacking the gregariousness and easy charm of his father, he was less comfortable in social situations, a failing that can be an obstacle to an officer's advancement. He wasn't withdrawn or unapproachable, and he didn't shrink from social obligations. He just didn't seem entirely at ease when his career required something more than strict, tireless dedication to the task at hand.

My mother was indispensable to my father. She had adapted to Navy life with few regrets, and acquired an abiding affection for the whole of the culture she had entered upon marriage, once remarking that she was "tailor-made" for the Navy. Her vivacious charm, beauty, and refinement assured her success in the social aspect of Navy life and more than compensated for my father's weaker possession of those graces. Her complete devotion to my father and his career contributed more to his success than anything else save his own determination.

The Navy in the years before the Second World War, the Navy my mother married into, was a small, insular world where everyone knew everyone else. "We were all in the same boat," my mother says of those days. "There wasn't any point for anyone to put up a false front." She means, of course, that few Navy families lived beyond their means. But they did live graciously, as graciously as circumstances allowed, assisting each other in a common effort to preserve the exacting social standards that were appropriate for an officer and his family in the small, prewar Navy.

Most families of naval officers lived on modest resources, a condition attributable to the meager salaries paid to officers in those days. Although my mother came from a wealthy family, our family lived, in accordance with my father's wish, on his income alone. Yet we never wanted for anything, and we believed we lived within a privileged society where refined manners made the relative poverty that most families shared inconspicuous.

In 1934, my father, a young ensign, was ordered to Hawaii to serve as a junior officer on a submarine. He brought his new bride with him, to what my mother called "paradise." Home to America's Pacific Fleet, Hawaii in the 1930s was the heart of Navy culture, where singular standards of social etiquette and personal and professional ethics were rarely breached.

Newly arrived officers, dressed in white uniforms, took their wives, who were attired in white gloves and hats, to call on the families of fellow officers every Wednesday and Saturday between four and six o'clock. The husband laid two calling cards on the receiving tray, one for the officer in residence and the other for the lady of the house. His wife offered a single card for her hostess, as it was inappropriate for an officer's wife to call on another officer. The visits never exceeded fifteen minutes. Within ten days, the officer and his wife who had been paid this homage returned the compliment by calling on the newly arrived couple at their home. The commanding officer was always called on first, followed by the executive officer. Their rank excused them from paying a return call.

When an officer had finished his tour he would complete another round of calls to bid good-bye, leaving his card with its upper left-hand corner turned down as a signal of his imminent departure.

Every Saturday night, my father and mother, dressed in formal attire, attended a party at the Pearl Harbor Submarine Club, after spending their afternoon at the Royal Hawaiian Hotel's four o'clock tea dance. The Beach Club at Waikiki, with its five-dollar monthly dues, was another venue for stylish socializing among the officers and their families. Though the exacting formality of this society seems pompous and excessive today, few who lived within its rules then thought it anything other than normal and appropriate. Even when they dined alone at home, my father dressed in black tie and my mother in a long evening gown.

One aspect of my parents' social life was unique to my father's branch of the service. The submarine service was a small component of the Navy and even more insular than the Navy at large. Small ships manned by small crews, submarines hosted a more intimate fraternity, less socially segregated by rank than those found aboard battleships and carriers. My parents were on familiar terms with the families of enlisted men on his submarine; officers and men attended parties at one another's homes and celebrated weddings and christenings together.

Submarine officers, like all naval officers, faithfully observed the professional distinctions governing their relationship to enlisted men, upon which the good order and discipline of the service depended. But living aboard ship in such small quarters bred an off-duty informality among officers and their enlisted shipmates. They were friends, and my father, like his father, valued those friendships highly.

More than the manners of polite society distinguished the life of a naval officer. His character was expected to be above reproach, his life a full testament to the enduring virtues of an officer and a gentleman. Those virtues were not necessarily as many as those required of clergy. An officer's honor could admit some vices, and many officers, my father and grandfather included, indulged more than a few. But honor would not permit even rare or small transgressions of the code of conduct that was expected to be as natural a part of an officer's life as was his physical description.

An officer must not lie, steal, or cheat—ever. He keeps his word, whatever the cost. He must not shirk his duties no matter how difficult or dangerous they are. His life is ransomed to his duty. An officer must trust his fellow officers, and expect their trust in return. He must not expect others to bear what he will not.

An officer accepts the consequences of his actions. He must not hide his mistakes, nor transfer blame to others that is rightfully his. He admits his mistakes openly, and accepts whatever sanction is imposed upon him without complaint.

For the obedience he is owed by his subordinates, an officer accepts certain solemn obligations to them in return, and an officer's obligations to enlisted men are the most solemn of all. An officer must not confer his responsibilities on the men under his command. They are his alone. He does not put his men in jeop-

ardy for any purpose that their country has not required they
serve. He does not risk their lives and welfare for his sake, but
only to answer the shared duty they are called to answer. He will
not harm their reputations by his conduct or cause them to suffer
shame or any penalty that only he deserves. My father once said,
"Some officers get it backwards. They don't understand that we
are responsible for our men, not the other way around. That's
what forges trust and loyalty."

An officer accepts these and his many other responsibilities
with gratitude. They are his honor. Any officer who stains his
honor by violating these standards forfeits the respect of his fellow officers and no longer deserves to be included in their ranks.
His presence among them is offensive and threatens the integrity
of the service.

Even in the small Navy world that disappeared with the
Second World War, some officers fell short of the demands of
honor. If they did so grievously, or repeatedly, or without
remorse and requital, they were, if not thrown out of the service,
so completely ostracized, so bereft of respect, that they would
usually leave of their own accord. If the Navy tolerated their conduct, it would shame everyone in the service.

My parents arrived in Hawaii in the aftermath of the infamous
Massie scandal, which had deeply shaken prewar Hawaiian society and the entire Navy community there. A young lieutenant,
Thomas Massie, who some time earlier had served on my father's
submarine, had committed an unpardonable breach of the code.
He was, reportedly, an intemperate and unlikable man, and his
petulant and difficult wife, Thalia Massie, one of three daughters
of a Kentucky bluegrass family of aristocratic pretensions, was
even less likable.

One evening, Massie and his wife drove with a few other officers and their wives to a nightclub in a rough part of Honolulu.
There the officer and his wife became very drunk. What happened next and why has never been determined with certainty.
What is known is that at some point the wife had left the nightclub without her husband. Her husband located her at home later

that evening, bruised and frightened and claiming to have been abducted and raped by as many as six native Hawaiian boys. She identified five boys who had been arrested that same evening for a traffic altercation as her assailants, and they were subsequently put on trial for the crime.

The evidence against the boys was far from conclusive. The jury was unable to reach a verdict, and a mistrial was pronounced. The accused were released on bail pending retrial. One month later, Lieutenant Massie persuaded two enlisted men from the submarine base to help him and his blue-blooded mother-in-law apprehend and murder one of the defendants. A short time later, Massie, his mother-in-law, and one of the enlisted men were stopped by police while racing through town in their car, curtains covering the windows, with the body of one of the boys wrapped in a tarp on the floor of the backseat.

The conduct of this officer shocked and outraged the rest of Hawaii's naval community, but not because the man had exacted mortal vengeance for his wife's rape. That showed poor judgment, perhaps, but given the nature of the alleged crime, the act was forgivable. What was unforgivable was that the officer had involved enlisted men in his crime, placing them in great jeopardy to help him avenge an offense that concerned only him and his wife. That was a grave breach of an officer's duty to his men.

There was a trial, and Massie, his mother-in-law, and the two enlisted men were convicted of manslaughter even though the famous defense attorney Clarence Darrow had defended them. They escaped justice, however. The Navy had intervened in the case to help in their defense, and, after their conviction, to help persuade the governor of Hawaii to commute their sentence from ten years to one hour. After the convicted vigilantes had served their hour in the governor's office, the Navy quickly sent them and Thalia Massie back to the States.

Many of his fellow officers felt shamed by Massie's conduct, and by the Navy's intervention in the matter. Initially, most officers believed the allegation of rape and their fellow officer's subsequent explanation of the killing as self-defense. They found it hard to believe an officer would lie. But most soon came to believe that he had indeed lied about the killing, and that he and his wife had probably lied about the rape as well. The discovery made the Navy's intervention on his behalf as unpardonable as the officer's use of enlisted men.

When my parents arrived, the scandal still dominated all conversation in every officer's home. The entire community seemed distressed over this singular violation of the standards they had always accepted as an unquestioned, ennobling way of life. And it was a long time before they recovered from the shock of it all.

My mother said that on the ship that returned him to the States, the disgraced Massie was observed to be frequently drunk and "making a natural fool of himself." She claims that some years later, he was incorrectly reported to have killed himself—an act that most of his fellow officers and their wives who had known of his crime and the damage it had done to the Navy's honor thought appropriate.

This was the Navy in which my father and grandfather felt so at home. They had entered its ranks already imbued with the notions of honor that distinguished a good officer. They were the standards passed down from one generation to another in their family. As boys, no less than as men, they did not lie, steal, or cheat, and they never shirked their duty. My brother once said that our father's word "had the constancy of Newtonian laws of physical motion." He added, "I have never met a more honest man than my father. I literally cannot think of a single time he did not tell the truth about something, as best he knew it."

My mother recalls playing gin rummy with my father once when she jokingly accused him of cheating. He reacted so strongly to the accusation, with such evident distress over the charge, admonishing her to "never say such a thing again," that she never did. Not even in jest.

The Navy revered my father's and grandfather's shared ideals and offered them adventure. It promised them the perfect life, and they were grateful to their last breath for the privilege.

Happy in his profession, my father worked every day, without exception. On Christmas morning, after we had opened our presents in front of the Christmas tree, he would excuse himself, change into his uniform, and leave for his office. I cannot recall a single instance when he came home from work earlier than eight o'clock in the evening.

As any other child would, I resented my father's absences, interpreting them as a sign that he loved his work more than his children. This was unfair of me, and I regret having felt that way. The most important relationship in my father's life had been his bond with my grandfather. That cherished bond influenced every major decision my father made throughout his life. Yet my grandfather had been absent from his family at least as often as my father was away from us, probably more often. He had done his duty as his country had asked him to, and his family understood, and admired him for it.

My father felt no shame in attending just as diligently to the responsibilities of his office, nor should he have. I am certain that he wanted to share with me the warm affection that he and his father had shared. But he wanted me to know also that a man's life should be big enough to encompass both duty to family and duty to country. That can be a hard lesson for a boy to learn. It was a hard lesson for me.

He worked hard to please his superiors and accepted every assignment as an opportunity to prove himself. Even when he viewed a new assignment as sidetracking him from his pursuit of important commands, he never betrayed the slightest hint of bitterness. "No matter what job you get," he told my mother, "you can make a good one out of it."

He once helped a friend get a prestigious position on an admiral's staff. My father thought him to be a born leader and expected great things from him in the Navy. But the man didn't like the long hours associated with the job. Nor did his wife, who openly resented the demands placed on young officers and their families.

Late one Sunday night, the admiral on whose staff my father's friend served called him to get the combination for a safe that contained classified documents he wanted to review. The young officer started to give him the combination over the phone, and the admiral cut him off abruptly. "Don't you dare give me that combination over the phone," he admonished his aide. Both my parents were shocked at their friend's careless regard for his professional responsibilities. My mother remarked, "Had it been Jack, he would have said, 'Sir, I'm on my way.'" It would never have occurred to my father to respond in any other way.

My father was devout, although the demands of his profession sometimes made regular churchgoing difficult. His mother, Katherine, was the daughter of an Episcopal minister, and she had ably seen to her son's religious instruction, no small feat in a home where the head of the household happily indulged a variety of vices.

My father didn't talk about God or the importance of religious devotion. He didn't proselytize. But he always kept with him a tattered, dog-eared prayerbook, from which he would pray aloud for an hour, on his knees, twice every day.

He drank too much, which did not become him. And I often felt that my father's religious devotion was intended in part to help him control his drinking. In the Navy in which my father came of age, men relaxed by drinking. The greater the burdens a man bore, the more he drank to relieve himself of them.

During the Second World War, when exhausted submarine crews finished a combat patrol in the Pacific, which typically lasted from six weeks to two months, they would come into port at Midway Island or Freemantle, Australia, for a month's "rest camp." These remote locations offered few natural or cultural distractions from the terrors of war. Midway's sole distinction was its claim to be home to a third of the world's population of gooney birds, large, awkward, and odd-looking fowl. Visiting sailors named the island Gooneyville. There is little else memorable about the place. To compensate for barren landscapes and somber circumstances, the Navy would see to it that the men had someplace to drink when the pleasure of playing baseball and horseshoes wore thin. In Freemantle, the Navy rented houses for the men and stocked them with cases of beer and liquor. The men, most of them kids in their teens and twenties, lacking anything better to do, would drink themselves senseless until their next patrol.

During one typically intoxicated evening while on leave at Midway, the officers of a recently arrived submarine tore up the officers' club when the bartender refused to serve them. For a time, they kept their destruction within reasonable limits. Then they discovered a plaque dedicated to the club that had been commissioned by the officers of another submarine in the days before submariners were banished from the place. Seeing this, and deeply aggrieved that the submariners' courtesy had been repaid with such a gross discourtesy, they took the plaque and tore the cabinet that contained it from the wall.

A short time later, a young ensign from the shore patrol arrived to restore order. After repeated unsuccessful attempts to ascertain which officer was in charge of the marauders, the ensign left to call for help. As he was placing the call a group of the officers walked over to him. One of them announced, "I'm in charge. Jack McCain, skipper of the *Gunnel*."

In a report the young ensign filed with the base commander the following day, he described how my father and his officers continued to ransack the officers' club until they were eventually persuaded to leave by the duty officer, who had arrived on the scene carrying his side arm. They took the offending plaque and the cabinet that had housed it along with several other pieces of furniture and drove off in a jeep and a weapons carrier they had stolen earlier in the evening. My father drove the jeep back to the old, dilapidated "Gooneyville Hotel," where he and his officers were quartered. He was accompanied by his executive officer, Joe Vasey, who recalled that when they arrived at their destination, my father "abruptly decided to drive through the main entrance into the lobby, overestimating by only an inch or so the width of the entrance."

My father then retired to his room. When the rest of the *Gunnel*'s officers arrived in the stolen weapons carrier, Vasey instructed them to return the confiscated furniture to the officers' club, which they did, heaving the large cabinet into a hallway and leaving it there in pieces.

The next morning, the Navy commodore in command at Midway called my father to his office and chewed him out for some time. Afterward, my father ordered his men to return the confiscated plaque to the officers' club.

During another leave, this time in Freemantle, my father and some of the men under his command barely escaped death after one of them had drunk himself so thoroughly witless that he threw a box of bullets into the fireplace of the house where they were drinking. The rounds cooked off and fired into walls and furniture as my father and his friends dove for cover.

When spirits were in short supply, submariners often drank the alcohol that was used to fuel torpedoes. My father once served as engineering officer on a submarine. His first day on the job, he discovered that his predecessor had drunk nearly all the torpedo alcohol aboard. His submarine was scheduled to stand for inspection that day, and he had to borrow a quantity of the alcohol from other submarine commanders to cover up the embarrassing deficit.

There was one rule about drinking that most submariners, my father included, considered inviolate. A submariner never drank aboard ship. Submarine warfare is as treacherous and mentally exacting as any form of warfare can be. It requires the combatants to be in full possession of their faculties at all times while under way. Accordingly, no matter how excessive their binge drinking was when ashore, my father and his crew stayed sober at sea.

My father returned from war with a great appetite for drink, which he overindulged until the very last years of his life. He didn't drink at work, and was never completely incapacitated by his weakness. But he would often ease his way into social settings by drinking too much. And, as with most people, drinking changed his personality in unattractive ways. When he was drunk, I did not recognize him.

On occasions, friends cautioned him that his drinking was harming his career, but he never let it get so out of hand that it ruined his fitness for command. His aspirations were dear to him, and his determination to achieve them more formidable than the allure of any vice.

Like his father, my father swore a lot, and subordinates often referred to him as "Good Goddam McCain." Also like his father, he was a chain-smoker, although he preferred enormous cigars to my grandfather's roll-your-own cigarettes.

As an ensign, he had served on a submarine commanded by Captain Herman Saul, whom my father regarded as an exemplary officer, and whose leadership style he tried to emulate. Saul taught my father the difficult technique of keeping a submerged submarine perfectly level, a skill my father mastered. Saul also introduced his protégé to the pleasure of smoking stogies, and my father, like his mentor, was seldom without one. The cigars performed an additional function later in his life, often serving as pointer and exclamation point for his well-regarded lectures on the history and importance of seapower.

As a submarine skipper, my father often let junior officers bring the ship into port so they could gain the experience necessary to operate a submarine competently. On one occasion, while my mother, sister, brother, and I watched from the pier, a young officer struggled to navigate my father's submarine through the strong river current coming into port at Groton, Connecticut. My father was standing in the conning tower, a cigar in his mouth, talking to his executive officer. He was not paying sufficient attention to his ship's progress.

It was clear to all of us watching onshore that the young ensign piloting the sub was going to drive her directly into the pier. When, at the last moment, my father finally recognized the approaching catastrophe, he turned excitedly to give the order "All engines stop." Unfortunately, as he drew a breath to bark out the order he inhaled his cigar and choked. A moment later, the submarine crashed into the pier, knocking down a lamppost, which landed on our car. My father calmly ordered the ensign to back the ship out and bring it in again, which he did without incident.

With his ship safely in port, my father went home with us and began a long and difficult argument with his insurance company over the credibility of his insurance claim for a car destroyed by a submarine.

My father developed his seapower lecture in midcareer, when he served as the Navy's first Chief of Information, and later as the Navy's senior liaison officer to the United States Congress. Both posts helped to broaden his circle of acquaintances outside the Navy. He became a frequent witness before congressional committees, experiences that he used to improve his lecture and polish his delivery. He acquired some of the skills of an accomplished military historian who moonlighted as a stage actor. Appreciative audiences gave him the nickname "Mr. Seapower."

My parents kept a house on Capitol Hill, where they entertained leading political and military figures. My mother's charm proved as effective with politicians as it was with naval officers. The political relationships my parents forged during this period contributed significantly to my father's future success. Among their friends was Carl Vinson, chairman of the House Armed Forces Committee. At my father's invitation, he ate his breakfast, prepared by my mother, at my parents' home on many if not most mornings when Congress was in session.

My father was not, however, a political admiral—a term of derision accorded to successful officers whose records lacked combat experiences comparable to those of the war fighters who disapproved of them. Moreover, my father, who surely valued the patronage of civilian commanders as necessary to his single-minded pursuit of four stars, nevertheless harbored a little of the professional military man's dislike for the sail-trimming and obfuscation of politics.

He was, as his father had been, a man of strong views who spoke his mind bluntly. This is as risky a habit in Navy politics as it is in civilian politics, and it often caused him trouble. Both McCain Senior and Junior believed war to be a ruthless endeavor, the purpose of which was to annihilate your enemy. A wise combat commander keeps a wary respect for his enemy's abilities, but neither my father nor my grandfather let his prudence temper his contempt for his country's enemies.

My grandfather's frequent insulting references to the personal qualities of the Japanese enemy were in accord with the conventions of the time, although when I read them today I wince at their racist overtones. I don't believe they were intended as racist screeds. But war, which occasions much heroism and nobility, also has its corruptions. That's what makes it so terrible, a thing worth avoiding if possible.

My grandfather, as combatants often do, needed to work up a powerful hate for his enemy. He once recommended of the Japanese "killing them all—painfully." Hate is an understandable reaction to the losses and atrocities suffered at the hands of the enemy. But hate also sustains the fighter in his devotion to the complete destruction of his enemy and helps to overcome the virtuous human impulse to recoil in disgust from what must be done by your hand.

My father rose to high command when communism had replaced fascism as the dominant threat to American security. He hated it fiercely and dedicated himself to its annihilation. He believed that we were locked inescapably in a life-and-death struggle with the Soviets. One side or the other would ultimately win total victory, and seapower would prove critical to the outcome. He was outspoken on the subject.

When he attained commands that required diplomatic skills, his candor occasionally lacked the rhetorical courtesies that attended the first attempts at détente. This often caused anxiety in the State Department, prompting complaints in cable traffic about Admiral McCain's indiscretion. It concerned some of his civilian and military commanders in the Pentagon as well, but it won him both admirers and detractors, despite the prominent antiwar sentiment in 1960s America. I imagine it also fortified that sense of himself that, as a boy, he derived from flouting conventions. Addressing the Naval Academy Class of 1970, he commented on the popular antiwar slogan "Make love, not war" that naval officers "were men enough to do both."

Few successful naval officers crest the heights of command without making enemies as well as friends along the way. My grandfather and father had their detractors in the Navy, some of whom may have disliked their highly personalized style of leadership, others their grasping ambition. But they were well respected by most of their fellow officers as resourceful, resilient, and brave commanders.

It was, however, the regard in which they were held by the enlisted men who served under them that gave them the greatest satisfaction. They both had great empathy for the ranks and went out of their way to show it.

An aide to Admiral Elmo Zumwalt, commander of U.S. naval forces in Vietnam, once recounted many years later an incident that typified my father's concern for his sailors. My father, who was Zumwalt's boss at the time, was in Vietnam on one of his regular visits to the field. Zumwalt decided to host a dinner for my father and several other senior American officials and ordered his young aide to arrange it. During the dinner, a Navy steward who was serving my father tipped a platter of roast beef au jus, and the juice spilled onto my father's head and shirt. "I got up in great embarrassment," the aide remembered, "to try to help Admiral McCain." But the admiral politely refused the young man's assistance as well as his offer of a clean shirt. "If I use your shirt, you'll just frame it," my father joked, "and tell everybody that this is a four-star admiral's shirt that you've been wearing. I can wear my own."

The next morning, as my father was preparing to leave the country, he called Admiral Zumwalt to instruct him not to punish the steward. "That was an accident last night and absolutely no fault of his. I know you won't let anything happen, but I just wanted to affirm my intent in the matter." The aide, who monitored Zumwalt's calls, never forgot the concern my father showed that morning for the welfare of a worried Navy steward. "It takes a very large man," he observed, "to remember something that small at six-thirty the next morning and to make sure that people didn't overreact. I was impressed."

To some of his most senior subordinates, my father could be a difficult and demanding boss. He kept his own counsel and would sometimes leave his subordinates in the dark about matters that directly concerned them. A few of them felt, perhaps with cause, that he did not treat them fairly. But his closest aides, men who worked with him and for him more than once during his career, loved him. And he was almost universally revered by those whose rank was the farthest beneath his own. They knew he held them in high esteem, and they returned the compliment.

To this day, several times a year I receive letters from men who once served in the ranks under my father's or grandfather's command. Some are from aides, who closely observed them for long periods of time under conditions of great stress. Others are from men who write to tell me of an occasion when my father or grandfather had boarded a ship commanded by a subordinate, and had ignored the welcoming party of ship's officers to walk immediately over to them and inquire after their welfare and that of their shipmates. I value these testimonials as much as my father and grandfather did. They are from men who at one time risked death at the order of the John McCain they wrote to praise.

CHAPTER SEVEN

The *Gunnel*

The day the Japanese sank the fleet in Pearl Harbor is one of my earliest memories. I was five years old. We were living in New London at the time. It was a Sunday morning, and my entire family was—for reasons I cannot recall—standing in the front yard of our small house. A black car passing our house slowed down and the driver, a naval officer, rolled down his window and shouted, "Jack, the Japs have bombed Pearl Harbor." My father left for the base immediately. I saw very little of him for the next four years.

He commanded three submarines during the war. The first command he held just briefly before being ordered on his first combat patrol. The second, the USS *Gunnel*, served as a reconnaissance and beacon ship for Operation Torch, the American invasion of North Africa. The *Gunnel* was ordered to leave New London at midnight on October 18 and proceed to waters off Fedala, French Morocco, about fifteen miles north of Casablanca, arriving there five days in advance of the invasion. Under strict orders to remain undetected at all costs, the *Gunnel* was to make landfall submerged, a dangerous and exacting maneuver, and, once there, to reconnoiter and photograph the beaches to determine the best landing sites.

By means of infrared searchlights invisible to the unaided eye, the *Gunnel* served as a lighthouse for the invading armada, keeping the ships on course for the landing beaches. An hour before midnight on November 7, the *Gunnel*'s signalman sighted the huge fleet cresting the horizon exactly on schedule. The *Gunnel* began flashing its designated signal, and throughout the night American ships took up their positions off the Moroccan coast and lowered their landing craft.

At dawn, the *Gunnel*'s secret mission complete, my father was ordered to fly the American flag, illuminate it with a spotlight, and proceed on the surface at top speed out of the congested area to safer waters near the Canary Islands.

Friendly fire, a misfortune of war today, was a much more frequent occurrence in earlier wars. In their first combat patrol, the crew of the *Gunnel* had a number of close calls when friendly ships and planes, in the fog of war, mistook my father's submarine for a German sub, as American submarines in war zones were an unfamiliar sight in 1942.

On their passage out of the invasion area, my father allowed his crew to stand topside in shifts to watch the naval barrage directed at the fortifications at Fedala and Casablanca. As my father and some of his crew stood mesmerized, watching the spectacular assault, the booming guns of American battleships firing one-ton shells toward the outgunned enemy, an American P-40 plane dropped out of the clouds and began strafing the *Gunnel*. My father ordered the sub to dive, and he and the other men on deck scrambled down the conning-tower hatch.

Fifteen minutes later, the *Gunnel* surfaced and was signaled by an American seaplane. "Good morning, sallow face, I am here to protect you." The plane escorted the *Gunnel* to safety for some time until it broke off to chase an approaching French plane away from the sub.

A little after noon that same day, an American bomber was spotted approaching the *Gunnel*. When the plane ignored the sub's signal, dipped a wing, and turned as if preparing for a dive-bombing, the executive officer, standing on the *Gunnel*'s bridge, ordered a crash dive. The sub descended at a dangerously steep angle as the bomb exploded so close that some of the crew were struck by flying paint chips knocked loose from inside the sub's conning tower by the force of the blast.

When the *Gunnel* reached its assigned station and patrolled waters off the Canaries, it was hunted for four days by German subs. On November 13, my father was ordered to make for a British submarine base at Roseneath, Scotland. En route three days later, the *Gunnel* was spotted and chased by a U-boat. Later that same day, one of the *Gunnel*'s four main engines broke down. Over the next nine days, the three remaining main engines stopped working.

When the last of its four engines gave out, the *Gunnel* was still a thousand miles from Scotland and sailing in extremely hazardous waters infested with German subs and patrolled by German aircraft. My father ordered his engineers to convert the auxiliary engine, normally used to power the sub's lights and air-conditioning, for propulsion.

Under full power, the *Gunnel* could make twenty knots on the surface and nine knots submerged. Powered by its auxiliary engine, the sub could make only five knots at best as it limped slowly toward Scotland, submerged by day and on the surface by night.

My father radioed his condition to naval authorities, and the *Gunnel* was redirected to a closer naval base, at Falmouth in southern England. The British offered to send an escort or a tug to tow the *Gunnel* to safety. According to the *Gunnel*'s torpedo officer, "Both offers were promptly and unequivocally declined by Captain McCain as he chomped down hard on his cigar."

Were the overworked auxiliary engine to break down, the *Gunnel* would be dead in the water. Use of the sub's lighting and fans was reduced to bare minimum. One of the machinist's mates placed a small statue of Buddha in front of the small engine and ordered passing crewmen to bow respectfully.

On November 19, still a week's voyage from Falmouth, my father sighted through the sub's periscope several ships' masts on the horizon. As three ships, antisubmarine escorts serving as a screen for an advancing convoy, drew closer, my father ordered battle stations. The *Gunnel*'s communications officer searched the ship recognition manuals but could find nothing that would identify the approaching ships as friendly.

At about three thousand yards, the three ships detected the *Gunnel*, and they advanced toward her. My father prepared his crew to fight. One of his officers recalls him declaring, "If those bastards drop depth charges we are going to give it to them." But just before the fight commenced my father recognized a British ensign flying on the closest ship.

My father ordered a red smoke-signal rocket launched from an underwater tube. The lead British warship ordered my father to surface with the *Gunnel*'s torpedo tubes pointed away from the ships. When he did so, the *Gunnel* found itself in the center of a triangle with the guns of all three British ships pointing at it. One of the British commanding officers hailed my father through a megaphone and announced, "Good thing you fired that red smoke. We were about to blast you out of the water."

Six days later, on Thanksgiving Day, the *Gunnel* reached Falmouth. After repairs, the sub proceeded to Roseneath. After further repairs, the *Gunnel* returned to the States, where it was outfitted in Portsmouth, New Hampshire, for combat duty in the Pacific.

Upon completion of his first combat mission, the thirty-one-year-old submarine skipper was commended by the Atlantic Fleet Commander in Chief. "Commander John S. McCain, by extremely skillful and daring handling of his ship, performed special missions which contributed materially to the successful execution of an extremely difficult landing of a large expeditionary force on a strange and poorly charted coast."

Although he had initially wanted to be an aviator, in later years my father would remark that his disqualification as a pilot had been a lucky twist of fate. He was proud to be a skipper in a service that was then and is now a select branch of the Navy. The submarine service places a high premium on the individual initiative of its commanders, especially in war. Long patrols, inconsistent communications with base command, battles often fought alone, fateful decisions left entirely to the skipper—the service suited my father's personality completely. "It's a unique life in submarines," he gratefully recalled. "You're on your own ... completely detached from the world."

He was a resourceful skipper, adept at devising imaginative improvements to his sub's war-fighting capabilities. He worked out a formula for targeting torpedoes at unseen enemy ships while submerged. He did it by taking sound bearings of the other ship and comparing his sub's course and speed to his estimate of the target's speed, thereby deriving the enemy's range and course. It was a remarkably accurate system, and my father credited a great many sunken enemy ships to its effectiveness.

He invented an electric firing device for the ship's guns. Until he improved the firing mechanism, the firing pin of submarine guns was released by depressing a foot pedal on the gun mount. The gunner had to apply a considerable amount of pressure to the pedal to get it to release the pin and fire a shell. Often the exertion by the gunner threw his aim off. My father rigged up a handheld firing button. All the gunner had to do was press a button held in his right hand, enabling him to keep a steadier aim while firing.

The officers and crew of the *Gunnel* called him Captain Jack. In the words of his executive officer, and friend of many years, retired Rear Admiral Joe Vasey, the men of the USS *Gunnel* "would do anything for their skipper."

My father made a point of knowing all about the personal lives of the men under his command. He daily wandered through the submarine's compartments, greeting and joking with his subordinates. He paused here and there to have a cup of coffee with the men, and to have them bring him up to date on the details of their lives back home.

There were eight officers and seventy-two enlisted men on board the *Gunnel*. My father knew the first names of every one of them. He knew who was married and who was single; how many kids they had; whose wives were pregnant and whether they were hoping for a boy or a girl. He knew what sports they favored; what they had done for a living before the war; what they wanted to do when they returned home. He knew what scared them and what made them angry. After the war, when any one of them contacted him for assistance, he did all he could to provide it.

FAITH OF MY FATHERS

Admiral Vasey, who worked for my father again when he reached the pinnacle of his career as Commander in Chief, Pacific, calls him "the greatest leader of men I have ever known."

My father and a few of his officers returned to the *Gunnel* one morning much the worse for wear after a long, raucous night ashore in Freemantle, Australia. The *Gunnel* was to leave on combat patrol that day. As they boarded the sub, my father turned to his exec and said, "Joe, muster the crew. I want to talk to these guys."

My father paced in front of the assembled crew, an unlit cigar protruding from the corner of his mouth, and exhorted them to martial glory. "Fellows, we're going off to fight the goddam Japanese. We're gonna find 'em and fight 'em wherever the hell they are. We're gonna fight these bastards, and we're gonna lick 'em. We're not gonna let these Japs hide from us. We'll fight 'em even if we have to go into their harbors to find them, and they're gonna be goddam sorry we did, I'll tell you that. Now, every man who wants to go with me, take one step forward, and anyone who doesn't, stay right where you are."

Laughing and roaring approval, every man of the *Gunnel* stepped forward and signaled his pride in following Captain Jack wherever he chose to lead him.

Many years later, in a commencement address he gave at the Naval Academy, he spoke of the all-important relationship between a skipper and the enlisted men under his command, the bluejackets, who were, he often said, the "backbone of the Navy." "When you step aboard ship and stand in front of your first division of bluejackets," he said, "they will evaluate you accurately and without delay. In fact, there is no more exacting method of determining an officer's worth. Furthermore, you can't fool bluejackets. They are quick to recognize the phony. If you lose the respect of these men, you are finished. You can never get it back."

My father never lost the respect of the men who sailed under his command. He taught them their duty, as they taught him his, and made them proud to carry it out. And he looked after them. Heading for Fremantle, Australia, for fuel during one patrol, the *Gunnel*'s officer of the deck sighted a bomber overhead. Knowing it was either an American or Australian plane, the officer exchanged prescribed recognition signals with the bomber indicating they were friendly.

A few moments after the plane passed overhead, it turned and made a run on the *Gunnel*. My father was on the bridge. As the plane menacingly approached, my father gave the order to dive. As his ship submerged, the plane released two bombs, which fell close by, shaking the *Gunnel* violently.

A few hours later, the *Gunnel* reached port. After the *Gunnel* tied up to the dock, my father asked the officer of the deck if he was sure he had given the bomber the right recognition signal. The young officer replied that he had. Angrily, my father had Joe Vasey bring him the two largest ensigns on board, one of whom had been an intercollegiate heavyweight wrestling champion. "Men, I want you to go find the bastards who did this to us, and take care of them. You got that?"

"Aye, aye, sir," the two hulking ensigns shouted, and then took off at a brisk pace to execute their skipper's order.

Some hours later, my father heard some kind of commotion on the dock and came up on deck to see what was happening. There he found the two ensigns he had ordered to avenge the *Gunnel*'s honor stumbling toward the ship, amid a crowd of Australian Army officers, all of whom were drunk, carrying beers in their hands and singing "Waltzing Matilda" loudly and off-key.

The two ensigns had apparently inquired of the Australians who were now escorting them back to ship where they might locate the offending bomber crew. Judging that the two men might come to more harm than good, the Australians pleaded ignorance about the crew's whereabouts, but promised to look into the matter if the ensigns would join them for a drink. The ensigns decided they surely had enough time to suspend their search briefly for a quick beer, and a good many beers later they found themselves part of the roving, boisterous chorus that now stood in the gaze of the much-amused skipper of the *Gunnel*.

My father was never one to begrudge any man under his command a much-deserved respite from war, and he gladly wrote off the ensigns' failure to carry out his orders to the greater good of improving Allied relations. No one laughed harder than he did at the drunken spectacle on the Fremantle dock. Long after the event, he would still joke with the wayward ensigns about how they had let their Australian brothers-in-arms get the better of them.

* * *

Patrolling the waters between Midway and Nagasaki on their second combat patrol, the crew of the *Gunnel* had their greatest success under my father's command as well as their first encounter with Japanese depth charges, one of the most harrowing experiences in naval warfare.

In the early evening of June 18, while hunting on the surface in the East China Sea just south of the Korean peninsula, the *Gunnel* sighted the masks and smokestacks of seven large Japanese freighters and two smaller vessels. The smaller boats, one a fishing trawler and the other probably a small destroyer, were serving as escorts. The ships were making full speed and changing course by forty to sixty degrees every ten minutes. By plotting their base course, the *Gunnel*'s navigation officer determined that the convoy was heading for Shanghai.

Unable to close with the fast-moving convoy while his submarine was submerged and making a top speed of only nine knots, my father decided to surface and, traveling at seventeen knots, get ahead of the convoy during the night. Over the next several hours the *Gunnel* raced to cut off the Japanese ships. By midnight it had reached its intended patrol site but had lost sight of the convoy.

Around five-thirty the morning of the 19th, the sub's radar picked up an enemy plane patrolling eight miles away. My father gave the order to submerge. When the *Gunnel* surfaced an hour later, the convoy was on the horizon, now steaming slowly. The *Gunnel* dove again and proceeded to close with the enemy at full speed, taking periscope observations every five minutes.

An hour and a half later, the *Gunnel* was within firing range of the freighters. My father fired three torpedoes from his bow tubes at the nearest ship, an old freighter of about eight thousand tons. A minute later, he fired three more from the bow at a second freighter. The first freighter was hit, and it sank within a few minutes while the *Gunnel* reached for the bottom.

At eighty feet the men of the *Gunnel* heard another torpedo explode. It had missed the second freighter but struck a third ship two thousand yards on the port side of the intended target. A moment later one of the convoy's two escort ships dropped the first of seven depth charges, each one detonating closer than the preceding one.

Joe Vasey described what it was like to be depth-charged: "You usually first heard the click of the detonator through the hull. But the explosion was the worst. It was like being in a steel container with someone hitting a giant sledgehammer against it. It can shake the whole bloody sub." Submarine crewmen prepared by bending their legs to absorb the impact. As Joe Vasey explained, many a submariner "had fractured legs from the shock of the deck plates and standing too rigidly."

The *Gunnel* had submerged 150 feet when the last of the seven depth charges exploded. One of the escorts, probably the trawler, was directly overhead. It dropped a grapnel over the side to try to hook the sub, a favorite tactic of commercial fishing vessels that were pressed into war service. The grapnel's chain dragged along the port side of the *Gunnel*, "rattling slowly and excruciatingly," my father recorded in his log, adding that "the chains of Marley's ghost sounded very much like that to old Scrooge."

My father ordered the *Gunnel* to descend to a depth of three hundred feet. The sub ran at that depth for four hours. Twice my father heard the enemy escort pass directly overhead. After an hour had passed without hearing anything from the enemy ship that was searching, its depth charges ready, for the *Gunnel*, my father came up to periscope depth. He sighted a Japanese warship about three thousand yards to his starboard, and immediately submerged again to three hundred feet.

A large Japanese naval base was located at Sasebo, less than a hundred miles to the east of the *Gunnel*'s position. In response to the *Gunnel*'s attack on the convoy, three destroyers had been sent out of Sasebo to hunt down and destroy the American sub. The approaching ship was one of them.

During its deep dive, it was necessary for the *Gunnel* to allow some water to flood in, making the sub heavier and enabling it to remain submerged at such a great depth. The *Gunnel* ran in this heavy condition for several hours, while the three destroyers hunted the sub with their sonar. When they were close, my father and his crew could hear distinctly through the sub's hull the destroyer's sonar pinging incessantly. The air was growing foul and the crew's nerves were strained to the breaking point. One of the *Gunnel*'s signalmen, Charles Napier, recalled fifty years later: "The Catholics were fingering their rosaries, other religious sailors were praying, and some were simply trying to figure how to get out of the situation."

Around nine o'clock that night, the *Gunnel*, its batteries dangerously low and its air banks nearly depleted, surfaced. The weary and frightened crew gasped clean air for the first time in sixteen hours.

Water from a leak in the conning tower had flooded the pump room and grounded out an air compressor and the air-conditioning plant. Intending to run on the surface while the crew made repairs, my father took the sub close to the area where he had sunk the freighter.

It was a cloudless night with bright moonlight and calm seas. At nine-thirty, a lookout spotted one of the Japanese destroyers 5,800 yards away. My father put the destroyer astern of the sub and gave the order for battle stations. He ordered every man off the bridge except for the quartermaster and himself and told the crew to make ready two of the stern torpedo tubes. He ran the *Gunnel* at full speed, making eighteen knots, but the destroyer made thirty knots, and closed rapidly.

At a little less than three thousand yards, the destroyer's guns opened up on the *Gunnel*, firing fused projectiles that passed over and on either side of the sub.

My father had ordered Joe Vasey, the *Gunnel*'s torpedo officer, to work out a firing solution for all four of the stern torpedo tubes. With shells fired from the destroyer's guns "getting uncomfortably close," exploding overhead and missing barely to the *Gunnel*'s port and starboard sides, my father yelled, "Goddammit, shoot, Joe, shoot." Vasey fired the two operable torpedoes "down the throat" of the destroyer as my father sounded the diving alarm.

When the *Gunnel* reached thirty-five feet, the first torpedo hit the destroyer. A few seconds later, five depth charges detonated simultaneously off the *Gunnel*'s stern. My father recorded the moment in his log, breaking his usual habit of restricting his official record to a dry recitation of the facts and avoiding dramatic embellishment: "The awesome sounds of exploding depth charges and collapsing bulkheads as the warship rapidly sank close astern of *Gunnel* was an unforgettable experience for all hands."

My father leveled the sub off at two hundred feet. When he picked up the two remaining destroyers on his sonar rapidly approaching, he took the *Gunnel* down to three hundred feet and commenced evasive tactics. The destroyers dropped eight more depth charges off the sub's stern. After six hours, the *Gunnel* surfaced very briefly to charge its batteries and air banks. Spotting the destroyers, my father took it down again. He remained submerged for the next eighteen hours with all auxiliary engines turned off, keeping the sub's noise at a minimum to avoid detection by sonar.

Running silent for such a long period was a perilous predicament for a submarine crew. You ran the risk of losing all power as the batteries, which could be charged only when the submarine was surfaced, ran down completely. The air grew unbreathable as the submarine's carbon dioxide absorbent was used up. This was the situation my father and his crew faced on the evening of June 20.

The air became so foul that crew members not needed at battle stations were ordered to rest in their bunks, where they would consume less oxygen. Earlier, the crew had felt a sense of hopelessness when the grapnel chain had scraped against the *Gunnel*'s side, knowing that if the hook grabbed onto something, depth charges would immediately be dropped directly onto the sub. Most of the crew, terrified, soaked with perspiration, had managed to control their emotions, and they responded to their skipper orders. Some of the younger crew members had wept, face-down in their bunks. Fear and poor air made a few men delirious, and one of them had to be strapped down.

The anxiety of those who were still in possession of their faculties after many hours submerged was growing into frantic desperation. Over the last two days they had endured the excitement of the chase and attack on the convoy, a hair-raising close call in a surface battle with an enemy destroyer, and the terror of repeated depth charge attacks. Now they were sweating out endless hours fathoms down, exhausted, slowly suffocating while their sub faced the imminent prospect of lying dead in the water.

The temperature inside the sub had reached 120 degrees. The humidity was 100 percent. Above them, two destroyers constantly patrolled, determined to locate and destroy the American submarine that had sunk their sister ship.

At eight-thirty that night, my father called all his officers to the wardroom. There the chief of the boat and chief electrician's mate informed them that the batteries would last only thirty to sixty minutes more, and that all the sub's good air was gone. The *Gunnel* would have to surface as quickly as possible. After receiving this discouraging report, my father informed his officers of his intentions.

The sub would surface slowly to reduce the likelihood that the blowing of its ballast tanks would be detected by the enemy's sonar. As soon as it surfaced, the ship's guns would be immediately manned and readied for battle. If either of the destroyers was in range, the *Gunnel* would shoot it out, and charge its batteries and air banks on the run.

My father offered one other course of action to his officers, a course he strongly opposed. If his officers did not unanimously concur with his decision to fight, he would order all classified information and materials destroyed, surface the sub, and scuttle her. All hands would jump overboard and hope for rescue, a remote hope at best, given that the Japanese skippers whom they would rely on for rescue were undoubtedly bent on vengeance and unlikely to be sympathetic.

To a man, my father's officers shouted their preference for a fight.

When they surfaced, they sighted the destroyers at a considerable distance and steaming away from the *Gunnel*. They gave no indication that they spotted the sub. My father reversed course and hurried away. The batteries for two of his diesel engines were recharged, and fresh air filled the ship.

Ten days after my father's submarine eluded the destroyers, it reached Midway. I suspect the men of the USS *Gunnel* were never so happy to see that desolate, uninteresting island.

My father received the Silver Star for this action. The citation praised his "conspicuous gallantry,... bravery under fire and aggressive fighting spirit."

After five combat patrols aboard the *Gunnel*, my father, now Commander McCain, took command of the USS Dentuda, which completed one patrol in the South China Sea before the war's end. During its only patrol, the Dentuda fought a gun battle with two Japanese patrol craft and an inconclusive submerged battle with a Japanese submarine.

It was as commander of the Dentuda that my father entered Tokyo Bay, exhausted from the strain of command in one of the more terrifying forms of combat, to enjoy his last reunion with the father whose example had led him to this life.

CHAPTER EIGHT

Four Stars

In 1965, my father reported for duty in New York, to serve as vice chairman of the delegation to the United Nations Military Staff Committee and as Commander of the Eastern Sea Frontier and the Atlantic Reserve Fleet.

He had distinguished himself in other commands since the Second World War and had enjoyed a notably successful career. He had commanded two submarine divisions. During the Korean War, as a captain, he served as second in command on the destroyer USS *St. Paul*. He was well regarded by influential leaders in Washington and had been given several important commands, the last being command of the Atlantic Fleet's Amphibious Force, when he directed the American invasion of the Dominican Republic.

In 1965, violent clashes between warring factions, one of which was believed to be a Communist front, had brought the Dominican Republic to the verge of civil war. President Johnson ordered my father to command the amphibious assault of Operation Steel Pike 1, the invasion and military occupation of the Caribbean nation. The operation was controversial. Critics judged it, with good reason, to be an unlawful intervention in the affairs of a sovereign nation. My father, typically, was undeterred by domestic opposition. "Some people condemned this as an unwarranted intervention," he observed, "but the Communists were all set to move in and take over. People may not love you for being strong when you have to be, but they respect you for it and learn to behave themselves when you are."

The operation was a success, and, at the time, it constituted the largest amphibious operation ever undertaken in peacetime. After its completion, he was awarded the Legion of Merit for attracting "worldwide attention to the highly mobile and devastating might" of the Navy and Marine Corps.

His subsequent assignment at the United Nations, however, was regarded by the Navy as a dead end and was expected to be his last. He was a three-star admiral, and the prospects for a fourth star were remote. But two years later he was ordered to London to assume command of all U.S. naval forces in Europe. A fourth star came with the job. He relieved the renowned Admiral John Thach, my grandfather's old operations officer and friend.

Within a year, he was given command of all U.S. forces in the Pacific, the largest operational military command in the world. The dominion of the Commander in Chief, Pacific Command (CINCPAC) is geographically immense, encompassing 85 million square miles, extending from the Aleutian Islands to the South Pole and from the west coast of North and South America to the Indian Ocean.

CINCPAC, Admiral Nimitz's wartime command, remains the U.S. Navy's second most prestigious office. Only the office of Chief of Naval Operations is a greater privilege, and, if truth be told, a good many officers would prefer running the Pacific Command to running the entire Navy. My father had achieved prominence in his beloved Navy that surpassed his father's storied career. The Washington Post reported his triumph under the headline navy cheers appointment of mccain.

Shortly after his new assignment was made public, my father received a letter from a retired sailor who had known my grandfather during the war. He wrote of how highly regarded my grandfather had been by the enlisted men under his command.

Dear Admiral,
Maybe I shouldn't be sending this to you, but I had to when I saw your name in this morning's paper. Commander of

<u>United States Forces in the Pacific.</u> I am an ex–carrier man, 1943–1946. Was Admiral John S. McCain your dad? I was a plank owner on the Wasp, and Admiral McCain was at our commissioning.... We had admirals on board before and after but Admiral McCain was liked by all the ship's company. It was a privilege to have served under him. They all speak of Admirals Halsey, Nimitz, Sprague, Spruance, Mitscher, and Bogan. But Admiral John S. McCain was tops with us. Every night about 8 p.m. he would walk around the flight deck with that salty-looking admiral's cap of his in his hands. He would stop and talk to us on our gun mount. Maybe you won't have time to read this. I don't send letters at all but when I heard of you and your command I just had to.

I imagine the old sailor's note, rejoicing in the professional triumph of the son of a Navy legend, must have moved my father very much. Though I was not privileged to witness his change-of-command ceremony, I have always believed that for that one moment, my father, so hard driven by his often oppressive desire to honor his father's name, looked on his career with tranquillity and satisfaction. He must have felt the old man's pride as he took his first salute as commander of the greatest military force in the world, with dominion over the waters where the answer "I've sent McCain" had once relieved an anxious predecessor.

Over a million soldiers, sailors, and airmen now answered to my father's orders. As CINCPAC, my father had command over the war in Vietnam. General Creighton Abrams, then commanding U.S. forces in Vietnam, was his subordinate; as was I, a lieutenant commander, held as a prisoner of war in Hanoi.

II

I heard the old, old men say,
'All that's beautiful drifts away
Like the waters.'

—William Butler Yeats,
"The Old Men Admiring
Themselves in Water"

CHAPTER NINE

Worst Rat

I was not quite two years old when my parents felt it necessary to instill in me a little self-restraint and my instruction in some of the colder realities of life began in earnest. During an otherwise tranquil early childhood, I had quite unexpectedly developed an outsized temper that I expressed in an unusual way. At the smallest provocation, I would go off in a mad frenzy, and then, suddenly, crash to the floor unconscious. Alarmed at this odd behavior and worried that I was suffering from a strange and possibly serious illness, my parents consulted a Navy physician for an explanation. The doctor assured them that the malady was not serious. It was self-induced. When I got angry I held my breath until I blacked out.

The doctor prescribed a treatment that seems a little severe by modern standards of child care. He instructed my parents to fill a bathtub with cold water whenever I commenced a tantrum, and when I appeared to be holding my breath to drop me, fully clothed, into it.

I do not recall at all these traumatic early encounters with the harsh consequences of my misbehavior, buried, as they must be, deep in my subconscious. But my mother assures me that they occurred, and went on for some time until I was finally "cured." Whenever I worked myself into a tiny rage, my mother shouted to my father, "Get the water!" Moments later I would find myself thrashing, wide-eyed and gasping for breath, in a tub of icy-cold water. Eventually, I achieved a satisfactory (if only temporary) control over my emotions. And as a side benefit, the treatment apparently instilled in me an early reverence for the principle of equal justice under the law. After my first few experiences with the dreaded immersion therapy, I would shout, "Get the water! Get the water!" whenever my older sister, Sandy, momentarily lost control of her temper.

My mother often despaired over the quality of our education. When asked today how her children were educated she is apt to respond that we were "raised to be completely ignorant."

The frequent relocations imposed on Navy families were the chief obstacle to a decent education. As soon as I had begun to settle into a school, my father would be reassigned, and I would find myself again a stranger in new surroundings forced to establish myself quickly in another social order. I was often required in a new school to study things I had already learned. Other times, the curriculum assumed knowledge I had not yet acquired.

Many of the base schools I attended were substandard institutions. Sometimes the school building was nothing more than a converted aircraft hangar. The classes mixed children of varying ages. We might have one teacher on Monday and a different one on Tuesday. On other days, we lacked the services of any teacher at all. My first purpose during my brief stay in these schools was to impress upon my classmates that I was not a person to suffer slights lightly. My second purpose was to prove myself as an athlete. When I was disciplined by my teachers, which happened regularly, it was often for fighting.

My parents worried a great deal about our irregular schooling. Once, when we were transferred to Long Beach, California, my father resolved to improve upon the educational circumstances to which we had grown accustomed. He drove to the rectory of a Catholic parish and pleaded with the monsignor to allow us to attend the parish school. He even offered to convert to Catholicism if that was necessary. The good monsignor admitted us without obliging my parents to abandon their church.

My mother's complaint not withstanding, I enjoyed my early education. I enjoyed it for the very quality that caused my parents to despair—its informality. Until I was sent at fifteen to a boarding school, I relied on the members of my family to be my principal instructors. My mother assumed most of this responsibility, and she proved to be an imaginative and amusing educator.

Like wealthy parents who "finish" their children's education with a tour of the European continent, my mother saw our frequent cross-country trips to join my father as an opportunity to supplement our irregular schooling. She was forever routing our journeys through locations that offered a site of historical significance or a notable institute of the arts or sciences.

When we passed through cities we searched for whatever the locals considered their most prominent attraction—art galleries, museums, churches, buildings designed by celebrated architects, natural phenomena, and the homes of historical figures. I recall being greatly impressed with Carlsbad Caverns, the Grand Canyon, the Petrified Forest, the high bluffs and Civil War history of Natchez, Mississippi, and the venerated shrines of American heroes, especially Washington's Mount Vernon and Andrew Jackson's Hermitage. They were all memorable events in my childhood, and I recall them today with gratitude.

We once spent a night in El Paso, Texas, so that my mother could take us across the border to Juárez, Mexico, the next day. She wanted us to see a cathedral that her father had taken her to see when she was a young girl; he had regaled her with stories of its difficult construction, how its enormous wooden beams had to be floated down the Colorado River. We arrived in Juárez to find the city much changed from my mother's recollection of it. She could not locate the cathedral, which she said had dominated the town when she saw it last. We became lost, and when we found ourselves in a rough neighborhood where the men were all dressed in zoot suits, she sensibly called off the search and beat a hasty retreat for the border.

My mother went about these tours with her usual direct, enthusiastic approach to life and her extraordinary self-confidence. The difficulties we encountered en route seldom proved superior to her problem-solving skills. And when her children posed a problem to her progress, we too proved inferior to her resolve.

I earned my reputation as a "hell-raiser"—my mother's term—in high school and at the Naval Academy. But, appropriately, it was in my mother's mobile classroom that I gave the first indication that I was headed in a troubling direction. On an exhausting trip from Washington to Coronado, my mother had become exasperated with Sandy and me. We had been quarreling for hours on end. Reaching back from the front seat to throw a banana at me for making a smart-aleck reply to her most recent rebuke, she accidentally hit Sandy. When I laughed at her for missing her target, my mother grabbed the first object in reach, an empty aluminum thermos, and flung it at me, hitting me on the brow, knocking me temporarily mute, and denting the thermos.

Having now reached the end of her maternal patience, she resolved to hasten our arrival in Coronado. We diverted from our course so that we could stop in College Station, Texas. Upon arriving there, my mother located the dean of students at Texas A&M and appealed to him to help her find a student who was in need of transportation to California and would agree to travel with us and share the driving. We checked into a hotel that evening, and my mother wrote to my father to inform him that for the first time in my life I had been "a real pain in the neck." Apparently she had forgotten by this time my brief period of defiance as a two-year-old, which had ended in complete surrender to parental authority. After the cold-water treatment had subdued my incipient rebelliousness, I possessed for the next ten years a rather meek disposition.

The next morning two students arrived to take my mother up on her offer. As the trip progressed, my mother charmed our new companions. One of them remarked how fortunate we were to have such an attractive and clever mother. The compliment was too much for me, as I was still angry over the previous day's swift and unexpected punishment. Holding up the damaged thermos and pointing to my head, I replied, "Oh yeah, you think she's so great. Look what she did to me." My denunciation prompted gales of laughter from my mother. She laughed about it intermittently for most of the remainder of the trip, as did our new traveling companions. And she still laughs when reminded of the incident today.

I became my mother's son. What I lacked of her charm and grace I made up for by emulating and exaggerating other of her characteristics. She was loquacious, and I was boisterous. Her exuberance became rowdiness in me. She taught me to find so much pleasure in life that misfortune could not rob me of the joy of living. She has an irrepressible spirit that yields to no adversity, and that part of her spirit she shared with us was as fine a gift as any mother ever gave her children. My father, as she will admit if asked, always came first with her. She loved him deeply, and made his life whole, mending as best she could the breaches in his life, the times when doubt and insecurity would cloud his sense of his destiny. Even today, many years after his death, my mother still keeps a card on which, after his passing, she wrote down a list of the things my father had found pleasure in, from his favorite meal to his favorite music, as well as a list of the things he had disliked. But although there was never any doubt about the primacy my father enjoyed in my mother's affections, her heart has always been large enough to encompass her children with as much love and care as any mother's child has ever enjoyed.

When I was young, similarities between my mother and me were more apparent than were those between my father and me. My father and I probably seemed in many respects, at least superficial ones, very different people. My keen-eyed brother in his observations on our family's domestic life often remarked on our father's and my contrasting dispositions in those long-ago days. We were, he thought, mirror opposites. My father was taciturn, while I was noisy. My father was shy, while I "loved working a crowd." My father "was often quiet at the dinner table, while the rest of us raised hell, argued, until Dad would intervene—always on my mother's behalf. John was either fiercely immersed in the squabble or the root cause of it."

My father was a more learned man than his grades at the Naval

Academy indicated. He taught physics at the Academy for two years and was regarded as an able instructor. He had many intellectual interests, but he especially loved history and English literature. An "outstanding command of the English language," he often remarked, "will stand you in good stead as time moves on." He was an avid reader of Toynbee and Spengler. He could recite great lengths of poetry from memory. He loved Edgar Allan Poe, Kipling, Dante, Tennyson, and Lewis Carroll. But his favorite poem was Oscar Wilde's ode to the British Empire, "Ave Imperatrix," which he quoted from at length in his lectures on seapower:

> The fleet-foot Marri scout, who comes
> To tell how he hath heard afar
> The measured roll of English drums
> Beat at the gates of Kandahar.

He was a great admirer of the British Empire, crediting it with keeping "a relative measure of peace" in the world for "someplace in the neighborhood of two centuries."

He read and reread the biographies of historical figures whose lives, he felt, would always be an inspiration to others. "I heard some man make a statement one time not so long ago," he once recalled of a popular futurist, "that reading the lives of great men was somewhat a waste of time because this was past history. Well, this is stupid on the face of it, because one of the real factors of life is what you learn from reading about the lives of great men, because there are certain fundamentals of human relationships that never change."

Alfred Thayer Mahan, the great naval historian, author of the seminal work on the importance of naval expansion, The Influence of Sea Power upon History, was my father's inspiration and his passion. He quoted from Mahan's book often and at length, not only in his seapower lectures but to almost anyone he thought could profit from Mahan's wisdom. He talked about Mahan to me quite often, during his occasional attempts to help steer me toward a successful naval career.

My paternal grandmother was a well-educated woman of gifted intellect and refined manner. She had been an instructor of Latin and Greek at the University of Mississippi, where she taught my grandfather. Bookish and eight years his senior, she won the devotion of the much coarser but widely read naval officer. Throughout their union, they indulged together their shared love of literature, reading aloud to each other whenever time allowed. That my father was well versed in the classics is undoubtedly a tribute to both his parents: his mother, the scholarly taskmaster; his father, the rough adventurer who in glamour resembled the fictional heroes who had enlivened the provincial world of his Mississippi childhood. Together they instilled in my father their love of literature and learning, encouraged his imagination, gave him responsibilities early in life, and fortified him with their values. As a schoolboy, he got in trouble once for telling his classmates a tall tale about having seen a bear on the way to school. His mother excused the lapse, remarking, "All little boys must have an imagination. Don't worry, he'll know about honesty and the truth."

It was while I was in my grandmother's care that I began to develop my own interest in literature. I spent the summer of 1946 with my widowed grandmother and her daughter, my Aunt Katherine, at their house in Coronado. My grandmother was a composed, straightlaced woman who kept a formal house. I still recall quite vividly their maid summoning me to tea and supper every day, at precisely four and seven, by ringing a bell. If I lingered too long at whatever activity I was preoccupied with and arrived a minute or two past the appointed hour, my grandmother would dismiss me very politely from her presence. She would observe that she had looked forward to dining with me, but as I had failed to arrive promptly, she would have to forgo the pleasure of my company until the next meal. She never yielded to any of the elaborate excuses I devised to coax her into allowing an exception to her daily routine.

The room I occupied in my grandmother's house was fur-

nished with my father's boyhood belongings. It contained a substantial collection of the authors he had favored as a boy. I spent
most of the summer reading one volume after another. Among
the authors who most impressed me in that summer of unsuper-
vised study were Mark Twain, Robert Louis Stevenson, James
Fenimore Cooper, Edgar Rice Burroughs, and Booth Tarkington.
I was also taken with the tales of King Arthur's court. These
works instilled in me a lifelong love of reading. And, with their
straightforward moral lessons, they reinforced my sense of right
and wrong and impressed upon me the virtue of treating people
fairly.

Among the Stevenson volumes was a collection of his poetry.
It included the poem he wrote for his own epitaph, "Requiem."

> Under the wide and starry sky
> Dig the grave and let me lie:
> Glad did I live and gladly die,
> And I laid me down with a will.
> This be the verse you grave for me:
> Here he lies where he longed to be;
> Home is the sailor home from the sea,
> And the hunter home from the hill.

In his brief life, Stevenson had been quite an adventurer, wandering the continent of Europe, and later the Americas and the South
Pacific. He had lived in the capitals of Europe, in the Adirondacks
of upstate New York, and in Monterey, California. He spent the
last years of his life in a house he had built in Western Samoa, a
location as remote from the cold austerity of his native Scotland
as could be imagined. He is buried there on a low hill overlooking the Pacific.

Stevenson is recalled in biographies as a restless, striving man.
Crediting a tropical grave as the place "he longed to be" struck me
as a brave declaration of self-determination. I thought the poem
the perfect motto for all who lived a life according to their own
lights, and a moving tribute to the lives of strong-willed, valorous

men like my grandfather and father. I read it as an exhortation to "be your own man." It influenced my childhood aspiration to find adventures, pursue each one avidly, and, when it had run its course, find another.

Like my father and grandfather, I lacked as a boy the physical size to appear imposing on first acquaintance. Together with the challenges of my transient childhood, my small stature motivated me to prove quickly to new schoolmates that I could stand up for myself. The quickest way to do so was to fight the first kid who provoked me.

Whether I won or lost those fights wasn't as important as establishing myself as someone who could adapt to the challenges of a new environment without betraying apprehension. I foolishly believed that fighting, as well as challenging school authorities and ignoring school regulations, was indispensable to my self-esteem and helped me to form new friendships.

The repeated farewells to friends rank among the saddest regrets of a childhood constantly disrupted by the demands of my father's career. I would arrive at a new school, go to considerable lengths to make new friends, and, shortly thereafter, be transplanted to a new town to begin the process all over again. Seldom if ever did I see again the friends I left behind. If you have never known any other life, these experiences seem a natural part of existence. You come to expect friendships to last but a short time. I believe this breeds in a child a desire to make the most of friendships while they last. The relationships make up with intensity what they lack in length. That's one of the benefits of an itinerant childhood.

On the other hand, you never lose the expectation that friendships come and go and should not be expected to do otherwise. That fatalistic expectation is reinforced later in life when war imposes a sad finality on relationships grown extremely close under difficult conditions. Even when you are an adult, when passing time and changing circumstances separate you from old friends, their absence seems unremarkable and in accord with the normal course of things.

This is not to say that I value my friends less than other people value theirs. On the contrary, I have made friends with many people over the years, and whether I see them or not, whether they are still living or not, their friendship honored me, and honors me still. Many of my friendships exist only in memory. But they are memories I cherish for the lessons they taught me and the values they imparted to me, gifts that proved invaluable in later years.

At each new school I arrived eager to make, by means of my insolent attitude, new friends to compensate for the loss of others. At each new school I grew more determined to assert my crude individualism. At each new school I became a more unrepentant pain in the neck.

These are the attitudes I brought to Episcopal High School in Alexandria, Virginia, when I enrolled there, Class of '54. My parents had resolved to put an end to our haphazard education and arranged for my sister, my brother, and me to attend private boarding schools. I was sent to Episcopal to prepare for my unavoidable appointment to the United States Naval Academy three years later.

* * *

I liked EHS more than I liked my previous schools. No doubt my memory of it has softened over time as it became mixed with nostalgia for the pleasurable vanities of youth—vanities that the Naval Academy worked hard to suppress in its resolve to make a man of me. I did not at first acquaintance recognize Episcopal and its antique traditions as hospitable. Unlike my classmates, I arrived without any allegiance to those traditions, having had no share of them in my roving childhood. The traditions in which I was raised were peculiar to military families, and the dimensions of my small Navy world had mapped the limits of experience for most of my earliest friends.

When I entered Episcopal I encountered another small world, but one so unfamiliar to me that I thought it exotic. The Episcopal High School Class of 1954 was all male and all white.

But more than the racial bigotry and gender segregation of the times distinguished the class from the rest of our generation. Most of the students came from families who lived south of the Mason-Dixon line and east of the Mississippi River, and their fathers, grandfathers, and great-grandfathers had preceded them at the school. Almost all were sons of wealthy men. None but me were sons of professional officers in the armed services.

The Navy has, of course, its own aristocracy, but not one that seemed to me as exclusive, mannered, and fixed as the aristocracy from which EHS drew its ranks. Most of my classmates were so settled in their society that they had an air of serenity uncommon in the young. They were not snobs. But they had envisaged the whole of their futures before they came to EHS, and what they had foreseen was so pleasant an existence that the certainty of it made them very self-assured young men.

After graduation, about half of my class would enroll in the University of Virginia, an arcadia of genteel Southern learning. The other half would venture north to one or another Ivy League school where wealthy children from North and South mixed and the friction of differing regional cultures was eased by their common appreciation for refined living. When they had completed their education, many of my classmates returned to their families and settled into careers in their fathers' businesses, law firms, and medical practices.

I, too, had a clear sense of how my life would unfold after I left Episcopal. I, too, was destined to join my father's business. But I knew my life would diverge from those of my classmates as sharply as my childhood had differed from theirs. I was on leave from the Navy while I attended high school. And the Navy expected me to return when I graduated.

I cannot recall any other student at EHS who expected to enter military service. Some would be drafted into the Army. I am sure they accepted that responsibility without complaint, and served honorably. But no one in the Class of '54 except me anticipated a career in the armed forces.

The most pervasive military influence at the school was the

heroic legends taken from the annals of Civil War history. More precisely, they were the stories of Confederate heroes. There is a memorial at the school that commemorates those students who were among the fallen in the Civil War. It's a long list. You would be hard-pressed to find among those honored dead the name of anyone who gave his last full measure of devotion to the Union. More Episcopal graduates died in the Civil War than in any subsequent war in our nation's history.

EHS gave me a sense of what life could be like were I somehow to elude a Navy career. On a school holiday, some friends and I visited Princeton University. Long afterward, I would daydream about enrolling at Princeton, joining one of its stately eating clubs, and sharing in the romance of a place that seemed to me to offer equal parts of scholastic excellence and gracious leisure. But I was never so enthralled by the attraction of such a life that I deluded myself into sincerely believing it would be mine. I was bound for the Naval Academy, and while I seldom discussed with my high school friends the fate that awaited me, I knew that were we ever to meet again, they would find me in uniform.

My father never ordered me to attend the Naval Academy. Although I am sure we must have talked about it from time to time, I cannot recall the conversations. There are no scenes in my memory of sitting in my father's study listening to him expound on the virtues of an Academy education, or explain the reasons why I must follow him to Annapolis as he had followed his father. Neither do I recall any arguments with my parents about my wanting to consider an alternative future. I remember simply recognizing my eventual enrollment at the Academy as an immutable fact of life, and accepting it without comment.

I remember my parents frequently commenting on it to their friends. "He's going to the Naval Academy," they would casually remark, not with the evident satisfaction one derives from a welcome discovery of a child's potential, but as if they were discussing an inheritance that had been marked for my eventual possession. It was as if they were saying, "Someday this house will be Johnny's"—which, in a way, was what they meant.

My father and grandfather believed they had discovered the perfect life for a man. To them, the Navy was the most accommodating profession for good men who craved adventure. They never imagined possessing a greater treasure than a life at sea, and they regarded it as a legacy they were proud to bestow on their descendants, who, they assumed, would be appropriately grateful.

EHS offered me more than a glimpse at a different culture. It shared certain aspects of service academies. Life there was regimented. Jackets and ties were worn at all times. Students attended chapel every morning. On Sundays, we held morning services at the church on Seminary Hill and evening services at the chapel. The academics were superb and serious. But athletics were accorded equal importance in our education. Classes were held in the morning, including Saturday morning. We broke for lunch at twelve-thirty. The afternoons were devoted to athletic training.

Demerits were handed out for every infraction, large and small, of school regulations, and I piled them up. I was chronically late for class. I kept my room in a near permanent state of disorder and filth. I mocked the dress code by wearing a ratty old jacket and tie with a pair of infrequently laundered Levi's. And I despised and resisted the caste system that first-year students were obliged to endure with good humor.

EHS was not a military academy, but it borrowed a few traditions from Southern service academies. Like the Virginia Military Institute and the Citadel, Episcopal imposed on first-year students the designation "rats." Rats were expected to submit to a comparatively mild form of hazing. Mild or not, I resented the hell out of it. And my resentment, along with my affected disregard for rules and school authorities, soon earned me the distinction of "worst rat."

My hazing increased to correspond to the disrespect with which I treated school customs, and my ever-lengthening catalog of demerits was addressed with ever-longer punishments. But neither my offenses nor their consequences were so serious that they caused a permanent estrangement to develop between me and the staid society that I imposed upon.

My initial entry into EHS society was rough. I was one of the smaller boys in my class, a fact that upperclassmen, annoyed by my obdurate refusal to show a rat's humility, took to be further evidence of arrogance on my part, or arrogance that was all the more insufferable to them because neither social connections nor physical stature justified it. Despite my Confederate ancestors and my family's Southern origins, my heritage was perceived as rootless and not particularly distinguished—a perception confirmed by my conspicuous lack of a Southern accent.

These circumstances might have made for a lonely three years, but I managed to make friends and find a place for myself without pretending to share in the culture from which EHS students were drawn. I was good at sports, and athletics were my passage through my difficult first weeks at the school. I played football in the fall. I wrestled in the winter. I played tennis in the spring. I wasn't an exceptional athlete, but I was good enough to earn the respect of my teammates and coaches.

Eventually, I would use my reputation both as a credible athlete and as a troublemaker to earn a modest distinction as a leader of sorts at Episcopal—a leader of a few troublemakers, but a leader nonetheless. I was part of a small cadre of students who satisfied our juvenile sense of adventure by frequently sneaking off-campus at night to catch a bus for downtown Washington, and the bars and burlesque houses on 9th Street.

Our exploits there were tame compared to my more reckless conduct at the Naval Academy. But because we exaggerated them for the benefit of our rule-abiding classmates we were granted some prestige for our daring, and for the welcome fallacy that our excursions were somehow leading us to romantic opportunities that were only imagined in our all-male society.

The school hosted two dances a year, and for most students these were the only opportunities during the school year to enjoy the company of girls. To give the impression that you were regularly pursuing liaisons outside the school's walls with women you were unlikely to meet at a school dance was a sure route to notoriety on campus. That the impression was, for the most part, contrived did not overly concern us. We deluded ourselves into believing the most salacious rumors about our behavior.

I had good friends at Episcopal. Memory often accords our high school years the distinction of being among the happiest, most relaxed of our lives. I remember Episcopal in that light, and the friendships I formed there make up the better parts of my remembrance. But there was one unexpected friendship that enriched my life at EHS beyond measure.

Were William B. Ravenel the only person I remember from high school, I would credit those days as among the best of my life. His influence over my life, while perhaps not apparent to most who have observed its progress, was more important and more benevolent than that of any other person save members of my family.

Mr. Ravenel headed the English department at EHS, and he coached the junior varsity football team, on which I played. He had been a star running back at Davidson College and had a master's degree in English from Duke University. Stocky and compact, he still had the appearance and manner of an athlete but without the callowness that often marks men who live in the shadow of their long-ago successes on the playing field.

Like most men of his generation, Mr. Ravenel had known far greater danger than that posed by a tough defensive line. He had served in Patton's tank corps during the Third Army's aggressive advance across Europe and had survived its hard encounters with Hitler's panzer divisions. He was a lieutenant colonel in the Army Reserve, the only master at the school who still served in the military.

With his craggy face and athlete's build, he was a rugged-looking man. He seemed to his students to be as wise and capable as any man could expect to be. He loved English literature, and he taught us to love it as well. He had a way of communicating with his students that was uniquely effective and personal. He made us appreciate how profound were the emotions that animated the characters of Shakespeare's tragedies. Macbeth and Hamlet, in his care, were as compelling and revealing to boys as they are to the most learned and insightful scholar. He wasn't Mr. Chips, but he was as close to that ideal teacher as anyone is ever likely to find. No other master had half as much of our respect and affection. My class dedicated our senior yearbook to him. He was, simply, the best man at the school; one of the best men I have ever known.

Demerits required the offender to march ceaselessly around the long circle drive in the front of the school or to tend the yard of a master's house. It was my good fortune to have received for my many transgressions assignment to work in Mr. Ravenel's yard. Perhaps the school authorities knew they were doing me a favor—knew that Mr. Ravenel was best able to repair the all too evident flaws in my character.

I don't know if it was their benevolence or providence that brought me to his attention. Neither do I understand why it was that Mr. Ravenel took such an interest in me, seeing in me something that few others did. But that he did take an interest in me was apparent to all. And as he personified the ideal of every student, Mr. Ravenel's regard for me signaled my classmates that I had some merit despite the fact that they and I had to strain to see it.

I discussed all manner of subjects with him, from sports to the stories of Somerset Maugham, from his combat experiences to my future. He was one of the few people at school to whom I confided that I was bound for the Academy and a Navy career, and to whom I confessed my reservations about my destiny.

In the fall of my senior year, a member of the junior varsity football team had broken training and been found out. I cannot recall the exact nature of the offense, but it was serious enough to merit his expulsion from the team. Mr. Ravenel called a team meeting, and most of the players argued that the accused be dropped from the team. I stood and offered the only argument for a less severe punishment.

The student in question had, in fact, broken training. But unlike the rest of us, he had chosen at the start of the year not to sign a pledge promising to abide by the training rules faithfully.

Had he signed the pledge, he would have been expelled from school, because violating the pledge constituted an honor offense. Had he signed it, I wouldn't have defended him. But he had not. Moreover, he had not been caught breaking training, but had confessed the offense and expressed his remorse freely, without fear of discovery. I thought his behavior was no less honorable than that of a student who signed the pledge and adhered to its provisions.

So did Mr. Ravenel. But he kept his own counsel for most of our discussion, preferring, as was his way, to let his boys reason the thing out for ourselves.

At the start, most of my teammates wanted to hang the guy. But I argued that he had made a mistake that he sincerely regretted, and, uncoerced, had admitted the infraction. His behavior warranted no further disciplinary action. As I talked, I noticed Mr. Ravenel nodding his head. When some of the other guys started to come around to my point of view, Mr. Ravenel closed the discussion by voicing support for my judgment. The team then voted to drop the matter.

After the meeting broke up, Mr. Ravenel approached me and shook my hand. With relief evident in his voice, he told me we had done the right thing, and thanked me for my efforts. He allowed that before the meeting he had been anxious about its outcome. He had hoped the matter would be resolved as it had been, but was uncertain it would. Still, he had not wanted to be the one who argued for exoneration; he wanted the decision to be ours and not his. He said he was proud of me.

I have never forgotten the confidence his praise gave me. Nor have I ever forgotten the man who praised me. Many years later, when I came home from Vietnam, Mr. Ravenel was the only person outside of my family whom I wanted to see. I felt he was someone to whom I could explain what had happened to me, and who would understand. That is a high tribute to Mr. Ravenel. For I have never met a prisoner of war who felt he could explain the experience to anyone who had not shared it.

I regret that I was never able to pay him that tribute. Mr.

Ravenel had died of a heart attack two years before my release. He lived for only fifty-three years. His early death was a great loss to his family, friends, and students, and to everyone who had been blessed with his company; a loss I found difficult to accept.

I was often accused of being an indifferent student, and given some of my grades, I can appreciate the charity in that remark. But I was not so much indifferent as selective. I liked English and history, and I usually did well in those classes. I was less interested and less successful in math and science. My grades at Episcopal were divided along those lines. Overall, my academic record there could be fairly described as undistinguished, but acceptable. I graduated a member in adequate if not good standing of the Class of 1954. One of my closest friends at the school, Rives Richey, said later, "If they'd rated everybody in the class for likely to succeed, I guarantee you he'd have been in the bottom ten, without any question."

A few months prior to graduation, I had taken the Naval Academy entrance exams. I had applied myself, after having been enrolled by my father in a course at an Academy preparatory school, and did surprisingly well, even on the math exam. At graduation there was no longer even the slightest doubt that I would follow my father and grandfather to Annapolis. And on June 28, after a short vacation with some friends at Virginia Beach, my father drove me to the Academy to begin my plebe summer.

In those days an officer escorting his son to the Naval Academy was thought to be an event charged with symbolic importance, a solemn rite of passage. Yet I don't remember it so. I had so long expected the day, so often envisioned the drive, that the actual event seemed more familiar than remarkable. I remember being nervous, and my father offering me typical words of encouragement. But nothing occurred in that one-hour trip that affected my long-held paradoxical image of the Academy, a place I belonged at but dreaded.

CHAPTER TEN

Plebe

To my surprise, I liked it at first. I liked almost every minute of it until that time when my education at the Naval Academy began in earnest. I liked it until plebe summer concluded with the return of the upperclassmen from their vacations, eager to commence their campaign to humiliate, degrade, and make miserable me and every other plebe they encountered.

During plebe summer, Academy life had been sort of a highly organized camp: sports, pleasant company, and, compared to what awaited us after Labor Day, rather benign leadership from the few upperclassmen and junior officers who supervised us. I made friends easily. I boxed, wrestled, ran the obstacle course, and marched in formation. I did well enough in all of these activities that I briefly showed an enthusiasm for the place that my superiors mistook for an indication that I was an emerging class leader. They made me a company commander that summer. It was one of the very few occasions when I distinguished myself in a positive way at the Academy.

Coming out of plebe summer, I had, in Academy parlance, good grease, which meant I showed a natural aptitude for the service and possessed embryonic leadership qualities. The grease would last about a week past summer's end. For a short time in my last year at the Academy, I would again possess good grease. But that was to be an anomaly in a long history of transgressions and improprieties.

The Academy that welcomed the Class of '58 was essentially

unchanged from the days of my father's and grandfather's classes. The Academy prided itself on the continuity of its traditions,
linking tomorrow's officers with the heroes of an honored past.
It wasn't until the 1970s that the Academy, at the prodding of
the influential Admiral Rickover, agreed to substantive changes
in its core curriculum and even some of its more venerable customs.

When I arrived there, the Reina Mercedes, where my father
had been obliged to reside his last year, was still visible in the
Yard. The curriculum was the same. There were no electives.
Everyone took the same courses, which included a good number
of rather outdated offerings such as a stupefyingly dull class in
Navy boilers, the purpose of which was lost on midshipmen living in the nuclear age.

Every plebe was issued a copy of *Reef Points*, a book of Navy
legends and maxims that plebes were expected to quickly memorize. The first passage I was expected to commit to memory, as it
had been expected of my father and grandfather, was John Paul
Jones's "Qualifications of the Naval Officer":

It is by no means enough that an officer of the Navy should
be a capable mariner. He must be that, of course, but also a
great deal more. He should be as well a gentleman of liberal education, refined manners, punctilious courtesy, and the
nicest sense of personal honor.

He should be the soul of tact, patience, justice, firmness
and charity. No meritorious act of a subordinate should
escape his attention or be left to pass without its reward,
even if the reward is only a word of approval. Conversely,
he should not be blind to a single fault in any subordinate,
though at the same time, he should be quick and unfailing
to distinguish error from malice, thoughtlessness from
incompetency, and well meant shortcoming from heedless
or stupid blunder.

In one word, every commander should keep constantly before

him the great truth, that to be well obeyed, he must be perfectly esteemed.

* * *

In this well-ordered, timeless world, with its lofty aspirations and grim determination to make leaders and gentlemen of schoolboys, plebes who possessed minor eccentricities might be tolerated somewhat, but arrogant nonconformists encountered open hostility. Recognized as belonging in the latter category, I soon found myself in conflict with the Academy's authorities and traditions. Instead of beginning a crash course in self-improvement so that I could find a respectable place in the ranks, I reverted to form and embarked on a four-year course of insubordination and rebellion.

Once the second and first classes returned, the unexpected happiness I had experienced in my first weeks at Annapolis rapidly disappeared in the strain of surviving the organized torment that is plebe year. From that moment on, I hated the place, and, in fairness, the place wasn't all that fond of me, either.

Now, more than forty years after my graduation from the Naval Academy, I understand the premise that supported the harsh treatment of plebes. I may have even grasped it at the time I experienced it, but was simply reluctant to accept its consequences personally. Service academies are not just colleges with a uniform dress code. Their purpose is to prepare you for one profession alone, and that profession's ultimate aspiration is a combat command. The Academy experience is intended to determine whether you are fit for such work, and if you are, to mold your natural ability into the attributes of a capable officer. If you aren't, the Academy wants to discover your inaptitude as quickly as possible. The period of discovery is your plebe year, when you are subjected to as much stress as the law and a civilized society will allow. The agents of the Academy's will are the upperclassmen, most of whom relish the assignment.

One-quarter of the plebes who entered the Academy with me had decided or were told to find another line of work by the time our class graduated. Most of them left during our plebe year, unable to cope with the pressures, having failed to lose their individuality in the corporate identity. Upperclassmen had driven them out.

Of course, nothing in peacetime can replicate the dire experiences of war. But the Academy gives it a hell of a try. The workload imposed on you by instructors is daunting but by itself is probably not enough to break all but the least determined plebe. It is the physical and mental hazing by upperclassmen that makes the strain of plebe year so excruciating. It seems mindless and unrelenting.

We were expected to brace up, sit or stand at rigid attention with our chins tucked into our neck, whenever upperclassmen came into view. Our physical appearance was expected to conform to a code with rules so numerous, esoteric, and pointless that I thought them absurd. We were commanded to perform dozens of menial tasks a day, each one intended to be more demeaning than the last, and made all the more so by the heap of verbal abuse that would accompany it. We were ordered to supply encyclopedias of obscure information to any silly son of a bitch who asked a question. When we did not know an answer, which, of course, our interrogators hoped would be the case, we were made to suffer some further humiliation as punishment for our ignorance.

As bad as my plebe year seemed, it was a considerably more civilized experience than it had been for my grandfather and father. My father, who was two years younger and much smaller than I when he entered the Academy, had been hazed cruelly and suffered much worse treatment than that which awaited me twenty-seven years later. But he accepted his trial with better humor and more courage than would I. Even as a boy, my father exhibited a fierce resolve to prove himself the equal of any man.

Rear Admiral Kemp Tolley, who was an upperclassman at the Academy when my father was a plebe, described the merciless treatment accorded my father by Tolley's roommate. He explained the "preferred method" used by "sadistically inclined" midshipmen to punish plebes—a broom with its bristles cut to just below its stitching. "A man pulled that thing back as hard as he could, like a baseball bat, and whacked you with it when you were bent over. The first time it hit you, you just couldn't believe that a broom could do that. It jolted your backside right through the top of your head."

Kemp had a roommate, "one of these sadists," who delighted in using the broom on my father whenever my father was unable to recite one or another of the "utterly useless things" a plebe was supposed to have memorized, things like the day's lunch menu or the names of various British battleships. As pictured in Kemp's account, my father was a pathetic physical specimen, a "little runt" who "looked like a wretched little animal that had just got out of the water with its fur still wet." But he compensated for his lack of stature with extraordinary courage. "In order to protect himself," Kemp said, "he was tougher than hell.

"[O]ld Jack would bend over, and my roommate would hit him—three or four or five times. Then he would say, 'Do you want another one? Are you going to learn it the next time?'

"And Jack would say, 'Hit me again, sir. I can take it.' And he would tell him that until my roommate would give up, even though tears were coming out of his eyes. That was the kind of guy he was. Jack McCain was not, in my personal opinion, one of the brightest naval officers that ever lived, but he certainly was one of the guttiest."

The practices of plebe year described in Admiral Tolley's account of my father's ordeal exceed the severity of my experience, but I despised my upperclass tormentors nonetheless. And although I lacked my father's courage, I tried in my own way not to yield my dignity to their abuse.

It was a trying time. That was the point, of course. Though I may now understand the purpose of that punishing year, even grant the necessity of learning to tolerate the barely tolerable, I nevertheless hated every minute of it. And I resented everyone who inflicted it on me. I dislike even the memory of it. But, like most graduates of the Academy, my hate for the experience does not constitute regret. It rests in memory, paradoxically, with my appreciation, gratitude really, for the privilege of surviving it, and for the honor of that accomplishment.

At moments of great stress, your senses are at their most acute; your mind works at a greatly accelerated pace. That's the purpose, I take it, of plebe year—not simply to test your endurance, but to show that you can function exceptionally well, as a leader must function, in concentrated misery. I began to glimpse this truth about midway through my plebe year when added to contempt for imperious upperclassmen was my burgeoning pride in not succumbing to their design to see me bilge out.

I resisted not by refusing the hazing but by letting my resentment show, and by failing to conform fully to the convention of a squared-away midshipman. I tried to balance my insolence on just the other side of intolerable, but I worked hard to expose a trace of my resistance. I wanted the lords of the first and second class to know my compliance was grudging and in no way implied my respect for them. I did not accept that they were entitled to my deference, as Academy custom held, for the minor accomplishment of having lived for a year or two longer than I had. Nor did I accept that the abuse they had suffered in their plebe year now gave them the moral authority to abuse me. The Academy granted them that authority, and I wanted to remain at the Academy. I did not want to break. So I suffered their tyranny to the extent necessary to avoid bilging out. But no more than that.

A civilian observer might have judged my appearance to be as neat as that of any other midshipman, but by the exacting standards of the Academy I was a slob. My roommates and I kept our personal quarters in less than acceptable order. My ritual obedience to an upperclassman's commands was perfunctory, or, at least, I hoped there was something in my manner that gave the impression that I lacked proper enthusiasm for the task. These are small rebellions, to be sure. But they were noted, and I was pleased that they were.

One second classman in particular tested my self-control, and I had a hard time suppressing the urge to respond to his assaults on my dignity in a way that would have hastened my departure from the Academy.

Henry Witt (false name) was the son of a chief petty officer. I was a captain's son. Witt never tired of reminding me that our respective stations at the Academy reversed the order of our fathers' relationship in the Navy. "My father is a chief, and yours is a captain. Isn't that strange, McCain," he observed as I discharged the commission he had given me at the start of the year. He had instructed me to enter his room every morning at five-thirty, close the window he left open at night, turn up his radiator, and perform various other small tasks to make comfortable the advent of his day.

There was in Witt's edgy hostility resentment not evident in the affected disdain upperclassmen typically held for plebes. He had a bitterness about him that apparently stemmed from an imagined injustice. Perhaps he admired his father very much, and resented the officers whom his father was obliged to obey, thinking them lesser men, and perceiving in the exercise of their authority a self-importance that demeaned his father's dignity. Maybe he had felt ill at ease his plebe year among so many officers' sons, and his insecurity had embittered him. Or he might have just been a jerk who enjoyed humiliating people.

I never learned what experience lay at the heart of Witt's contempt for me, but whatever it was, I hated its expression like hell, because I believed it implied an assumption that my grandfather and father were the kind of shallow officers who let rank determine their regard for sailors. They were not that kind of officer. They took great care with their men. They often put more faith in the judgment of their chiefs than in that of their fellow officers. They were fair judges of character, good commanders who measured their respect for a man according to his merit and not his station. And had they ever seen me locate my self-regard in class distinctions, they would have quickly expressed their disappointment in me.

Witt did not know my father or grandfather, and he should not have assumed anything about their character. Nor, for that matter, should he have assumed anything about mine. Also implicit in his scorn was an assumption that he had merited his appointment to the Academy, while I was merely the Navy's version of a fraternity legacy. Had my father and grandfather been accountants, it is unlikely I would have sought appointment to the Academy. But it was their example, and my father's expectation, that led me there, not their influence in the Navy. I had passed the same exams as Witt had.

I disliked him intensely, as did my friends. "Shitty Witty the Middy," we called him, and behind his back we ridiculed his pretensions, which was, he probably assumed, exactly how we would have reacted had he treated us decently.

The following year, Witt's last at the Academy, my friends and I, still resentful of his mistreatment of us during plebe year, seized opportunities to avenge our injured pride. The reprisals amounted to nothing serious, small inconveniences really. But we felt they balanced the book with Witt, and recovered whatever degree of our self-respect had been a casualty in the previous year's encounters with him.

After graduation, the second most anticipated event of a midshipman's last year at the Academy was the first class's training cruise. In June, eager midshipmen would embark, sometimes in barely seaworthy ships, for a six-week cruise to exotic ports. During the cruise, it was presumed, they would learn the essentials of life at sea, though often they only acquired a taste for the excesses of leave in foreign ports.

Every midshipman was assigned a cruise box to stow his gear in during the summer cruise. At graduation, the box was sent to his first duty station. My friends and I got hold of Witt's cruise box and changed the address to a fraternity at an Ivy League school, where it arrived some days later, never to be recovered by its puzzled owner.

It's hard to credit our trivial revenge on Witt as anything more than the sort of puerile mischief that kids often aggrandize as acts of justice. We took the pranks more seriously than their effects warranted, just as I accorded far more gravity to Witt's assaults on my dignity than they warranted. Had I really possessed the sturdy sense of honor I prided myself on, I would have suffered his harassment with equanimity.

I made this observation only a few years after my first encounter with Witt, when I learned he had been killed. He was serving as a flight instructor at a naval air station in the South and had flown his T-28 to the town where his father had retired from the Navy. As he flew in front of his parents' house and unwisely attempted a dangerous maneuver, he lost control of his plane and crashed while his parents watched.

Considering all the adversity that a human being confronts in a lifetime, what had passed between Witt and me was nothing. I was embarrassed that I had taken his abuse so seriously. My animosity dissolved into regret after I learned of his death. I assumed his death had been caused by an impulse to impress his father. It was an impulse a great many other midshipmen and I understood.

CHAPTER ELEVEN

Low Grease

Although my friends and I seethed at the treatment we received from upperclassmen, our main nemesis was our company officer, Captain Ben Hart (false name), a red-faced, muscular, bullnecked Marine who had played on the Academy football team some years earlier. His father was a Marine colonel, and Captain Hart had been raised to revere the protocols of command.

He was probably in his late twenties when we knew him, although he seemed much older to us. He was tightly wound, the kind of guy who never appeared relaxed. I don't think he possessed even an anemic sense of humor. It was hard to imagine him out of uniform. He was a stickler for rules and regulations and exhibited the overeagerness of a junior officer trying too hard to allay his own insecurities. Every day when his wife dropped him off at work, he bade her goodbye with a crisp salute while standing at attention.

Hart wasn't highly regarded by the other officers at the Academy, but he was fiercely determined to command respect from his subordinates. He intended to bring any miscreant in his company quickly to heel. I was one of the miscreants he had in mind.

A group of midshipmen who shared a common conceit that we were rebels against the established order had formed a small club and anointed ourselves the Bad Bunch. My roommates Frank Gamboa, Jack Dittrick, and I were the chief instigators of the group's mischief, but membership often included a few conspicuously squared-away midshipmen. Chuck Larson, one of my best friends at the Academy, was a member who joined in many of our misadventures. In the fall semester of our last year, he was selected brigade commander, the top leadership post for midshipmen, and president of our class. He went on to a spectacularly successful career in the Navy, wearing four stars as Commander in Chief, Pacific (my father's last command), and as Superintendent of the Naval Academy.

Our exploits were well known to most midshipmen, as well as to Academy authorities. We were hardly as daring as we regarded ourselves, but we managed to defy most of the rules without committing any breach of the honor code. We were in search of a good time, which led us over the Academy walls on many an evening.

Nothing serious ever occurred in our nightly revels outside the Yard. Mainly we drank a lot of beer, occasionally we got in fights, and once in a while we found girls willing to give us the time of day. However, most of our activities were proscribed by the Academy, and the fact that we were never caught in the act only intensified the anger of our superiors. It drove Captain Hart crazy.

Failing to apprehend us in the commission of a serious offense, but aware of the notoriety we enjoyed in our class, Captain Hart scrupulously called us to account for smaller infractions of Academy regulations and punished us more severely than required. By so doing, he hoped to prove to the rest of our company that we had not escaped justice for our more egregious threats to the brigade's good order and discipline. I spent the bulk of my free time being made an example of, marching many miles of extra duty for poor grades, tardiness, messy quarters, slovenly appearance, sarcasm, and multiple other violations of Academy standards.

My reputation as a rowdy and impetuous young man was not, I am embarrassed to confess, confined to Academy circles. Many upstanding residents of lovely Annapolis, witnesses to some of our more extravagant acts of insubordination, disapproved of me as thoroughly as did many Academy officials. Neither did I often find more appreciative audiences on the road.

During my second year at the Academy, I met and began dating a girl from a Main Line suburb of Philadelphia. The following summer, she called me at my parents' house on Capitol Hill, where I was spending my leave, and invited me to visit her family for a few days. I instantly accepted the invitation, grateful for a little relief from what had been a pretty monotonous leave.

On the agreed-upon day, I bade good-bye to my parents for the weekend and departed Washington's Union Station on the train to Philadelphia. Some hours later, I arrived at Philadelphia's 30th Street Station, where I was supposed to catch the next commuter train for her town. I had a few minutes to kill before my train left, so I decided to have a quick beer in the station's bar.

As I settled on a bar stool, dressed in my white midshipman's uniform, I drew the attention of several friendly, inebriated commuters, who graciously offered to buy me a beer. I welcomed the offer and their company. We chatted amiably as I, eager to be on my way, quickly drained my glass. Not wishing to appear discourteous, however, I cheerfully consented when they pressed me to accept another drink, and several others after that.

I missed the first train, and then two others, before I politely refused my new friends' entreaties to continue drinking and made my way unsteadily through the station to catch the last train of the evening that would carry me to my girlfriend's hometown. After arriving there, I hailed a cab, and finally I arrived, several hours behind schedule, at my destination.

As I ascended the long staircase that led to the front door of her house I was aware that I was probably not in ideal condition to be introduced for the first time to her family. Nevertheless, I believed I could manage the task without betraying the extent of my insobriety.

At the top of the stairs, I noticed that the front door was open. Knocking on the screen door, I was beckoned inside as my girlfriend and her mother and father rose from their chairs to greet me. When I reached for the door handle, I lost my balance and fell through the screen and into a heap on the floor of the entry hall. My startled hosts helped me to my feet, and after I spent a few moments dusting myself off and clumsily straightening my uniform, they led me into the living room.

My unorthodox entry must have aroused her father's suspicions that I was perhaps not the suitable escort for their daughter they had expected the United States Naval Academy to provide. I cannot recall much of the conversation that ensued in their warm and brightly lighted living room. Whatever I said, and the manner in which I said it, apparently confirmed my host's suspicions. After little more than a quarter hour of their hospitality, he abruptly thanked me for paying them a visit and wished me a safe journey home.

I took this gesture as an indication that my weekend visit was to be substantially abbreviated. Politely, I asked if someone would be kind enough to call me a cab, and a few minutes later I was on my way back to Philadelphia to catch a late train for Washington.

When I arrived in the early morning of the next day, my surprised mother greeted me with: "What happened? I thought you were going away for the weekend."

"Mother, I don't want to talk about it," I replied sullenly, and headed for my room, and a few hours' sleep.

I never saw the girl or her family again.

A combination of academic performance and grease grade determined a midshipman's class standing. The company officer assigned your grease grade. Hart considered my aptitude for the service to be the poorest in the company. In fact, by Hart's reckoning I possessed no aptitude at all. He never failed to give me the low grease, which, combined with my spotty academic record, always kept me somewhere near the very bottom of the class standings.

I must take most of the responsibility for my poor relationship with my company officer. We were a poor match from the start: Hart was a meticulous, by-the-book junior officer who was unfailingly deferential to his superiors, and I was an arrogant, undisciplined, insolent midshipman who felt it necessary to prove my mettle by challenging his authority. In short, I acted like a jerk, and gave Hart good cause to despise me.

The encounter that set the stage for our four years of discord occurred early in my plebe year. My roommates and I had returned to our room late one morning to find my bed (or "rack," in Academy jargon) unmade, the sheets and cover balled up in the center of the mattress. That was not the condition I had left it in when earlier that morning I had gone to my first class. I might not have been scrupulous about obeying many Academy regulations, but I usually managed to make my bed in the morning. Apparently, Captain Hart considered the manner in which I performed this morning ritual to be below Academy standards, and had stripped my bed to show his dissatisfaction.

I don't recall which disturbed me more, the fact that he had stripped my bed or simply the idea of Hart prowling around in my room when I was not there. Whatever the cause, I instantly lost my temper and what little self-restraint I possessed in those days. Disregarding my roommates' pleas to forget the insult, I marched immediately to Hart's office to confront him. I knocked on his door, and entered before he gave me leave to do so. Without any prefatory remark, and with only the sloppiest of salutes, I declared my indignation:

"Captain, please don't do that again. I am too busy to make my bed twice a day."

My honor avenged, I turned on my heel and left his office before I had been dismissed or reprimanded by my shocked company officer. My behavior was inexcusable. Such impertinence was not tolerated at the Academy, least of all when the offender was nothing more than a troublemaking plebe. I should have paid a terrible price for my outburst. But Hart took no action and never said a word to me about it. I am sure it intensified his contempt for me and steeled his determination to purge me from his company. Today, when I remember this incident, I am ashamed of myself, but at the time, Hart's failure to respond immediately and forcefully to my insubordination caused me to respect him even less.

It is fair to say that Hart hated us. He had acute tunnel vision as he focused, often to the exclusion of all else, on our flawed characters. He knew what we were doing, and he was consumed by an intense desire to apprehend us in midcrime. With any luck, he would rid the Academy of our odious presence. He couldn't stand the sight of us, and believed me to be the worst of a very bad lot. At times, his loathing was comical.

Every company officer was obliged to host the members of his company in their last year, inviting them in small groups to dine at his quarters. The implicit purpose of the custom was to provide us with a little practical training in the social graces before we began our careers as officers who would be expected to know our salad fork from our soup spoon.

No doubt Hart had by this time wearied somewhat of chasing us, but his contempt for Frank, Jack, and me was still palpable. Nevertheless, he couldn't contrive a legitimate reason to refuse us our moment at the Hart dinner table. Accordingly, the three of us and our other, more respectable roommate, Keith Bunting, were invited to join Captain and Mrs. Hart for dinner on a pleasant spring evening in 1958. We anticipated the experience with a mixture of amusement and dread. We did not find very appealing the prospect of spending several hours awkwardly pretending to enjoy the company of a man who clearly despised us. But on the other hand we expected the evening to have enough entertainment value to provide material for a few jokes when it was over.

Before the event we laughed while conjuring up the image of our earnest company officer temporarily suspending his blind hatred of us to help us grasp the rudiments of gentlemanly deportment; watchfully presiding over the table; fussing over deficiencies in our table manners; noting whether we navigated the cutlery correctly and whether we paid the lady of the house the proper amount of formal deference; weakly attempting clever repartee; raising his glass aloft and booming, "Gentlemen, the Academy," or "the Corps." As it turned out, the captain had planned a considerably less ostentatious affair than we had imagined.

At the appointed hour, Captain Hart picked us up at Bancroft

Hall, and drove us in silence to his home, where we presumed
Mrs. Hart awaited our presence at her table. When we arrived at
his quarters, we naturally headed toward the front door. Hart
commanded us to stop. "No, gentleman, come around here," he
ordered. He led us around the house to the backyard, where a pic-
nic table had been set for dinner. The grill had been lighted. Hart
entered his kitchen through the back door. He returned a
moment later with hot dogs, beans, and a few bottles of Coca-
Cola. We ate the meal in silence, quickly. No formalities were
observed. No toasts to the Academy or the Corps. No strained
attempts at witty dinner conversation. No Mrs. Hart. A half hour
after we arrived, he loaded us back into his car and returned us to
Bancroft. Quite an etiquette lesson.

To Hart's severe disappointment, I managed to remain at the
Academy despite what he perceived as my seditious intentions.
For all my antics, I avoided accumulating the number of demerits
required to discharge a midshipman from further service. My
grades were usually poor, but, as I had at Episcopal, I showed
greater aptitude for English and history, subjects I enjoyed.

The eminent naval historian E. B. Potter was one of my pro-
fessors, and I liked him and his classes very much. For my term
paper in one of Professor Potter's classes, I chose to write about
my grandfather. In preparing the research for the paper, I had
written Admiral Nimitz to ask for his impressions of him.

I received a very prompt and generous response from the then
elderly national hero. He wrote me that my grandfather had been
a great man who had contributed significantly to our victory in
the Pacific, but he devoted most his letter to a detailed account of
the days he and my grandfather had sailed around the Philippines
on the Panay as very young men at the beginning of their long
and distinguished careers.

I recall the term paper only with embarrassment for its clumsy prose and poor scholarship. But I still feel pride when I remember the kind and generous regard that the old admiral lavished on
my grandfather's memory, and that I faithfully recorded for
Professor Potter, who had written extensively about both men

and knew more about my grandfather's career than I did.

Unfortunately, the curriculum at the Academy was weighted preponderantly toward math and the sciences. Indeed, in those days, all midshipmen were obliged to major in electrical engineering. I struggled with it, possessing no special calling to the trade. Nevertheless, as I was adept at cramming for exams, and blessed with friends who did not seem to mind too much my requests for urgent tutorials, I managed to avoid complete disaster. I got by, just barely at times, but I got by.

CHAPTER TWELVE

Fifth from the Bottom

I am sure my disdainful contemporaries and disapproving instructors believed I would become a thoroughly disreputable upperclassman were I somehow to escape expulsion during my plebe
year. Most of the time, my behavior only confirmed their low
regard for me. For a moment, though, I came close to confound-
ing their expectations. That moment began when I boarded the
USS *Hunt* to begin my first-class cruise to Rio de Janeiro in June
of 1957.

The *Hunt* was an old destroyer. It had seen better days. It
seemed to me a barely floating rust bucket that should have been
scrapped years before, unfit even for mothballing. But I was ignorant, a sailor's son though I was, and I overlooked the old ship's
grace and sea-worthiness. I assumed the *Hunt* was suitable only
for the mean task of giving lowly midshipmen a rustic experience
of life at sea. I was wrong.

We lived in cramped quarters in the aft of the ship. We kept
the hatch open to cool our quarters with the breeze blowing off
the Chesapeake Bay. Once the *Hunt* left the bay and entered the
Atlantic, the seas grew heavier and seawater washed in through
the hatch. We lived in the pooled water for several days. The
rough seas sent a good number of us running for the lee side to
vomit. We had restricted water hours on the cruise, which meant
there was only enough water to allow us to drink from the ship's
water fountains during a three-hour period every day. We took
saltwater showers.

We spent a third of the cruise in the engineering plant, a grim place that seemed, to the untrained eye, a disgrace. The boilers blew scorching hot air on us while we spent long hours in misery learning the mysteries of the ship's mechanics. That the ship sailed at all seemed to us a great testament to the mechanic's mates' mastery of improvisation. It was a hell of a vessel to go to sea in for the first time.

We spent another third of the cruise learning ship's navigation, and the last third on the bridge learning how to command a ship at sea.

The skipper was Lieutenant Commander Eugene Ferrell. He seemed to accord the *Hunt* affection far out of proportion to her virtues. More surprisingly, he seemed to have some affection for me. He expressed it in eccentric ways, but I sensed his respect for me was greater than I had lately been accustomed to receiving from officers. I appreciated it, and I liked him a lot.

I spent much of the cruise on the bridge, where the skipper would order me to take the conn. There is a real mental challenge to running a ship of that size, and I had little practical experience in the job. But I truly enjoyed it. I made more than a few mistakes, and every time I screwed up, the skipper would explode, letting loose an impressive blast of profane derision.

"Dammit, McCain, you useless bastard. Give up the conn right now. Get the hell off my bridge. I mean it, goddammit. I won't have a worthless s.o.b. at the helm of my ship. You've really screwed up this time, McCain. Get the hell out of here!"

As I began to skulk off the bridge, he would call me back. "Hold on a second. Come on back here, mister. Get over here and take the conn." And then he would begin, more calmly, to explain what I had done wrong and how the task was done properly. We would go along pleasantly until I committed my next unpardonable error, when he would unleash another string of salty oaths in despair over my unfitness for the service, only to beckon me back for a last chance to prove myself worthy of his fine ship.

It was a wonderful time. I enjoyed the whole experience. As I detected in Ferrell's outbursts his sense that I showed some promise, I worked hard not to disappoint him, and I learned the job passably well. I was rarely off his bridge for much of the cruise. No other midshipman on the *Hunt* was so privileged.

Inspired by the experience, I began to consider becoming an officer in the surface Navy, with the goal of someday commanding a destroyer, instead of following my grandfather into naval aviation. I told Ferrell of my intentions, and he seemed pleased. Fine gentleman that he is, he never rebuked me after I abandoned my briefly held aspirations for a destroyer command and returned to my original plan to become an aviator. Many years later, he wrote me, and recalled a chance encounter we had sometime in the early sixties. "I was surprised but pleased to see that you were wearing two stripes and a pair of gold wings. Your grandfather would have been very proud of you."

Years later, while serving as a flight instructor in Meridian, Mississippi, I realized that I had adopted, unintentionally, Lieutenant Commander Ferrell's idiosyncratic instruction technique. I took pride in the fact.

When a Navy ship at sea needs to refuel or take on supplies and mail, it must come alongside and tie up to a refueling or replenishing ship while both vessels are under way. The maneuver is difficult to execute even in the calmest seas. Most skippers attempt it cautiously, bringing their ship alongside the approaching vessel very slowly.

But the most experienced ship handlers are bolder, and pride themselves on their more daring form. They come alongside at two-thirds or full speed, much faster than the other ship. At precisely the right moment they throw the engines in reverse, and then ahead again at one-third speed. It's a spectacular thing to see when it's done right. An approximate image of the maneuver is a car traveling at sixty miles an hour as it approaches a parallel parking space; the driver slams on the brakes and pulls cleanly, without an inch to spare, into the spot.

Eugene Ferrell was a gifted ship handler, and he never considered coming alongside another ship in any other fashion, unless, of course, a green midshipman had the conn. I had watched him perform the task several times, and had admired his serene composure as he confidently gave the orders that brought the rushing *Hunt* abruptly but gracefully into place, moving at exactly the same speed as her sister ship. A seaman would fire a gun that shot a line to our bow. Soon the two ships, several lines now holding them in harness, would sail the ocean together for a time, never touching, but in perfect unison. It was a grand sight to behold.

One beautiful afternoon, the flagship of the destroyer division to which the *Hunt* was attached, flying the ensign of the commanding admiral, approached us for the purpose of replenishing the *Hunt*'s depleted stores. Lieutenant Commander Ferrell gave me the conn, and without a trace of apprehension, bade me bring her alongside the admiral's flagship.

Ferrell told me to bring her up slowly, but offered no rebuke when I gave the order "All engines ahead two-thirds." At precisely the right moment, I ordered, "All engines back full." A few moments later, again well timed, I ordered, "All engines ahead one-third." Thrillingly and to my great relief, the *Hunt* slipped into place so gracefully that any observer would have thought the skipper himself, master ship handler that he was, had the conn.

Ferrell was proud of me, and I was much indebted to him. He had given me his trust, and I had had the good fortune to avoid letting him down. After the two ships were tied up, he sent a message to the admiral. "Midshipman McCain has the conn." The impressed admiral sent a message to the Superintendent of the Naval Academy, informing him of my accomplishment.

Many years later I learned that Ferrell had been a student and admirer of my father's. Perhaps that explains his kindness toward me. Whatever the reason for the care he took with me, I was grateful for it. His confidence in me gave me more confidence in myself, and greater assurance that I belonged at sea than I had ever experienced in the rigid, disapproving world of the Academy. Eugene Ferrell was the man who taught me the craft of my father and grandfather. He gave me cause to love the work that they had loved. Debts such as that you incur for life. I sailed for Rio de Janeiro a more contented young man than I had ever been before.

Liberty in Rio. My imagination could not have embellished the good time we made of our nine days in port, indulging in the vices sailors are infamous for, as if we had been at sea for months instead of weeks. After some excessive drinking, nightclubbing, and little or no sleep, I had exhausted my appetite for the joys of liberty and intended to return to ship. Chuck Larson persuaded me to accompany him to a party at a grand house on Sugarloaf Mountain. There I met and began a romance with a Brazilian fashion model, and gloried in the envy of my friends.

We danced on the terrace overlooking the bay until one o'clock in the morning, when I felt her cheek was moist.

"What's the matter?" I asked.

"I'll never see you again," she replied.

I told her that we would remain in town for eight more days, and that I would gladly spend as much time in her company as she would grant me. But she rebutted my every assurance with "No, I can never see you again."

"Are you engaged?"

"No."

"Look, I'm going to be down at the gate of the shipyard at one o'clock tomorrow afternoon. I'll be there, and I want you to be there, too."

She said nothing in reply, and an hour later she left the party with her aunt, who served as her constant companion and chaperone.

The next afternoon, I left the ship at about twelve-thirty and waited for her at the place I had designated. An hour passed, and she had not arrived. Another hour and still she had not appeared. An hour after that, I forlornly prepared to abandon all hope. Just as I was preparing to return to the ship in a state of deep despondency, she pulled up in a Mercedes with gull-wing doors. She honked the horn, and I jumped in, ecstatic.

I spent every free moment with her for the rest of my stay in Rio. She was very beautiful, stylish, and gracious—common attributes in her wealthy and socially prominent family. She took me to dinners and receptions where I toasted my extraordinary good fortune in the company of cabinet members, generals and admirals, wealthy aristocrats, and, on one occasion, the president of Brazil.

We spent my last evening on liberty together. She drove me to my ship the next morning. I emerged from under the open gull-wing door and kissed her to a chorus of rowdy cheers from my shipmates. I accepted their approval with an affected sheepish humility.

When we returned to Annapolis, I had a few weeks' leave, which I used to fly right back to Rio to continue my storybook romance. By the following Christmas, the distance between us, and our youthful impatience and short attention spans, brought an end to our affair. But it resides in my memory, embellished with age, of course, among the happier experiences of my life.

On the return cruise we made port in the Virgin Islands and at Guantanamo Bay, Cuba, where we received further instruction in the rituals of shore leave. Guantanamo in those pre-Castro days was a wild place. Everyone went ashore and headed immediately for huge tents that had been set up on the base as temporary bars, where great quantities of strong Cuban beer and an even more potent rum punch were served to anyone who professed a thirst and could afford a nickel a drink.

The officers' club boasted the same menu in slightly more comfortable surroundings. We drank there for a good while, serenaded by a Pat Boone record. A music lover had evidently come ashore and filled the O club's jukebox with as many nickels as he could scrounge, choosing but one selection, "Love Letters in the Sand," which played over and over again. Returning to the ship, my friends and I were delighted to discover that the throng of sailors and Marines crowding the landing had taken a dislike to one another and had begun fighting. The shore patrol arrived and waded into the riot of whites and khaki vainly trying to separate the opposing forces. It was bedlam. We loved it.

On the cruise back to Annapolis I returned to my place on the bridge and happily resumed my one-on-one tutorial in the elements of expert ship handling. Two officers who were attached to the Academy but were not officers in my company had been assigned to the cruise to evaluate our performance. They gave me the best marks, reporting that I had shown a very high aptitude for the service. I had the high grease.

Captain Hart was astonished. He was convinced there had been a terrible error, perhaps a case of mistaken identity. First-class cruise had turned out to be the best time of my young life.

Inspired by my success on the USS *Hunt*, I resolved to make something of myself in my last year at the Academy. I studied hard and maintained a respectful attitude toward my superiors. I set up a tutoring system for plebes who were struggling academically. I managed the battalion boxing team, which won the brigade championship. My grades were improving, and I stayed well out of trouble. I had become, for a brief time, a squared-away midshipman whom any company officer could be proud of—any company officer save mine.

In January, I went to Captain Hart's office to receive my grease grade, which I was confident would elevate me for the first time from the bottom regions of the class standings where I had dwelled in infamy for three years. Hart began by noting my improved behavior. "Keep this up, son, and you'll have something to be proud of." When I asked where he had placed me in the company, he mumbled an answer that I couldn't make out.

"Where, sir?"

"At the bottom," he whispered.

"Where?"

"At the bottom."

Rising from my chair, I glared at Hart, who remained seated. "You can expect nothing more from me, Captain," I said as I left his office, slamming the door so hard behind me that I thought its opaque glass window would break.

Any other officer would have shouted at me, "Get back in here and sit down, mister! Where do you get off barking at me like that?" Not Captain Hart. He never spoke of the interview. He knew he had wronged me. For the first time, I had wanted something from him, had felt I'd earned it. And he, dogged to the end, had gotten his revenge.

True to my word, I returned to the habits of my first three years, accumulating demerits by the dozen, waiting out, indifferently, my last few months at the Academy.

A month after my interview with Hart, my room was chosen for a surprise inspection. It didn't pass. Only one roommate is responsible for keeping the room in some semblance of order, the job rotating among four roommates on a monthly basis. The surprise inspection occurred on my watch.

"Room in gross disorder" was the charge. The customary punishment for such an offense was fifteen demerits and three hours of extra duty. I received seventy-five demerits. A midshipman was allowed only 125 demerits his last year. Any more and he bilged out. I was already carrying forty demerits when the inspector arrived. It was a practical impossibility to last more than three months without collecting another ten. The slightest mistake, the most insignificant oversight, would get me kicked out in the last few weeks before graduation. My fate, I thought, was sealed.

I telephoned my parents. My father was at sea, so I informed my mother that I was coming home. I explained the circumstances, and that my expulsion was imminent. I might as well come home now, I argued, and not waste a few days or weeks waiting for the ax to fall.

My mother wisely cautioned me not to make an irrevocable decision until I had an opportunity to talk to my father. In the meantime, she advised me to talk things over with my wrestling coach, Ray Schwartz, a friend of my parents and a good man. Mr. Schwartz commiserated with me about my difficult predicament, and agreed that I had been punished excessively for a minor infraction. But he, too, advised me to withhold any decision until I had discussed the situation with my father. A day or two later, I received a summons from the Commandant of the Naval Academy, Captain Shin. My mother had called him.

"What's this I hear about you leaving?" he asked.

"I have too many demerits, sir," I replied.

"Why?"

"Because I have been punished unfairly, sir."

I then explained how the sentence had far exceeded the pre-scribed penalty, and that I thought the action was unjust. My complaint seemed only to irritate him. He said I was spoiled, a charge that I greatly resented.

"Whatever you say, sir, but it's still not fair."

He leveled a scornful gaze at me and told me to leave.

The commandant was neither the first nor the last person to accuse me of being spoiled, implying that my parents had greased my way in the world. Witt had been the first to do so when he derided me for being a captain's son. Later in my career, as I rose through the ranks, some would attribute my advance to my admi-ral father's benefaction. I suppose it is an accusation that many children of successful parents learn to ignore. I never did, howev-er. I grew red-faced and angry every time some know-it-all told me how easy a life my father had made for me. The life my father led me to has been a richly rewarding one, and I am grateful to him for it. But "easy" is not the first adjective that comes to mind when describing it.

My father was only a captain when I was at the Naval Academy, a rank that surely didn't grant him the influence to compensate for my shortcomings. Later in my life, when my father wore stars on his shoulder, he would, indeed, influence my career, but in ways my detractors did not appreciate. He had met the standard his father had set. It was my obligation and my priv-ilege to try to uphold it.

A week or two after Captain Shin instructed me to leave his presence, I was informed that the punishment for my disordered room had been reduced to thirty demerits and seven days of con-finement. I was relieved to comply with the order.

A month or so after the room inspection incident, I had yet another close brush with disaster. The ever vigilant Captain Hart believed he had at last discovered a violation that would result in my swift expulsion from the Academy.

In September of my last year, my roommates and I, along with four roommates in the room next to ours and two other midshipmen on our floor, chipped in to buy a television set. In those days, Academy regulations enjoined midshipmen from keeping electrical appliances of any kind in their rooms. Even hot plates were considered contraband. I remember a few midshipmen would take back to their rooms bread and cheese from the mess hall after the evening meal, and sell cheese sandwiches to the rest of us. It was a thriving industry, much appreciated by me and every other hungry midshipman who was denied the convenience of devices to store or prepare food.

Mindful of but undeterred by the regulation, our small syndicate had decided we would risk the wrath of our superiors for the pleasure of watching the Friday-night fights on our own television. We each pitched in ten dollars and bought a used black-and-white television with a twelve-inch screen. We kept the set hidden in a crawl space in our room, located behind a wooden panel. The panel could be easily removed by hand, and we would bring the set out to watch the fights on Friday, Maverick on Sunday, and other popular television programs of the time.

We lived in Bancroft Hall, the Academy's only dormitory, which at the time had not been changed in any of its particulars since the turn of the century. The floors in Bancroft Hall were referred to, in ship nomenclature, as decks. We lived on the top deck, the fourth. We soon drew considerable numbers of top-deck residents to our room to join our forbidden television viewing. On Friday nights, it was standing room only.

In every hall of every deck, a third-year midshipman served as the mate of the deck. The mate's job was to receive and deliver messages to the midshipmen in residence there and, generally, to stand as a sentinel for his part of the deck to ensure that nothing untoward happened on his watch. The mate on our hall stood at a podium directly across the hall from my room. We pressed him into service as our lookout on evenings when we were crowded around our television set. He kept an eye out for company officers who would have loved to discover our blatant disobedience and rapped a warning on my door when one approached.

As upperclassmen, we no longer had to worry about being disciplined or harassed by other midshipmen as we had been during our plebe year. We also took comfort in knowing that our indiscretions would be kept confidential within the brigade and not reported to unsuspecting officers. The most sacrosanct principle governing a midshipman's behavior was the unwritten rule "Never bilge a classmate," which required midshipmen to overlook any violation of the rules by a fellow midshipman short of honor code violations.

Brigade discipline was supervised by four authorities, the most senior being the officer of the watch, an office that was rotated monthly among company officers. Those midshipmen with the highest grease in the brigade rotated daily as the midshipman of the watch, while a group of the more promising plebes served as their assistants.

My pal Chuck Larson, whose exemplary scholastic record and obvious aptitude for command had won him the highest office a plebe could hold, brigade commander, was serving as the midshipman of the watch. Academy officials would have been disappointed to discover their prized midshipman among those gathered around the television in my room to watch a boxing match, shirking the duties of his office to enjoy a few minutes of illicit fun with some of the more disreputable midshipmen at the Academy.

In the middle of our viewing, the mate of the deck rapped on my door to warn us that the officer of the watch was approaching. We quickly returned the television set to its hiding place and stuffed the midshipman of the watch, dressed in his formal blue uniform and wearing his sword, along with his startled plebe, into my closet. The rest of us opened up textbooks and earnestly affected the appearance of dutiful midshipmen gathered together in a study group. Fortunately, the officer never bothered to enter our room. Had he done so, our atypical studiousness surely would have aroused his suspicion.

A few days later, when I returned to my room after classes had ended for the day, I found a message on my desk ordering me to report to Captain Hart. Hart's office was five doors down from my room. Responding to my summons, I knocked on his door, entered, stood at attention, and announced myself: "Midshipman McCain, First Class, sir."

Sitting there with a look of considerable satisfaction, Hart allowed himself a rare smile as he threw a Form 2 across his desk to me and inquired, "Do you want to sign this now?" A Form 2 was the standard notification that a midshipman had been put on report. A midshipman was required to sign the form acknowledging his offense.

I picked up the form and read the line where the offense was reported: "electrical equipment, unauthorized use of," and on the line below, "television set."

While all the midshipmen on the fourth deck were at class, Hart had taken the opportunity to closely inspect our quarters. So thorough was the inspection that Hart had entered the rooms' crawl spaces, which adjoined each other. When he reached our room and discovered the contraband hidden in our crawl space, he must have silently exulted in his good fortune, believing that the day of judgment was finally at hand for the sorriest midshipman in his company.

The penalty for the offense was thirty demerits and seven days' confinement. The demerits I had already accumulated took me perilously close to the limit, and again I faced certain expulsion. I thought over my situation for a moment while Hart waited contentedly for my response.

"Sir, this isn't necessarily mine," I finally replied.

"What do you mean?" he asked.

"The television, it isn't necessarily mine."

"Whose is it?" the now less content and incredulous Captain Hart responded.

"I'll let you know in a very short time."

A puzzled look overtook the captain's smile, and he dismissed me with an order to report back quickly with an answer.

I returned to my room and called the television's ten owners together. I explained the situation, and that I had to bring Hart an answer right away. "Only one of us is going to get the demerits," I said, "and we have to choose who, right now." We settled the question as we always settled things in those days, with a "shake around." Over my objection, my friends, aware of my perilous situation at the Academy, excused me from participating.

In unison, each man hit his right fist three times into the palm of his other hand. On the third strike, each stuck out some of the fingers of his right hand. We then counted off the sum of the nine men's extended fingers, one number per man, with the last number falling on the man who would confess ownership of the television. As luck and fate would have it, the man turned out to be Henry Vargo.

Henry Vargo was a model midshipman. Studious, disciplined, respectful, Henry hardly ever bothered to watch the television. He had joined in its purchase only to help us out, to be one of the guys. Henry did not possess very many demerits, so the punishment he was about to receive wouldn't pose much of a problem for him. As added compensation, we magnanimously said that Hart would have to give the television back at the end of the year and Henry could keep it.

Smiling with satisfaction and relief, I returned to Hart's office to reveal the culprit.

"Midshipman McCain, First Class, sir."

"Well?"

"Sir, the television set belongs to Midshipman Vargo."

"Midshipman Vargo!" he bellowed in disbelief.

"Yes, sir, Midshipman Vargo."

Fighting to stop from smiling, I watched Hart's face flush red with anger. Finally, he dismissed me—"Get out of here, McCain."

I left him and walked back to my room, much relieved to have evaded, for the last time, Hart's wrath and his four-year quest to bring me to justice.

* * *

A few months later I sat amid a sea of navy whites, fifth from the bottom of my class, listening to President Eisenhower confer our degrees, exhort us to noble service on behalf of the Republic, and commission me an ensign in the United States Navy.

Eisenhower's remarks were not particularly memorable, owing to a combination of his flat delivery and our impatience to begin celebrating our liberation. Although he wasn't much of a speaker, we all admired the President. I remember wishing at one point during commencement that my dismal performance at the Academy had earned me an even lower place in the class standings.

In those days, only the first one hundred graduates in the class were called to the dais to receive their diplomas from the President. Graduation was conferred on the rest of us by company. John Poindexter graduated first in our class, an honor he had well earned. He walked proudly to the podium to receive his diploma and a handshake from the President of the United States, which the President bestowed on him with a brief "Well done and congratulations."

The midshipman who graduates last in his class is affectionately called the anchorman. When the anchorman's company was called, he was cheered by the whole brigade and hoisted onto the shoulders of his friends. Eisenhower motioned him up to the dais, and to the crowd's loud approval personally handed him his diploma; both President and anchorman smiling broadly as the President patted him on the back and chatted with him for a few minutes. I thought it a fine gesture from a man who understood our traditions.

I was proud to graduate from the Naval Academy. But at that moment, relief was the emotion I felt most keenly. I had already been accepted for flight training in Pensacola. In those days, all you had to do was pass the physical to qualify for flight training, and I was eager to embark on the life of a carefree naval aviator.

My orders left me enough time to take an extended holiday in Europe with Jack, Frank, and another classmate, Jim Higgins. We bummed a ride to Spain on a military aircraft from Dover Air Force Base in Delaware. We spent several enjoyable days in Madrid, then boarded a train for Paris. Four days after we arrived, my friends left Paris for Copenhagen and the World's Fair. I remained behind, waiting to meet my new girlfriend, the daughter of a tobacco magnate from Winston-Salem, North Carolina. We were in Paris during the summer of de Gaulle.

At the time, France was fighting a war to hold on to its Algerian colony, and its conspicuous lack of military success had caused the collapse of the French Fourth Republic. Terrorist bombings and other unpleasantness associated with the war had driven many Parisians out of the city to seek refuge in the French countryside. We had the city to ourselves, and we enjoyed it immensely.

Near the end of our stay, we stood in a throng of cheering Parisians along the Champs Elysées as two long, noisy lines of motorcycle policemen led the way to the Arc de Triomphe for de Gaulle's motorcade. The general and now president of the infant Fifth Republic stood erect in the backseat of his convertible limousine nodding at the overwrought crowds as they chanted, "Algerie Française, Algerie Française."

Four years after returning to power, and despite his solemn promise that Algeria would be forever French, de Gaulle granted the colony's independence. Nevertheless, he cut a hell of a figure that day, standing there so impassive and noble-looking while his nation's adoration washed over him. I was a kid at the time, and the general's grandeur made a great impression on me. In truth, I remain just as impressed four decades later.

I suppose to most people who knew me at Annapolis, my entire career at the Naval Academy is aptly summarized by the anecdotes I have recorded here. Most of my reminiscences feature the frivolous escapades with which I once established my reputation as a rash and prideful nonconformist.

In truth, I was less exceptional than I had imagined myself to be. Every class has its members who aspire to prominence by unconventional means. My father and grandfather had enjoyed only slightly less tarnished reputations at the Academy. My father, perhaps mindful of his own performance, rarely chastised me for falling well short of an exemplary midshipman's standards. In fact, I don't recall the subject of my record at the Academy ever being extensively discussed by either of my parents.

There was one occasion when my father registered his disapproval over my conduct at the Academy. One evening in our second year, my roommates and I were in the middle of a water balloon fight, adding to our room's usual disarray. We suspended our activity when someone knocked on the door. Frank opened the door to find an officer facing him with a disdainful look on his face as he appraised our room's unacceptable condition and the four of us standing in our skivvies soaking wet. My roommates greeted our unexpected guest by briskly standing at attention. I greeted him by saying, somewhat quizzically, "Dad?"

After an awkward second or two, he ordered, "As you were, gentlemen," and as my roommates began to exhale, he added, "This room is in gross disorder. John, meet me downstairs in five minutes." With that, he turned on his heels and left. I met him less than five minutes later, and he proceeded to lecture me, observing, "You're in too much trouble here, Johnny, to be asking for any more." That single incident is the only time I can remember my father upbraiding me for my dismal performance as a midshipman.

My behavior was not something that particularly worried my father. I believe he assumed that, like him, I would be absorbed into the traditions of the place whether I wished to or not, and that when the time arrived for me to face a real test of character, I would not disappoint him. He had seen many an officer who enjoyed the reputation of a rake—indeed, he had been one himself—rise to the occasion in the most dire situations, and exhibit courage and resourcefulness that confounded earlier detractors. He expected no less from me.

Even as I spent my years as a junior officer in the same profligate manner I had spent my Academy years, I cannot recall his severely rebuking me. America had fought two wars during his career, and he was certain there would soon be another one. He knew I would fight, and I think he trusted me to do my duty when my moment arrived. I don't know if I deserved his trust, but I am proud to have had it.

If I had ignored the less important conventions of the

Academy, I was careful not to defame its more compelling traditions: the veneration of courage and resilience; the honor code that simply assumed your fidelity to its principles; the homage paid to men who had sacrificed greatly for their country; the expectation that you, too, would prove worthy of your country's trust.

Appearances to the contrary, it was never my intention to mock a revered culture that expected better of me. Like any other midshipman, I had wanted to prove my mettle to my contemporaries, and to the institution that figured so prominently in my family history. My idiosyncratic methods, if you can call them that, amounted to little more than imaginative expressions of the truculence I had used at other schools and in other circumstances to fend off what I had identified, often wrongly, as attacks upon my dignity.

The Academy, despite the irritating customs of plebe year and the encumbrances it placed on the individualist, was not interested in degrading my dignity. On the contrary, it had a more expansive conception of human dignity than I possessed when I arrived at its gates. The most important lesson I learned there was that to sustain my self-respect for a lifetime it would be necessary for me to have the honor of serving something greater than my self-interest.

When I left the Academy, I was not even aware I had learned that lesson. In a later crisis, I would suffer a genuine and ruthless attack on my dignity, an attack that, unlike the affronts I had exaggerated as a boy, left me desperate and uncertain. It was then I would recall, awakened by the example of men who shared my circumstances, the lesson that the Naval Academy in its antique way had labored to impress upon me. It changed my life forever.

CHAPTER THIRTEEN

Navy Flyer

My early years as a naval officer were an even more colorful extension of my rowdy days at the Academy. At flight school in Pensacola, and then at advanced flight training with my pal Chuck Larson in Corpus Christi, Texas, I did not enjoy the reputation of a serious pilot or an up-and-coming junior officer.

I liked to fly, but not much more than I liked to have a good time. In fact, I enjoyed the off-duty life of a Navy flyer more than I enjoyed the actual flying. I drove a Corvette, dated a lot, spent all my free hours at bars and beach parties, and generally misused my good health and youth.

At Pensacola, I spent much of my off-duty time at the legendary bar Trader John's. On Friday and Saturday nights, after happy hour at the officers' club had ended, almost every unmarried aviator in Pensacola headed for Trader John's. It was a vast, cavernous place that was packed shoulder to shoulder on the weekends, as was the back room where local girls, trained as exotic dancers, entertained rowdy crowds of aviators. Pensacola has since designated the place a historic landmark in recognition of its former infamy when it was the scene of some of the wildest revelry the state of Florida had ever experienced.

After graduation from the Academy, our class was divided between those newly commissioned ensigns who intended to extend their carefree bachelorhood and those who had left the commencement ceremony to immediately enter the blessed state of matrimony. A good number of my classmates, including several of my closest friends, had married their girlfriends before taking up their first duty assignment, and this difference in our married status unfortunately created a social division between us.

At Pensacola, married ensigns and their wives mostly socialized together. Married couples had to rent homes off base and had less disposable income than their unmarried friends. I and the other residents of the base's bachelor officers' quarters, with more money to waste and mindful that the amusements we sought were likely to offend the sensibilities of our married friends' respectable young wives, kept largely to ourselves.

Walt Ryan was one of my closest friends from the Academy, a charter member of the Bad Bunch. He, too, had been accepted into pilot training at Pensacola, but because he had married after graduation, I saw less of him than I would have preferred. His wife, Sarah, was a lovely, well-mannered girl whom I liked very much. I saw them both occasionally, and always enjoyed their company, but on most weekends I kept less civilized company.

At some point during my time at flight school, I had begun dating a local girl whom I had met at Trader John's. She made her living there, under the name Marie, the Flame of Florida. She was a remarkably attractive girl with a great sense of humor, and I was quite taken with her. Since her work kept her busy on Friday and Saturday nights, our dates occurred on Sunday evenings when the bar was closed.

Most Sundays we went to the movies and had a nice dinner afterward. One Sunday, however, on our way downtown we passed Walt Ryan's house, where I recognized the cars of several other married friends. I impulsively decided to pull over and join the party uninvited, telling Marie that I wanted to introduce her to some of my friends. Always a good sport, Marie agreed to my suggestion.

Most of my friends' wives were from privileged families and had been educated at distinguished Eastern schools. Marie, the Flame of Florida, had a more interesting biography, more in the "graduated from the school of hard knocks" genre. The young wives she was about to meet would be decorously attired and unfailingly genteel. Marie was dressed somewhat flamboyantly that evening, as was her custom.

Walt and Sarah greeted our surprise visit with their usual graciousness, inviting us in without too much hesitation, offering us drinks, and introducing us to the six or so other couples gathered in their home. After the introductions and a few inane pleasantries were exchanged, the conversation seemed to become a little awkward, at times lapsing into long silences.

Marie sensed that the young wives, while certainly not rude to her, were less than entirely at ease in her presence. So she sat silent, not wishing to impose on anyone or intrude in the conversations going on around her. After a while, she must have become a little bored. So, quietly, she reached into her purse, withdrew a switchblade, popped open the blade, and, with a look of complete indifference, began to clean her fingernails.

My startled hosts and their guests stared at her with looks that ranged between disbelief and alarm. Marie seemed not to notice, and concentrated on her task. A short time later, recognizing that our presence had perhaps subdued the party, I thanked our hosts for their hospitality, bid good-bye to the others, and took my worldly, lovely Flame of Florida to dinner.

I crashed a plane in Corpus Christi Bay one Saturday morning. The engine quit while I was practicing landings. Knocked unconscious when my plane hit the water, I came to as the plane settled on the bottom of the bay. I barely managed to get the canopy open and swim to the surface. After X rays and a brief examination determined I had not suffered any serious injury, I returned to the quarters Larson and I shared. I took a few painkillers and hit the sack to rest my aching back for a few hours.

My father learned of the accident immediately and asked a friend, the admiral in charge of advanced flight training, to check on me. Chuck Larson and I had adjoining rooms in the bachelor officers' quarters. We had moved both our beds into the same room and used the second room to entertain in. The room was, of course, in a constant state of "gross disorder."

When the admiral contacted by my father arrived, I was asleep and Chuck was shaving. He pounded on the door while Chuck, unaware that a distinguished visitor was at our door, shouted at him to "hold his horses." He opened the door to our guest, snapped a salute, and stood nervously while the admiral surveyed the wreckage that was our quarters. Groggily, I thanked the admiral for his concern. Neither he nor my father needed to have bothered. I was out carousing, injured back and all, later that evening.

I began to worry a little about my career during my deployments on several Mediterranean cruises in the early sixties. I flew A-1 Skyraiders in two different squadrons on carriers based in Norfolk, Virginia: on the USS *Intrepid* for two and a half cruises in the Mediterranean; and on the nuclear-powered USS *Enterprise* for one short and one long Mediterranean cruise.

The A-1 was an old, propeller-driven plane; it was a very reliable aircraft and a lot of fun to fly. We would sometimes take them on twelve-hour flights that were quite enjoyable, flying low, and admiring the changes of scenery over the long distances we flew.

The pilots in the squadrons were a close-knit group. We enjoyed flying together, as well as one another's company while on shore leave in Europe. I found plenty of time to revel in the fun that European ports offered a young, single flyer; spending holidays on Capri, risking my wages in the casinos of Monte Carlo. However, by my second cruise on the *Intrepid*, I had begun to aspire to a reputation for more commendable achievements than long nights of drinking and gambling. I had started to feel a need to move on, a natural impulse for me, born of the migrant's life I had led since birth.

Like my grandfather and father, I loved life at sea, and I loved flying off carriers. No other experience in my life so closely approximated the exploits of the brash, daring heroes who had captivated my schoolboy's imagination during those long afternoons in my grandmother's house. Ever since reading about the storied world of men at arms, I had longed for such a life. The Navy, especially with a war on, offered the quickest route to adventure if I could manage to avoid committing some career-ending mistake.

Once, when I thought I was about to flunk out of the Academy, I had contemplated joining the French Foreign Legion. I wrote to an address in New Orleans for information about how to join the legendary force. I received a nice brochure. While reading it, I discovered that the Legion required nine years of obligated service. I decided to try to stick it out in the Navy. Now I accepted that any adventure that might come my way would almost surely be found while I wore a Navy uniform. The Navy was stuck with me, and I with it, and I decided to make the best of my circumstances.

Remembering the satisfaction of my days on Commander Ferrell's bridge, I volunteered for bridge watches and qualified as an "officer of the deck under way," proving capable of commanding a carrier at sea. Already enjoying a reputation for large living as colorful as that of my legendary forebears, I began to give my superiors some reason to think I might eventually prove myself, if not as gifted an officer as my father and grandfather, perhaps competent enough not to squander my legacy.

As I was one of the few bachelors in my squadron, I volunteered on three occasions to spend my leave attending escape and evasion school to prepare myself for the possibility of being shot down in combat. I also volunteered because I found the course to be a pretty good time.

One course took place during a large Army exercise in Bavaria, Germany. A number of other pilots and I were released at night in the middle of the Black Forest. We wore our flight suits and were allowed only those belongings that a pilot would normally possess when he ejected during a combat mission, which amounted to a few C rations.

We were given a map and instructed to find our way, undetected, to a designated safe area. Soldiers participating in the exercise were ordered to hunt us down. The Army also broadcast over the radio a reward offer to any German civilians who found us and reported our whereabouts to the authorities. An Air Force pilot and I teamed up and began a careful trek through woods filled with eager soldiers.

It took five days to reach the safe area. There was plenty of water around, and although we were hungry, we enjoyed ourselves. The forest was beautiful, and the summer weather was pleasant. Several mornings we awoke under the shelter of a large fir tree to the sound of German families out for an early-morning stroll through the woods (Germans are great walkers). We hustled quickly and quietly away lest some lucky, unsuspecting German seize the opportunity to add to the family's wealth.

My Air Force friend and I were the only pilots to avoid capture and reach our designation. When we arrived, Special Forces soldiers picked us up and took us to a lovely inn on a lake in a small German village called Unterdeisen, where we remained until the exercise was completed two days later. The inn was run by a former Luftwaffe pilot, who took us flying in glider planes. We whiled away the rest of the time drinking beer, admiring the scenery, and watching deer come down to the lake to drink.

As we had not been captured (nor was I captured during two other similar exercises I participated in), we were not subjected to simulated interrogations or any other unpleasantness associated with being captured in war. When the exercise was over, we were taken to Special Forces headquarters in Bad Tolz, where we were debriefed and attended lectures and films about what we might expect were we ever to have the bad luck to be prisoners of war.

In those days, the military emphasized escape and evasion more than it dwelled on life in a prison camp. However, an Air Force major who had been a POW in Korea was brought in to brief us on his experiences, and I shared quarters with him for the two days I remained at Bad Tolz. He told us that while he had not experienced a great deal of torture as a POW, American prisoners in Korea had been kept isolated, and on near-starvation rations.

What I remember most from my conversations with him was my astonishment at learning that this congenial, well-adjusted former POW had been kept in solitary confinement. I commended him for his physical and mental courage, and remarked that I seri-

ously doubted I could have survived such a long stretch in solitary. He told me I would be surprised what suffering a man could
endure when he had no alternative.

While at Bad Tolz, I and the pilot I had escaped and evaded
with met two college girls from the States who were spending the
summer in Europe. Since the *Intrepid* wasn't due in port for
another ten days, we joined them on their drive through southern
Germany to Italy, ending our brief time as fugitives with a very
pleasant holiday. There was little we had experienced during our
Bavarian excursion that approximated the experiences of pilots
who were hunted and captured in a real war.

There were occasional setbacks in my efforts to round out my
Navy profile. My reputation was certainly not enhanced when I
knocked down some power lines while flying too low over southern Spain. My daredevil clowning had cut off electricity to a great
many Spanish homes and created a small international incident.

While I was stationed at Norfolk during my service on the
Intrepid and *Enterprise*, a few pilots in my squadron and I lived in
Virginia Beach in a beach house known far and wide in the Navy
as the infamous "House on 37th Street." We enjoyed a reputation
for hosting the most raucous and longest beach parties of any
squadron in the Navy. On the whole, however, I made steady, if
slow, progress toward becoming a respectable officer.

In October 1962, I was just returning to home port at Norfolk
after completing a Mediterranean deployment aboard the
Enterprise. The air wing of a carrier always leaves the ship just
before she comes into home port. My squadron had flown off the
Enterprise and returned to Oceana Naval Air Station while the
ship put in at Norfolk. While at Oceana we would train out of
land bases until the *Enterprise*'s next deployment.

A few days after our return, we unexpectedly received orders
to fly our planes back to the carrier. Our superiors explained the
unusual order by informing us that a hurricane was headed our
way. The explanation only aroused our curiosity further, since
none of us had heard any forecast of an approaching storm, nor
did putting to sea strike us as a reasonable course of evasion.

Nevertheless, we flew all our planes back to the carrier within twenty-four hours and headed out to sea. In addition to our A-1s, the *Enterprise* carried long-range attack planes, which typically had a hard time managing carrier takeoffs and landings. We embarked on our mysterious deployment without them.

As the *Enterprise* passed Cherry Point, Virginia, a Marine squadron of A-4s approached and attempted to land. I watched the scene from up in the air tower. Several of the Marine pilots experienced considerable difficulty trying to land. Our air boss turned to a representative of the Marine squadron and said we didn't have time to wait for all their planes to land; some of them would have to return to their base. The Marine replied that his planes were already below bingo fuel, which meant that they did not have sufficient fuel to return to base and had to land on the *Enterprise*.

I was quite puzzled by the apparent urgency of our mission—we'd been hustled back in one day, leaving some of our planes behind; the Marine squadron had been ordered to join us with only enough fuel to land or ditch. The mystery was solved a short while later when all pilots were assembled in the *Enterprise*'s ready room to listen to a broadcast of President Kennedy informing the nation that the Soviets were basing nuclear missiles in Cuba.

The *Enterprise*, sailing at full speed under nuclear power, was the first U.S. carrier to reach waters off Cuba. For about five days, the pilots on the *Enterprise* believed we were going into action. We had never been in combat before, and despite the global confrontation a strike on Cuba portended, we were prepared and anxious to fly our first mission. The atmosphere aboard ship was fairly tense, but not overly so. Pilots and crewmen alike adopted a cool-headed, business-as-usual attitude toward the mission. Inwardly, of course, we were excited as hell, but we kept our composure and aped the standard image of a laconic, reserved, and fearless American at war.

After five days the tension eased, as it became apparent the crisis would be resolved peacefully. We weren't disappointed to be denied our first combat experience, but our appetites were whetted and our imaginations fueled. We eagerly anticipated the occasion when we would have the chance to do what we were trained to do, and discover, at last, if we were brave enough for the job.

We remained in the Caribbean for another two or three months. We did a lot of heavy flying, landing at various Caribbean nations, and our accident rates began to increase. Our commanders arranged for the pilots to get some R&R, and I soon found myself boarding a carrier Onboard delivery plane for four days of fun in Montego Bay, Jamaica.

Shortly after I got back to the ship from my Jamaican holiday, the *Enterprise* left the Caribbean and returned to port in Norfolk. A little while later, I embarked on my last Mediterranean cruise, an event that marked the end of my days as a completely carefree, unattached, and less than serious Navy flyer.

My newly formed professional aspirations were not as far-reaching as were my father's as he diligently pursued flag rank, single-minded in his intention to emulate his famous father. Certainly I would have been proud to achieve the feat myself, but I doubt I ever allowed myself to daydream about someday wearing an admiral's stars.

I had, by this time, begun to aspire to command. I didn't possess any particular notion of greatness, but I did hold strong notions of honor. And I worried that my deserved reputation for foolishness would make command of a squadron or a carrier, the pinnacle of a young pilot's aspiration, too grand an ambition for an obstreperous admiral's son, and my failure to reach command would dishonor me and my family.

Despite my concerns, I resolved to follow the conventional course to command. With the country at war, that course led to Vietnam. The best way to raise my profile as an aviator, perhaps the only way, was to achieve a creditable combat record. I was eager to begin.

More than professional considerations lay beneath my desire to go to war. Nearly all the men in my family had made their reputations at war. It was my family's pride. And the Naval

Academy, with its celebration of martial valor, had penetrated
enough of my defenses to recall me to that honor. I wanted to go
Vietnam, and to keep faith with the family creed.

When I was a young boy, I would often sit quietly, unob-
served, and listen to my father and his friends, who had gathered
in our home for a cocktail or dinner party, reminisce about their
wartime experiences. They talked about battles on sea and land,
kamikaze attacks, depth-charge attacks, Marine landings on fiercely defended Pacific atolls, submerged battles between submarines,
gun battles between ships of the line—all the drama and fury of
war that most kids went to the movies to experience.

But the men in my house who spoke about war did so with an
unstudied nonchalance, a style reserved for commanders who had
long ago proved whatever martial virtues their egos required them
to possess. They did not bluster or brag or swap war stories to
impress each other. They talked about combat as they talked
about other experiences in the service. They talked about the lessons of leadership they learned and how they could apply them to
current situations.

They talked about how their commanding officers had performed in battle, who had been the most capable and steady leaders, and who had not measured up to the demands of their offices.
It was evident in the way my father's friends talked about my
father, especially those who had served on submarines with him,
that they revered him as a fighting commander. They treated him
differently, more respectfully, than they did one another. They
often regaled a party with descriptions of my father biting down
hard on an unlit cigar in the middle of a fight, unafraid and
intensely focused on destroying the enemy.

They talked about how the men under my father's command
had been affected by combat, and how my father had inspired
their confidence in his leadership. They remembered how my
father had quieted his crew's fear by making clear to them that he
cared about them, respected them, and would show them the way
to fight the Japanese without getting them all killed. They made
military life seem more exciting and attractive to me.

They were proud veterans of an epic war, and they never felt the need to exaggerate their experiences. They took dramatic license only with stories about their days away from combat, when they were sent to distant, sometimes exotic, more often bleak refuges for a few weeks' respite from war. Midway Island loomed large in their personal folklore of war, and they seemed to take a curious pride in having endured its charmless environs, a pride they displayed more openly than their pride as conquerors of a formidable enemy. My father often sang to us, and sometimes quietly to himself, the ditty he had sung so often in war, "Beautiful Midway," seeming to recall in its incantation some memorable irony of battle.

> Beautiful, beautiful Midway,
> Land where the gooney birds play.
> We're proud of our predecessors,
> Who kept the Japs at bay.
> We live in the sand and skavole,
> Down where the sea breezes blow.
> There will always be a Midway,
> The goddammdest place I know.

He also often recounted, with more humor than embarrassment, an occasion early in the war when he and my grandfather were both briefly on leave and had accepted my invitation to address the students at my grade school in Vallejo, California. Both men liked the idea of appearing before a group of admiring kids as father and son warriors and bringing tales of courage and adventure to impressionable schoolkids. My grandfather spoke first, my father in the front row watching him. He had become accustomed during the war to public speaking and had inspired a number of audiences with stories from the Solomon Islands campaign. He would bring them to their feet with tales about great naval battles; about the gallant Marines who held their ground and beat the Japanese in the enemy's preferred form of warfare, jungle fighting; and about his intrepid pilots at Henderson Field, who persevered through savage bombing and shelling.

This time, however, was different. The tender youth of his audience seemed to distract him, and rendered his usually robust delivery a little flat. His found it difficult to give his usual rousing call to arms, filled as it was with ridicule and scorn for the enemy, and laced extensively with profanity for punctuation and emphasis. He had always prided himself on his rough ways, as a man for whom salty language had always been a perfectly serviceable means of communication. Now he was knocked off his stride as he searched for ways to commend to a group of children their fathers' courage in language their mothers would approve.

My father watched his father's discomfort with obvious amusement, at times laughing out loud as the old sailor struggled to find some way to hold his audience's attention without resorting to impolite language. Further confounded by his son's delight in his dilemma, he abruptly ended his remarks without ever having hit his high notes. But his wit had not entirely deserted him. He concluded his speech by gesturing toward my father, who had expected to give the audience a riveting description of his battles beneath the sea. "Now, children, my son will sing 'Beautiful Midway' for you," my grandfather said as he grinned and winked at my father.

Crestfallen, my father did as he was instructed and sang to my schoolmates his favorite tune, but in a soft, low voice and with none of his usual enthusiasm. We all watched with puzzled looks on our faces. I perked up a little at the end when I thought I heard my father change the last line of the song from "the goddammdest place I know" to the "gosh-darnedest place I know." After he finished, he hurried away, escorted by his grinning father, who clapped him on the back and complimented him on his performance.

My father never had to sit me down and explain the nature of an officer's life to me, to spell out the demands and expectations that came with the uniform. As the son of a professional officer, I had abundant opportunity to observe the long absences, hard work, and frequent upheavals that attended a military career. I knew firsthand the dominance the Navy's priorities held over family considerations.

But it was war, the great test of character, that made the prospect of joining my father's profession attractive, and I was very curious about my father's knowledge of it. I listened intently to every conversation about war that my father and his friends had in my presence. I admired them as they relaxed with drinks in hand, their thoughts turned again to the days when their dreams of adventure had become harshly real and the last attributes of their youth had been lost in the noise and gun smoke of battle. I hoped that I, too, would know days when I would learn that courage was finding the will to act despite the fear and chaos of battle.

One summer, on leave from the Academy, I went to see my father in his study in our house on Capitol Hill and asked him to tell me about his experiences in the Second World War. He set aside what he was reading and described in detail, but in a very businesslike manner, his war.

He began with his combat patrol in the Atlantic, when the *Gunnel* had reconnoitered the North African coast. He told me about losing power in all his ship's engines, save the auxiliary engine, and how nerve-racking was the *Gunnel*'s slow progress to Scotland and safety. He described bleak Midway Island, and how ironic it seemed that men were sent to such a desolate, inhospitable place to recover from the hardships of war. He recounted the terrifying hours he had spent submerged as exploding depth charges unrelentingly shook his submarine. He talked about his narrow escape after sinking the destroyer, how they had been hunted relentlessly by its sister ships. He described how badly his crew had been affected by the experience, and the measures he had taken to prevent them from wasting oxygen and losing their minds. He talked warmly about the friendships he had formed during the war, and how important they were to enduring the strain and deprivations that war imposes on a commanding officer.

He told me all about his war, letting the facts speak for themselves. My father respected the facts of war. He felt no need to embellish them to make a point or to make any obvious pronouncements like "Let this be a lesson to you, boy." He assumed his story, briefly but honestly told, would answer my curiosity, and that I would derive from it what lessons I should.

Implicit in his assumption was his respect for me, and I was grateful to have it. I was not a member of the audience attending his seapower lectures. I was the son and grandson of Navy officers, and I had his trust that I would prepare myself for my turn at war.

I had known less of my father's attention than had many of my friends whose fathers were not as deeply involved in their work or absent as often as my father was. My father could often be a distant, inscrutable patriarch. But I always had a sense that he was special, a man who had set his mind to accomplishing great things, and had ransomed his life to the task. I admired him, and wanted badly to be admired by him, yet indications of his regard for me were more often found in the things he didn't say than in the things he did.

He wasn't purposely sparing with praise or encouragement, but neither did he lavish such generous attention on his children. He set an example for us, an example that took all his strength and courage to live. That, I believe, is how he expressed his devotion to us, as his father had expressed his devotion to him.

He assumed that I had the qualities necessary to live a life like his; that I would be drawn by some inherited proclivity to a life of adventure. He trusted that when I met with adversity, I would use the example he had set for me just as he had relied all his life on his father's example.

The sanctity of personal honor was the only lesson my father felt necessary to impart to me, and he faithfully saw to my instruction, frequently using my grandfather as his model. All my life, he had implored me not to lie, cheat, or steal; to be fair with friend and stranger alike; to respect my superiors and my subordinates; to know my duty and devote myself to its accomplishment without hesitation or complaint. All else, he reasoned, would be satisfactorily managed were I to accept, gratefully, the demands of honor. His father had taught him that, and the lesson had served him well.

"There is a term which has slipped somewhat into disuse," he remarked late in his life, "which I always used till the moment I retired, and that is the term 'an officer and a gentleman.' And those two imply everything that the highest sense of personal honor implies."

* * *

For nine months after leaving my squadron on the *Enterprise*, I served on the staff of the Chief of Air Basic Training in Pensacola. A job on an admiral's staff is considered a plumb assignment for an ambitious junior officer, and I was lucky to have it. But I was more eager to build my reputation as a combat pilot, and I looked for any opportunity to hurry the day when I would deploy to Vietnam.

One day, I got word that Paul Fay, Undersecretary of the Navy at the time, was coming to visit. After a round of meetings, Fay wanted to play a little tennis to relax. I was asked to play with him. After tennis, we went swimming at the officers' club. I took the opportunity to ask the undersecretary if he could help get me a combat tour in Vietnam.

Navy pilots rotate tours of sea and shore duty. I had left my squadron immediately after my last deployment in the Mediterranean. Fay knew that I had just begun my rotation on shore duty, but he promised to see what he could do. A few weeks after Fay returned to Washington, I got a call from one of his aides informing me that I would be sent to Vietnam, but not before I had finished my current rotation. I decided to put in for a transfer to Meridian, Mississippi, where, as a flight instructor at McCain Field, I could fly more in preparation for my combat tour.

Because Meridian was a remote, isolated location that offered few obvious attractions for pilots at play, I was reasonably serious about my work, and I became a better pilot. My fitness reports began to reflect these first signs of maturity. My superiors began to notice in me faint traces of qualities associated with capable officers. They once selected me as instructor of the month.

We worked long hours at Meridian, twelve or more hours a day. Every day began with the morning briefing at five-thirty, followed by the first of three training flights. After our third flight, we ended the long day with a debriefing. Meridian was a dry town at the time, and besides the officers' club, the only place where alcohol could be found was at an old roadhouse located outside the city limits. The county sheriff had come to the base one day, announcing at the gate that he had come to demand that alcohol no longer be served at the O club. He was refused entry. It was, as one pilot put it, "a hard town to have any fun in."

Given the challenge that our colorless circumstances posed to our imaginations, however, my fellow officers and I expended considerable energy devising entertainments to make time pass quickly and pleasantly. We organized a number of legendary bacchanals that abide, fondly, in the memory of many middle-aged, retired, and nearly retired Navy and Marine officers under the name of the legendary Key Fess Yacht Club.

Early in my time at McCain Field, a base beautification project had been launched by our well-intentioned commanding officer, at the behest of his wife and the wives of other senior officers. The plan to improve our plain surroundings included the construction of several man-made lakes. Bulldozers dug large holes in the base's clay soil, which stood empty until enough rainfall filled them with water to give them, it was hoped, a natural appearance. Sadly, they looked more like swamps than lakes, and they stank like a swamp as well.

One particularly unattractive and malodorous lagoon, called Lake Helen in honor of the CO's wife, lay just off the back of the BOQ, a prospect most of us regarded with bemusement as we walked along the outdoor corridors along which the doors to our rooms were located. Living among us at the time was a Marine captain who worked in an administrative capacity at the base. He was a man with a great thirst, which he attempted to slake virtually around the clock. He set up a bar on a card table in his room, and day and night we would hear him beckon any passerby, from young ensigns to room stewards, into his quarters for "a drink before din-din."

Late in the evening, we would often find him outside his room, leaning precariously on the balcony railing, cursing the eyesore that was Lake Helen. He had taken an intense dislike to the offending lagoon and would rage at it profanely for hours. Refusing to acknowledge its given name, he called it Lake Fester. Planted in the middle of the lake was a small island, nothing more than a little mound of dirt with a few spindly trees perched there pathetically. Our hard-drinking Marine neighbor called it Key Fess. And soon most of the residents of the BOQ referred derisively to the lake and its ridiculous island by those names.

One evening, several of us were bemoaning the sorry condition of our social life when someone came up with the brilliant idea of forming the Key Fess Yacht Club. The next weekend, attired in yachting dress of blue jackets and white trousers, we commissioned the club. We had strung lights on the trees of Key Fess and draped banners and flags over the BOQ's railings. We elected the club's officers, choosing Lake Fester's chief critic, the Marine captain, as the club's first commodore. I was elected vice commodore. We christened an old aluminum dinghy the *Fighting Lady*, and as "Victory at Sea" blasted over loudspeakers, we launched her ceremoniously on her maiden voyage to Key Fess, with the new commodore standing comically amidships, hand tucked inside his jacket like Washington crossing the Delaware.

Over the next several months, the weekend revels of the Key Fess Yacht Club became famous in Meridian and throughout the world of naval aviation. Huge throngs of people could now be found every Saturday night on the shores of Lake Fester, throwing themselves wholeheartedly into the evening's festivities. We held a toga party in the officers' club one night, replacing all its furniture with the mattresses from our rooms, which I still remember as one of the most exhausting experiences of my life. We often paid bands to come in from Memphis and entertain us.

Some of the club's members dated local girls, who spread the word in sleepy Meridian about our riotous activities, and soon a fair share of the town's single women were regular guests at our parties. One Sunday morning, BOQ residents were awakened by cries of help coming from Key Fess. Someone had rowed a few young ladies out to Key Fess the night before and stranded them there. We rowed the *Fighting Lady* out to rescue them. Despite their weariness, they still managed to give full vent to their anger, complaining bitterly about the mosquito bites that covered them.

Aviators from both east and west coasts began showing up for the fun. An admiral even flew in from Pensacola one Saturday to see for himself what all the fuss was about. Eventually, our commodore received orders to transfer to another base. I was elected the new commodore. Aviators flew in from everywhere to attend the huge party celebrating the change of command. We had put Naval Air Station, Meridian, on the Navy's map.

Despite the demands of my office as commodore of the Key Fess Yacht Club, I managed to devote at least as much energy to my job as I did to my extracurricular activities. Correspondingly, my reputation in the Navy improved. Anticipating my forthcoming tour in Vietnam, and confident that I could perform credibly in combat, I had begun to believe that I would someday have command of a carrier or squadron. I finally felt that I had settled into the family business and was on my way to a successful career as a naval officer.

I was also in the middle of a serious romance with Carol Shepp of Philadelphia, a relationship that added to my creeping sense that I might have been put on earth for some other purpose than my own constant amusement.

I had known and admired Carol since Academy days, when she was engaged to one of my classmates. She was a divorced mother of two young sons when we renewed our acquaintance shortly before I left for Meridian. She was attractive, clever, and kind, and I was instantly attracted to her, and delighted to discover that she was attracted to me.

Carol would occasionally visit me at Meridian and good-naturedly join in the weekend's festivities. But most weekends during our brief courtship, I abjured the social activities at Meridian, preferring Carol's company to the usual revelry at the Key Fess Yacht Club. On Friday afternoons, I would take a student pilot on a four-hour training flight to Philadelphia, refueling at Norfolk on the way. I would arrive at seven or eight o'clock in the evening. Carol would be waiting at the airfield to pick me up, and we would go out to dinner.

Connie Bookbinder, whose family owned Bookbinder's Restaurant, had been Carol's college roommate, so every evening we dined there on lobster and drank with friends. On Saturdays we would go to a football game at Memorial Stadium or a college basketball game at the Pallestra. We would enjoy some other entertainment on Sunday before I flew back to Meridian on Sunday night.

We had been dating for less than a year when I realized I wanted to marry Carol. The carefree life of an unattached naval aviator no longer held the allure for me that it once had. Nor had I ever been as happy in a relationship as I was now. I was elated when Carol instantly consented to my proposal.

We married on July 3, 1965. My marriage required that I relinquish my office as commodore of the yacht club, which I did without regret. The party held to celebrate my retirement was a memorable one.

Carol's two sons, Doug and Andy, were great kids, and I quickly formed a strong affection for them. I adopted them a year after our marriage, and I have been a proud father ever since. A few months later, Carol gave birth to our beautiful daughter, Sidney.

That December, I flew to Philadelphia to join my parents at the Army-Navy football game. My mother had brought Christmas presents for Carol and the kids, and I stowed them in the baggage compartment of my airplane on the return flight to Meridian. Somewhere between the Eastern Shore of Maryland and Norfolk, Virginia, as I was preparing to come in to refuel, my engine flamed out, and I had to eject at a thousand feet. The

Christmas gifts were lost with my airplane.

This latest unexpected glimpse of mortality added even greater urgency to my recent existential inquiries and made me all the more anxious to get to Vietnam before some new unforeseen accident prevented me from ever taking my turn in war.

So it was with some relief that I received my orders at the end of 1966 to report to Jacksonville, Florida, where I would join a squadron on the USS *Forrestal* and complete Replacement Air Group (RAG) training. I trained exclusively in the A-4 Skyhawk, the small bomber that I would soon fly in combat missions. Later that year, we sailed through the Suez Canal, on a course for Yankee Station in the Tonkin Gulf and war.

III

In me there dwells
No greatness, save it be some far-off touch
Of greatness to know well I am not great.

—Alfred, Lord Tennyson,
"Lancelot and Elaine"

CHAPTER FOURTEEN

The *Forrestal* Fire

Tom Ott had just handed me back my flight helmet after wiping off the visor with a rag. Tom was a second-class petty officer from Hattiesburg, Mississippi, and a fine man. He had been my parachute rigger since I came aboard the USS *Forrestal* several months earlier to begin RAG training off Guantanamo Bay. A parachute rigger is responsible for the maintenance and preparation of a naval aviator's equipment. Tom had heard me complain that I often found it difficult to see through my visor. So he always came on deck before launch to clean it one last time.

I was a thirty-one-year-old A-4 pilot, and like most pilots I was a little superstitious. I had flown five bombing runs over North Vietnam without incident, and I preferred that all preflight tasks be performed in the same order as for my previous missions, believing an unvarying routine portended a safe flight. Wiping off my visor was one of the last tasks executed in that routine.

Shortly before eleven on the morning of July 29, 1967, on Yankee Station in the Tonkin Gulf, I was third in line on the port side of the ship. I took my helmet back from Tom, nodded at him as he flashed me a thumbs-up, and shut the plane's canopy. In the next instant, a Zuni missile struck the belly fuel tank of my plane, tearing it open, igniting two hundred gallons of fuel that spilled onto the deck, and knocking two of my bombs to the deck. I never saw Tom Ott again.

Stray voltage from an electrical charge used to start the engine of a nearby F-4 Phantom, also waiting to take off, had somehow fired the six-foot Zuni from beneath the plane's wing. At impact, my plane felt like it had exploded.

I looked out at a rolling fireball as the burning fuel spread across the deck. I opened my canopy, raced onto the nose, crawled out onto the refueling probe, and jumped ten feet into the fire. I rolled through a wall of flames as my flight suit caught fire. I put the flames out and ran as fast as I could to the starboard side of the deck.

Shocked and shaking from adrenaline, I saw the pilot in the A-4 next to mine jump from his plane into the fire. His flight suit burst into flames. As I went to help him, a few crewmen dragged a fire hose toward the conflagration. Chief Petty Officer Gerald Farrier ran ahead of me with a portable fire extinguisher. He stood in front of the fire and aimed the extinguisher at one of the thousand-pound bombs that had been knocked loose from my plane and were now sitting in the flames on the burning deck. His heroism cost him his life. A few seconds later the bomb exploded, blowing me back at least ten feet and killing a great many men, including the burning pilot, the men with the hose, and Chief Farrier.

Small pieces of hot shrapnel from the exploded bomb tore into my legs and chest. All around me was mayhem. Planes were burning. More bombs cooked off. Body parts, pieces of the ship, and scraps of planes were dropping onto the deck. Pilots strapped in their seats ejected into the firestorm. Men trapped by flames jumped overboard. More Zuni missiles streaked across the deck. Explosions tore craters in the flight deck, and burning fuel fell through the openings into the hangar bay, spreading the fire below.

I went below to help unload some bombs from an elevator used to raise the jets from the hangar to the flight deck and dump them over the side of the ship. When we finished, I went to the ready room, where I could check the fire's progress on the television monitor located there. A stationary video camera was recording the tragedy and broadcasting it on the ship's closed-circuit television.

After a short while, I went to sick bay to have my burns and shrapnel wounds treated. There I found a horrible scene of many men, burned beyond saving, grasping the last moments of life. Most of them lay silently or made barely audible sounds. They gave no cries of agony because their nerve endings had been burned, sparing them any pain. Someone called my name, a kid, anonymous to me because the fire had burned off all his identifying features. He asked me if a pilot in our squadron was okay. I replied that he was. The young sailor said, "Thank God," and died. I left the sick bay unable to keep my composure.

The fires were consuming the *Forrestal*. I thought she might sink. But the crew's heroics kept her afloat. Men sacrificed their lives for one another and for their ship. Many of them were only eighteen and nineteen years old. They fought the inferno with a tenacity usually reserved for hand-to-hand combat. They fought it all day and well into the next, and they saved the *Forrestal*.

The fire on the flight deck was extinguished that first afternoon, but the last of the fires still burned belowdecks twenty-four hours later. By the time the last blaze was brought under control, 134 men were dead or dying. Dozens more were wounded. More than twenty planes were destroyed. But the *Forrestal*, with several large holes in its hull below the waterline, managed to make its way slowly to Subic Naval Base in the Philippines.

It would take almost a week for the *Forrestal* to reach Subic, where enough repairs would be made to the ship to enable it to return to the States for further repairs. It would take two more years of repairs before the *Forrestal* would be seaworthy enough to return to duty. All the pilots and crew who were fit to travel assumed we would board flights for home once we reached the Philippines. It appeared that my time at war was to be a very brief experience, and this distressed me considerably.

Combat for a naval aviator is fought in short, violent bursts. Our missions last but an hour or two before we are clear of danger and back on the carrier playing poker with our buddies. We are spared the sustained misery of the infantrymen who slog through awful conditions and danger for months on end. Some pilots like the excitement of our missions, knowing that they are of short duration, but most of us concentrate so fiercely on finding our targets and avoiding calamity that we recall more vividly our relief when it's over than we do our exhilaration while it's going on.

I did not take a perverse pleasure in the terror and destruction of war. I did not delight in the brief, intense thrill of flying combat missions. I was gratified when my bombs hit their target, but I did not particularly enjoy the excitement of the experience.

Nevertheless, I was a professional naval officer, and the purpose of my years of training had been to prepare me for this moment. As the crippled *Forrestal* limped toward port, my moment was disappearing when it had barely begun, and I feared my ambitions were among the casualties in the calamity that had claimed the *Forrestal*.

A distraction from my despondency appeared on the way to Subic in the person of R. W. "Johnny" Apple, the *New York Times* correspondent in Saigon. Serving as a pool reporter, he arrived by helicopter with a camera crew to examine the damaged ship and interview the survivors. When he finished collecting material for his report, he offered to take me back to Saigon with him for the daily press briefing irreverently referred to as the "Five O'Clock Follies." Seeing it as an opportunity for some welcome R&R, I jumped at the invitation. I passed a few days there pleasantly, wondering about my future, and beginning a lifelong friendship with Johnny.

Shortly after I returned to the *Forrestal*, an officer from the carrier USS *Oriskany* addressed my squadron to ask if any of us would consider volunteering for combat duty aboard his ship. The *Oriskany* had lately lost a number of pilots, and the squadron was considerably undermanned. A few others and I signed up.

The year before the *Forrestal* fire, the *Oriskany* had also suffered a terrible disaster at sea when a magnesium flare had ignited a blaze that nearly destroyed the ship. The *Oriskany* fire was not as great a holocaust as the fire that had engulfed the *Forrestal*. Ordnance had not exploded in the blaze, and the fire was brought under control in four hours. But it was nevertheless a terrible calamity for the pilots and crew. Forty-four men had been killed. In addition, the carrier was suffering high casualties in 1967. The *Oriskany* was regarded as a dangerous place to live.

I was relieved at this unexpected change in my fortunes. The *Oriskany* was coming off Yankee Station for a few weeks, and my services would not be needed until it returned. I met Carol and the kids in Europe and spent a pleasant family holiday, visiting my parents in London and relaxing on the French Riviera. I was still waiting for my final orders when we returned to Orange Park, Florida, which was near my last squadron's home base in Jacksonville, and where my family would await my return from combat duty. In September, my orders came through. I was an eager thirty-one-year-old lieutenant commander in the Navy, no longer worrying excessively about my career.

Many of my parents' friends wrote to them after the *Forrestal* fire to express their concern for my welfare. My father wrote a brief response to all, informing them, "Happily for all of us, he came through without a scratch and is now back at sea."

CHAPTER FIFTEEN

Killed

On September 30, 1967, I reported for duty to the *Oriskany* and joined VA-163—an A-4 attack squadron nicknamed the Saints. During the three years of Operation Rolling Thunder, the bombing campaign of North Vietnam begun in 1965, no carrier's pilots saw more action or suffered more losses than those on the *Oriskany*. When the Johnson administration halted Rolling Thunder in 1968, thirty-eight pilots on the *Oriskany* had been either killed or captured. Sixty planes had been lost, including twenty-nine A-4s. The Saints suffered the highest casualty rate. In 1967, one-third of the squadron's pilots were killed or captured. Every single one of the Saints' original fifteen A-4s had been destroyed. We had a reputation for aggressiveness, and for success. In the months before I joined the squadron, the Saints had destroyed all the bridges to the port city of Haiphong.

Like all combat pilots, we had a studied, almost macabre indifference to death that masked a great sadness in the squadron, a sadness that grew more pervasive as our casualty list lengthened. But we kept our game faces on, and our bravado became all the more exaggerated when the squadron returned to ship after a mission with one or more missing pilots. We flew the next raid with greater determination to do as much damage as we could, repeating to ourselves before the launch, "If we destroy the target, we won't have to go back."

We had one of the bravest, most resourceful squadron commanders, who was also one of the best A-4 pilots in the war,

Commander Bryan Compton. In August, six weeks before I reported for duty, Bryan had led a daring raid on a thermal power plant in Hanoi. For the first time the Saints had been equipped with Walleye smart bombs, and their accuracy reduced the risk of killing great numbers of civilians when striking targets in densely populated areas. The Hanoi power plant was located in a heavily populated part of Hanoi and had consequently been off-limits to American bombers. Contrary to North Vietnamese propaganda and the accusations of Americans who opposed the war, the bombing of North Vietnam was not a campaign of terror and wanton destruction against innocent civilians. Pilots and their military and civilian commanders exercised great care to keep civilian casualties to a minimum. With the introduction of smart bombs, militarily significant targets that had previously been avoided to spare innocent lives could now be attacked.

Bryan Compton successfully petitioned for his squadron to receive smart bombs. Once the Saints were equipped with the new ordnance, he sought and received permission to bomb the power plant. He took just five other pilots from the squadron with him on the mission. Diving in from different points on the compass, through a terrible barrage of antiaircraft fire and surface-to-air missiles, five of the six A-4s hit their target. The mission was a huge success, but rather than leaving off the attack as soon as the bombs had struck their target, Bryan flew two more passes over the power plant, taking pictures of the bomb damage. For his courage and leadership of the raid, Bryan received the Navy Cross.

I was third pilot on another raid Bryan led, this time over Haiphong. During the raid, the plane of the number two pilot was shot down. None of us saw him eject. Bryan wanted to determine whether or not the missing pilot had managed to escape his destroyed aircraft and parachute safely to ground. He kept circling Haiphong at an extremely low altitude, about two thousand feet, searching in vain for some sign that the pilot had survived. We were taking a tremendous pounding from flak and SAMs. I was scared to death waiting for Bryan to call off the search and lead us back to the *Oriskany* and out of harm's way. To this day, I will swear that Bryan made at least eight passes before he reluctantly gave up the search. Bryan has since dismissed my account of his heroism as an exaggeration, claiming, "You can't trust a politician. They'll lie every time." But I remember what I saw that day. I saw a courageous squadron commander put his life in grave peril so that a friend's family might know if their loved one was alive or dead. For his heroics and his ability to survive them, the rest of the squadron regarded Bryan as indestructible. We were proud to serve under his command.

In the early morning of October 26, 1967, I prepared for my twenty-third bombing run over North Vietnam. President Johnson had decided to escalate the war. The *Oriskany*'s pilots were on line twelve hours a day, flying raids from midnight to noon or from noon to midnight. We would rest for twelve hours while another carrier took up the battle, and then return to combat for another twelve-hour shift. The Saints were now dropping on Vietnam 150 tons of ordnance a day. Until this moment we had found Johnson's prosecution of the war, with its frustratingly limited bombing targets, to be maddeningly illogical.

When I was on the *Forrestal*, every man in my squadron had thought Washington's air war plans were senseless. The night before my first mission, I had gone up to the squadron's intelligence center to punch out information on my target. Out came a picture of a military barracks, with some details about the target's recent history. It had already been bombed twenty-seven times. Half a mile away there was a bridge with truck tracks. But the bridge wasn't on the target list. The target list was so restricted that we had to go back and hit the same targets over and over again. It's hard to get a sense that you are advancing the war effort when you are prevented from doing anything more than bouncing the rubble of an utterly insignificant target. James Stockdale, the air wing commander on the *Oriskany* who had been shot down and captured in 1965, aptly described the situation as "making gestures with our airplanes."

Flying missions off the *Oriskany*, I often observed Soviet ships come into Haiphong harbor and off-load surface-to-air missiles. We could see the SAMs being transported to firing sites and put into place, but we couldn't do anything about them because we were forbidden to bomb SAM sites unless they were firing on us. Even then, it was often an open question whether we could retaliate or not.

We lost a pilot one day over Haiphong. Another pilot released his bombs over the place he thought the SAM had been fired from. When we returned to the *Oriskany*, the pilot who had avenged his friend was grounded because he had bombed a target that wasn't on Washington's list. We all squawked so much that our commanders relented and returned the enterprising pilot to flight status. But the incident left a bad taste in our mouths, and our resentment over the absurd way we were ordered to fight the war grew much stronger, diminishing all the more our already weakened regard for our civilian commanders.

In 1966, Defense Secretary Robert Strange McNamara visited the *Oriskany*. He asked the skipper for the strike-pilot ratio. He wanted to make sure the numbers accorded with his conception of a successful war, and he was pleased with the figures he received from the skipper. He believed the number of missions flown relative to the number of bombs dropped would determine whether or not we won the war in the most cost-efficient manner. But when President Johnson ordered an end to Rolling Thunder in 1968, the campaign was judged to have had no measurable impact on the enemy. Most of the pilots flying the missions believed that our targets were virtually worthless. We had long believed that our attacks, more often than not limited to trucks, trains, and barges, were not just failing to break the enemy's resolve but actually having the opposite effect by boosting Vietnam's confidence that it could withstand the full measure of American airpower. In all candor, we thought our civilian commanders were complete idiots who didn't have the least notion of what it took to win the war. I found no evidence in postwar studies of the Johnson administration's political and military decision-making during the war that caused me to revise that harsh judgment.

When the orders came down to escalate the bombing campaign, the pilots on the *Oriskany* were ecstatic. As the campaign heated up, we began to lose a lot more pilots. But the losses, as much as they hurt, didn't cause any of us to reconsider our support for the escalation. For the first time we believed we were helping to win the war, and we were proud to be usefully employed.

Today's attack on Hanoi was to be an Alpha Strike, a large raid on a "militarily significant" target, involving A-4s from my squadron and our sister squadron on the *Oriskany*, the "Ghost Riders," as well as fighter escorts from the carrier's two F-8 squadrons. It would be my first attack on the enemy capital. The commander of the *Oriskany*'s air wing, Commander Burt Shepard, the brother of astronaut Alan Shepard, would lead the strike. Our target was the thermal power plant, located near a small lake almost in the center of the city, that the Saints had destroyed two months earlier; it had since been repaired.

The day before, I had pleaded with Jim Busey, the Saints' operations officer, who was responsible for putting the flight schedule together, to let me fly the mission. The earlier raid on the power plant was the pride of the squadron, having earned Navy Crosses for Bryan and Jim. I wanted to help destroy it again. I was feeling pretty cocky as well. The day before, we had bombed an airfield outside Hanoi, and I had destroyed two enemy MiGs parked on the runway. Jim, who called me "Gregory Green-Ass" because I was the new guy in the squadron and had flown far fewer missions than had the squadron's veteran pilots, consented, and put me on the mission as wingman.

I was still charged up from the previous day's good fortune, and was anticipating more success that morning despite having been warned about Hanoi's extensive air defense system. The *Oriskany*'s strike operations officer, Lew Chatham, told me he expected to lose some pilots. Be careful, he said. I told him not to worry about me, that I was sure I would not be killed. I didn't know at the time that downed pilots imprisoned in the North referred to their shootdowns as the day they were "killed."

Hanoi, with its extensive network of Russian-manufactured SAM sites, had the distinction of possessing the most formidable air defenses in the history of modern warfare. I was about to discover just how formidable they were.

We flew out to the west of Hanoi, turned, and headed in to make our run. We came in from the west so that once we had rolled in on the target, released our bombs, and pulled out we would be flying directly toward the Tonkin Gulf. We had electronic countermeasure devices in our planes. In 1966, A-4s had been equipped with radar detection. A flashing light and different tone signals would warn us of imminent danger from enemy SAMs. One tone sounded when a missile's radar was tracking you, another when it had locked onto you. A third tone signaled a real emergency, that a launched SAM was headed your way. As soon as we hit land and approached the three concentric rings of SAMs that surrounded Hanoi, the tone indicating that missile radar was tracking sounded. It tracked us for miles.

We flew in fairly large separations, unlike the tight formations flown in World War II bombing raids. At about nine thousand feet, as we turned inbound on the target, our warning lights flashed, and the tone for enemy radar started sounding so loudly I had to turn down the volume. I could see huge clouds of smoke and dust erupt on the ground as SAMs were fired at us. The closer we came to the target the fiercer were the defenses. For the first time in combat I saw thick black clouds of antiaircraft flak everywhere, images familiar to me only from World War II movies.

A SAM appears as a flying telephone pole, moving at great speed. We were now maneuvering through a nearly impassible obstacle course of antiaircraft fire and flying telephone poles. They scared the hell out of me. We normally kept pretty good radio discipline throughout a run, but there was a lot of chatter that day as pilots called out SAMs. Twenty-two missiles were fired at us that day. One of the F-8s on the strike was hit. The pilot, Charlie Rice, managed to eject safely.

I recognized the target sitting next to the small lake from the intelligence photographs I had studied. I dove in on it just as the tone went off signaling that a SAM was flying toward me. I knew I should roll out and fly evasive maneuvers, "jinking," in fliers' parlance, when I heard the tone. The A-4 is a small, fast, highly maneuverable aircraft, a lot of fun to fly, and it can take a beating. Many an A-4 returned safely to its carrier after being badly shot up by enemy fire. An A-4 can outmaneuver a tracking SAM, pulling more G's than the missile can take. But I was just about to release my bombs when the tone sounded, and had I started jinking I would never have had the time nor, probably, the nerve, to go back in once I had lost the SAM. So, at about 3,500 feet, I released my bombs, then pulled back the stick to begin a steep climb to a safer altitude. In the instant before my plane reacted, a SAM blew my right wing off. I was killed.

CHAPTER SIXTEEN

Prisoner of War

I knew I was hit. My A-4, traveling at about 550 miles an hour, was violently spiraling to earth. In this predicament, a pilot's training takes over. I didn't feel fear or any more excitement than I had already experienced during the run, my adrenaline surging as I dodged SAMs and flak to reach the target. I didn't think, "Gee, I'm hit—what now?" I reacted automatically the moment I took the hit and saw that my wing was gone. I radioed, "I'm hit," reached up, and pulled the ejection seat handle.

I struck part of the airplane, breaking my left arm, my right arm in three places, and my right knee, and I was briefly knocked unconscious by the force of the ejection. Witnesses said my chute had barely opened before I plunged into the shallow water of Truc Bach Lake. I landed in the middle of the lake, in the middle of the city, in the middle of the day. An escape attempt would have been challenging.

I came to when I hit the water. Wearing about fifty pounds of gear, I touched the bottom of the shallow lake and kicked off with my good leg. I did not feel any pain as I broke the surface, and I didn't understand why I couldn't move my arms to pull the toggle on my life vest. I sank to the bottom again. When I broke the surface the second time I managed to inflate my life vest by pulling the toggle with my teeth. Then I blacked out again.

When I came to the second time, I was being hauled ashore on two bamboo poles by a group of about twenty angry Vietnamese. A crowd of several hundred Vietnamese gathered around me as I

lay dazed before them, shouting wildly at me, stripping my
clothes off, spitting on me, kicking and striking me repeatedly.
When they had finished removing my gear and clothes, I felt a
sharp pain in my right knee. I looked down and saw that my right
foot was resting next to my left knee, at a ninety-degree angle. I
cried out, "My God, my leg." Someone smashed a rifle butt into
my shoulder, breaking it. Someone else stuck a bayonet in my
ankle and groin. A woman, who may have been a nurse, began
yelling at the crowd, and managed to dissuade them from further
harming me. She then applied bamboo splints to my leg and right
arm.

It was with some relief that I noticed an army truck arrive on
the scene to take me away from this group of aggrieved citizens
who seemed intent on killing me. Before they put me in the truck,
the woman who had stopped the crowd from killing me held a
cup of tea to my lips while photographers recorded the act. The
soldiers then placed me on a stretcher, loaded me into the truck,
and drove me a few blocks to an ocher-colored, trapezoid-shaped
stone structure that occupied two city blocks in the center of
downtown Hanoi.

I was brought in through enormous steel gates, above which
was painted the legend "Maison Centrale." I had been shot down
a short walk's distance from the French-built prison, Hoa Lo,
which the POWs had named "the Hanoi Hilton." As the massive
steel doors loudly clanked shut behind me, I felt a deeper dread
than I have ever felt since.

They took me into an empty cell, in a part of the prison we
called the Desert Inn, set me down on the floor still in the stretcher, stripped to my underwear, and placed a blanket over me. For
the next few days I drifted in and out of consciousness. When
awake, I was periodically taken to another room for interrogation. My interrogators accused me of being a war criminal and
demanded military information, what kind of aircraft I had
flown, future targets, and other particulars of that sort. In
exchange I would receive medical treatment.

I thought they were bluffing, and refused to provide any information beyond my name, rank, serial number, and date of birth. They knocked me around a little to force my cooperation, and I began to feel sharp pains in my fractured limbs. I blacked out after the first few blows. I thought if I could hold out like this for a few days, they would relent and take me to a hospital.

For four days I was taken back and forth to different rooms. Unable to use my arms, I was fed twice a day by a guard. I vomited after the meals, unable to hold down anything but a little tea. I remember being desperately thirsty all the time, but I could drink only when the guard was present for my twice-daily feedings.

On about the fourth day, I realized my condition had become more serious. I was feverish, and was losing consciousness more often and for longer periods. I was lying in my own vomit, as well as my other bodily wastes. Two guards entered my cell and pulled the blanket down to examine my leg. I saw that my knee had become grossly swollen and discolored. I remembered a fellow pilot at Meridian who had broken his femur ejecting from his plane. His blood had pooled in his leg, and he had gone into shock and died. I realized the same thing was happening to me, and I pleaded for a doctor.

The two guards left to find the camp officer, who spoke some English. He was short and fat, with a strangely wandering right eye that was clouded white by a cataract. The POWs called him "Bug." He was a mean son of a bitch.

Desperate, I tried to bargain with him. "Take me to the hospital and I'll give you the information you want." I didn't intend to keep my word, reasoning that after my injuries had been treated, I would be strong enough to deal with the consequences of not holding up my end of the bargain.

Bug left without replying, but returned a short while later with a medic, a man the POWs called Zorba. Zorba squatted down and took my pulse. He turned to Bug, shook his head, and uttered a few words.

"Are you going to take me to the hospital?" I asked.

"No," he replied. "It's too late."

I appealed, "Take me to the hospital and I'll get well."

"It's too late," he repeated.

He and the doctor left my cell, and panic that my death was approaching briefly overtook me.

There were few amputees among the POWs who survived their imprisonment. The Vietnamese usually refused treatment to the seriously injured. I don't know whether they were negligent for purposes of cost efficiency, reasoning that Americans, unused to unsanitary conditions, were likely to develop fatal infections following an amputation, or if they refused us treatment simply because they hated us. Whatever the reason, a lot of men died who shouldn't have, the victims of genuine war crimes.

I lapsed into unconsciousness a few minutes after Bug and Zorba left me to my fate, a condition that blessedly relieved me of the terrible dread I was feeling. I was awakened a short while later when an excited Bug rushed into my cell and shouted, "Your father is a big admiral. Now we take you to the hospital."

God bless my father.

My parents were in London when I was shot down. They were dressing for a dinner party when my father received a telephone call saying that my plane had been shot down over Hanoi. My father informed my mother what had happened. They kept their dinner engagement, never mentioning to any of the other guests the distressing news they had just learned.

When they returned home, my father got a call from his boss, Admiral Tom Moorer, Chief of Naval Operations. Admiral Moorer was a friend and had decided to break the sad news to my father himself. "Jack, we don't think he survived."

My parents then called Carol, who had already been notified of my shootdown by the Navy. My mother told her to prepare for the worst: that I was dead, and they would have to find a way to accept that. My father, very matter-of-factly, said, "I don't think we have to."

After speaking with Carol, my parents placed calls to my sister and brother to break the bad news to them. Joe was working as a reporter for the *San Diego Tribune* at the time. He knew something was wrong when he answered the phone and both our parents were on the line.

Without any preliminaries, my mother said: "Honey, Johnny's been shot down."

"What happened?"

"He was hit by a missile and went down."

My brother's question hung in the air unanswered for a moment until my father explained: "His wingman saw his plane explode. They don't think he got out."

Joe began to cry, and then asked my father, "What do we do now?" He recalled my father answering in a soft, sad voice, "Pray for him, my boy."

The next day, October 28, Johnny Apple wrote a story that appeared on the front page of the *New York Times*: adm. mccain's son, FORRESTAL survivor, is missing in raid.

I was moved by stretcher to a hospital in central Hanoi. As I was being moved, I again lapsed into unconsciousness. I came to a couple of days later and found myself lying in a filthy room, about twenty by twenty feet, lousy with mosquitoes and rats. Every time it rained, an inch of mud and water would pool on the floor. I was given blood and glucose, and several shots. After several more days passed, during which I was frequently unconscious, I began to recover my wits. Other than the transfusion and shots, I received no treatment for my injuries. No one had even bothered to wash the grime off me.

Once my condition had stabilized, my interrogators resumed their work. Demands for military information were accompanied by threats to terminate my medical treatment if I did not cooperate. Eventually, I gave them my ship's name and squadron number, and confirmed that my target had been the power plant. Pressed for more useful information, I gave the names of the Green Bay Packers' offensive line, and said they were members of my squadron. When asked to identify future targets, I simply recited the names of a number of North Vietnamese cities that had already been bombed.

I was occasionally beaten when I declined to give any more

information. The beatings were of short duration, because I let out a hair-raising scream whenever they occurred. My interrogators appeared concerned that hospital personnel might object. I also suspected that my treatment was less harsh than might be accorded other prisoners. This I attributed to my father's position, and the propaganda value the Vietnamese placed on possessing me, injured but alive. Later, my suspicion was confirmed when I heard accounts of other POWs' experiences during their first interrogations. They had endured far worse than I had, and had withstood the cruelest torture imaginable.

Although I rarely saw a doctor or a nurse, I did have a constant companion, a teenage boy who was assigned to guard me. He had a book that he read at my bedside every day. In the book was a picture of an old man with a rifle sitting on the fuselage of a downed F-105. He would show me the picture, point to himself, and then slap me.

I still could not feed myself, so the boy would spoon-feed me a bowl of noodles with some gristle in it. The gristle was hard to chew. He would jam three of four spoonfuls in my mouth before I could chew and swallow any of it. Unable to force any more into my mouth, he would finish the bowl himself. I got three or four spoonfuls of food twice a day. After a while I really didn't give a damn, although I tried to eat as much as I could before the boy took his share.

After about a week in the hospital, a Vietnamese officer we called Chihuahua informed me that a visiting Frenchman had asked to look in on me, and had volunteered to carry a message back to my family. I was willing to see him, assuming at the time that my family probably believed I was dead.

As I later learned, the Vietnamese, always delighted when a propaganda opportunity presented itself, had already announced my capture, and helpfully supplied quotes from the repentant war criminal commending the Vietnamese people's strong morale and observing that the war was turning against the United States. And in an English-language commentary broadcast over the Voice of Vietnam, entitled "From the Pacific to Truc Bach Lake," Hanoi accused Lyndon Johnson and me of staining my family's honor.

Adding to the ever longer list of American pilots captured over North Vietnam was a series of newcomers. John Sidney McCain was one of them. Who is he? A U.S. carrier navy lieutenant commander. Last Thursday, 26 October, he took off from the carrier *Oriskany* for a raiding mission against Hanoi City. Unfortunately for him, the jet plane he piloted was one of ten knocked out of Hanoi's sky. He tried in vain to evade the deadly accurate barrage of fire of this city. A surface-to-air missile shot down his jet on the spot. He bailed out and was captured on the surface of Truc Bach Lake right in the heart of the DRV capital.

What were the feats of arms which McCain achieved? Foreign correspondents in Hanoi saw with their own eyes civilian dwelling houses destroyed and Hanoi's women, old folks and children killed by steel-pellet bombs dropped from McCain's aircraft and those of his colleagues.

Lt. Com. John Sidney McCain nearly perished in the conflagration that swept the flight deck of the U.S. carrier *Forrestal* last July. He also narrowly escaped death in Haiphong the Sunday before last but this time what must happen has happened. There is no future in it.

McCain was married in 1965 and has a ten-month-old daughter. Surely he also loves his wife and child. Then why did he fly here dropping bombs on the necks of the Vietnamese women and children?

The killing he was ordered to do in Vietnam has aroused indignation among the world's peoples. What glory had he brought by his job to his father, Admiral John S. McCain Jr., commander in chief of U.S. Naval Forces in Europe? His grandfather, Admiral John S. McCain, commander of all aircraft carriers in the Pacific in World War II, participated in a just war against the Japanese forces. But nowadays, Lt. Com. McCain is participating in an unjust war, the most unpopular one in U.S. history and mankind's history, too. This is Johnson's war to enslave the Vietnamese people.

From the Pacific to Truc Bach Lake, McCain has brought no reputation for his family in the United States. The one who is smearing McCain's family honor is also smearing the honor of Washington's United States of America. He is Lyndon B. Johnson.

Prior to the Frenchman's arrival, I was rolled into a treatment room, where a doctor tried to set my broken right arm. For what seemed like an eternity, he manipulated my arm, without benefit of anesthesia, trying to set the three fractures. Blessedly, the pain at its most acute rendered me unconscious. Finally abandoning the effort, he slapped a large and heavy chest cast on me, an act I can hardly credit as considerate on the part of my captors. The cast did not have a cotton lining, and the rough plaster painfully rubbed against my skin. Over time, it wore two holes in the back of my arm down to the bone. My other arm was left untreated.

Exhausted and encased from my waist to my neck in a wet plaster cast, I was rolled into a large, clean room and placed in a nice white bed. The room contained six beds, each protected by a mosquito net. I asked if this was to be my new room, and was told that it was.

A few minutes later, a Vietnamese officer, a Major Nguyen Bai, paid me a visit, accompanied by Chihuahua. He was the commandant of the entire prison system, a dapper, educated man whom the POWs had nicknamed "the Cat." The Cat informed me that the Frenchman who would arrive shortly was a television journalist, and that I should tell him everything I had told my interrogators. Surprised, I told the Cat I didn't want to be filmed.

"You need two operations on your leg, and if you don't talk to him, then we will take your cast off and you won't get any operations," he threatened. "You will say you are grateful to the Vietnamese people, and that you are sorry for your crimes, or we will send you back to the camp."

I assured him that I would say nothing of the kind, but believing that the Cat would send me back to Hoa Lo, and worrying that I could not endure the truck ride back, I agreed to see the Frenchman.

A few minutes later, François Chalais entered the room with two cameramen. He questioned me for several minutes, asking about my shootdown, my squadron, the nature of my injuries, and my father. I repeated the same information about my ship and squadron and told him I was being treated well by the doctors, who had promised to operate on my leg. Off camera, the Cat and Chihuahua were visibly displeased with my answers. Chihuahua demanded that I say more.

"I have no more to say about it," I replied.

Both Vietnamese insisted that I express gratitude for the lenient and humane treatment I had received. I refused, and when they pressed me, Chalais said, "I think what he told me is sufficient."

Chalais then inquired about the quality of the food I was getting, and I responded, "It's not like Paris, but I eat it." Finally, Chalais asked if I had a message for my family.

"I would just like to tell my wife that I'm going to get well. I love her, and hope to see her soon. I'd appreciate it if you'd tell her that. That's all I have to say."

Chihuahua told me to say that I could receive letters and pictures from home. "No," I replied. A visibly agitated Cat demanded that I say on camera how much I wanted the war to end so I could go home. Again, Chalais stepped in to help me, saying very firmly that he was satisfied with my answer, and that the interview was over. I appreciated his help.

Although I had resisted giving my interrogators any useful information and had greatly irritated the Cat by refusing his demands during the interview, I should not have given out information about my ship and squadron, and I regret very much having done so. The information was of no real use to the Vietnamese, but the Code of Conduct for American Prisoners of War orders us to refrain from providing any information beyond our name, rank, and serial number.

When Chalais had left, the Cat admonished me for my "bad attitude" and told me I wouldn't receive any more operations. I was taken back to my old room.

Carol went to see Chalais after he returned to Paris, and he gave her a copy of the film, which was shown in the States on the CBS evening news a short time later.

My parents saw it before it was broadcast nationally. A public affairs officer, Herbert Hetu, who worked for my father when my father was the Navy chief in Europe, had a friend who was a producer at CBS. His friend informed him that CBS had the film of my interview, and he offered to screen it for my parents. Hetu and my parents were in New York at the time. My father was scheduled to give a speech on the emerging strength of the Soviet Navy to the prestigious Overseas Press Club. It was an important and much-anticipated speech that he had been preparing for weeks.

Hetu viewed the film and decided not to show it to my father before he delivered his speech, fearing it would "uncork him." Instead, he persuaded his friend at CBS to hold the film until the morning, when my parents could view it. He then contacted my father's personal aide and told him: "After the speech, get with the admiral and tell him about this film. They're going to hold it and we'll take him over to CBS tomorrow. I'm sure he'll want to see it."

Hetu accompanied my parents to CBS the next day. He remembered my father reacting very emotionally to the film. "We took him over with Mrs. McCain, and I think I said to the admiral, 'I think you and Mrs. McCain ought to see this by yourselves. You don't want anybody else in there.' So that's the way they watched it, and it was a very emotional piece of film.... I think Admiral McCain and his wife looked at the film twice. His reaction afterward was very emotional, but he never talked to us about it. Some things are just too painful for words."

It was hard not to see how pleased the Vietnamese were to have captured an admiral's son, and I knew that my father's identity was directly related to my survival. Often during my hospital stay I received visits from high-ranking officials. Some observed me for a few minutes and then left without asking any questions. Others would converse idly with me, asking only a few innocuous questions. During one visit, I was told to meet with a visiting Cuban delegation. When I refused, they did not force the issue, either out of concern for my condition or because they were worried about what I might say. One evening, General Vo Nguyen Giap, minister of defense and hero of Dien Bien Phu, paid me a visit. He stared at me wordlessly for a minute, then left.

Bug arrived one day and had me listen to a tape of a POW denouncing America's involvement in the war. The POW was a Marine, a veteran who had flown in the Korean War. The vigor with which he criticized the United States surprised me. His language did not seem stilted, nor did his tone sound forced.

Bug told me he wanted me to make a similar statement. I told him I didn't want to say such things.

He told me I shouldn't be afraid to speak openly about the war, that there was nothing to be ashamed of or to fear.

"I don't feel that way about the war," I replied, and was threatened for what seemed like the hundredth time with a warning that I would be denied an operation because of my "bad attitude."

In early December, they operated on my leg. The Vietnamese filmed the operation. I haven't a clue why. Regrettably, the operation wasn't much of a success. The doctors severed all the ligaments on one side of my knee, which has never fully recovered. After the war, thanks to the work of a kind and talented physical therapist, my knee regained much of its mobility—enough, anyway, for me to return to flight status for a time. But today, when I am tired or when the weather is inclement, my knee stiffens in pain, and I pick up a trace of my old limp.

They decided to discharge me later that December. I had been in the hospital about six weeks. I was in bad shape. I had a high fever and suffered from dysentery. I had lost about fifty pounds and weighed barely a hundred. I was still in my chest cast, and my leg hurt like hell.

On the brighter side, at my request, the Vietnamese were taking me to another prison camp. Bug had entered my room one day and abruptly announced, "The doctors say you are not getting better."

The accusatory tone he used to relay this all too obvious diagnosis implied that I was somehow responsible for my condition and had deliberately tried to embarrass the Vietnamese medical establishment by refusing to recover.

"Put me with other Americans," I responded, "and I'll get better."

Bug said nothing in reply. He just looked at me briefly with the expression he used to convey his disdain for an inferior enemy, then withdrew from the room.

That evening I was blindfolded, placed in the back of a truck, and driven to a truck repair facility that had been converted into a prison a few years earlier. It was situated in what had once been the gardens of the mayor of Hanoi's official residence. The Americans held there called it "the Plantation."

To my great relief, I was placed in a cell in a building we called "the Gun Shed" with two other prisoners, both Air Force majors, George "Bud" Day and Norris Overly. I could have asked for no better companions. There has never been a doubt in my mind that Bud Day and Norris Overly saved my life.

Bud and Norris later told me that their first impression of me, emaciated, bug-eyed, and bright with fever, was of a man at the threshold of death. They thought the Vietnamese expected me to die and had placed me in their care to escape the blame when I failed to recover.

Despite my poor condition, I was overjoyed to be in the company of Americans. I had by this time been a prisoner of war for two months, and I hadn't even caught a glimpse of another American.

I was frail, but voluble. I wouldn't stop talking all through that first day with Bud and Norris, explaining my shootdown, describing my treatment since capture, inquiring about their experiences, and asking for all the details of the prison system and for information about other prisoners.

Bud and Norris accommodated me to the best of their ability, and were the soul of kindness as they eased my way to what they believed was my imminent death. Bud had been seriously injured when he ejected. Like me, he had broken his right arm in three places and had torn the ligaments in his knee—the left knee in his case. After his capture near the DMZ, he had attempted an escape, and had nearly reached an American airfield when he was recaptured. He was brutally tortured for his efforts, and for subsequently resisting his captors' every entreaty for information.

First held in a prison in Vinh before making the 150-mile trip north to Hanoi, Bud had experienced early the full measure of the mistreatment that would be his fate for nearly six years. His captors had looped rope around his shoulders, tightened it until his shoulders were nearly touching, and then hung him by the arms from the rafter of the torture room, tearing his shoulders apart. Left in this condition for hours, Bud never acceded to the Vietnamese demands for military information. They had to refracture his broken right arm and threaten to break the other before Bud gave them anything at all. He was a tough man, a fierce resister, whose example was an inspiration to every man who served with him. For his heroic escape attempt, he received the Medal of Honor, one of only three POWs in Vietnam to receive the nation's highest award.

Because of his injuries, Bud was unable to help with my physical care. Norris shouldered most of the responsibility. A gentle, uncomplaining guy, he cleaned me up, fed me, helped me onto the bucket that served as our toilet, and massaged my leg. Thanks to his tireless ministration, and to the restorative effect Bud and Norris's company had on my morale, I began to recover.

I slept a lot those first weeks, eighteen to twenty hours a day. Little by little, I grew stronger. A little more than a week after I had been consigned to his care, Norris had me on my feet and helped me to stand for a few moments. From then on, I could feel my strength return more rapidly each day. Soon I was able to stand unaided, and even maneuver around my cell on a pair of crutches.

In early January, we were relocated to another end of the camp, a place we called "the Corn Crib." We had neighbors in the cells on either side of ours, and for the first time we managed to establish communications with fellow POWs. Our methods were crude, yelling to each other whenever the turnkeys were absent, and leaving notes written in cigarette ash in a washroom drain. It would be some time before we devised more sophisticated and secure communication methods.

One day a young English-speaking officer escorted a group of older, obviously senior party members into our cell. Their privileged status was evident in the quality of their attire, which, although perhaps not elegant by Western standards, was far better than that worn by most Vietnamese of our acquaintance.

For a few moments after entering, the entire group just stared at me. Finally, the young officer began asking me questions in English, translating my answers for the assembled dignitaries.

"How many corporations does your family own?"

Puzzled by the question, I looked at him for a moment before asking, "What do you mean?"

"How many corporations does your family own? Your father is a big admiral. He must have many companies that work with your government."

Laughing at the absurd premise of the question, I replied, "You've got to be putting me on. My father is a military officer whose income is confined to his military salary."

When my answer had been translated, the crowd of high-ranking officials, all of whom had thrived in a system of government infamously riddled with corruption, smiled and nodded at each other, dismissing my protest as unimaginative propaganda. In their experience, admirals and generals got rich. Surely in a country as wealthy and undisciplined as the United States, military officers used their influence to profit themselves and their families.

Around that time, we began to notice that the Vietnamese were showing us unusual leniency. Our diet improved a little. For a few days we received large bunches of bananas. The Cat would often visit us and inquire about our health and how we were getting along.

No one invested much effort in interrogating us or getting us to make propaganda statements. Once we were instructed to write summaries of our military histories. We invented all the details. Mine contained references to service in Antarctica and as the naval attaché in Oslo, two places, I am sorry to say, I had never visited.

We were suspicious of the Vietnamese's motives, as we doubted that they had begun to take seriously their public commitments to a policy of humane treatment of prisoners. But initially we were at a loss to figure out their purpose.

We weren't in the dark for long. One evening in early February, Norris told us that the Vietnamese were considering releasing him along with two other prisoners. For a couple of weeks, the Vietnamese had regularly interrogated Norris. Unbeknownst to us, they had been quizzing Norris to determine whether he was willing and suitable to be included in their first grant of "amnesty." Bud advised him to reject the offer. The Code of Conduct obliged us to refuse release before those who had been captured earlier had been released.

The next day, Norris was removed from our cell. The day of his release, February 16, I was carried on a stretcher with Bud walking beside me to a room where we were to bid Norris goodbye. A crew was filming the departure ceremony. Bud asked if he had been required to make any propaganda statement or do anything else he might later on regret. Norris said that he had not, and we let the matter drop.

Some of the prisoners were pretty hard on Norris and the other two prisoners for taking early release. Norris had taken very good care of me. He had saved my life. I thought him a good man then, as I do today. I feared he had made a mistake, but I couldn't stand in judgment of him. I thought too well of him, and owed him too much to stand between him and his freedom. I wished him well as he departed, carrying a letter from me to Carol in his pocket.

CHAPTER SEVENTEEN

Solitary

Bud and I remained roommates for about another month. When the Vietnamese observed that I could get around on my crutches, they moved Bud to another cell. In April 1968, Bud was relocated to another prison, and I was moved into another building, the largest cellblock in the camp, "the Warehouse." I cannot adequately describe how sorry I was to part company with my friend and inspiration. Up until then, I don't believe I had ever relied on any other person for emotional and physical support to the extent I had relied on Bud.

Although I could manage to hobble around on my crutches, I was still in poor shape. My arms had not yet healed, and I couldn't pick up or carry anything. I was still suffering from dysentery, a chronic ailment throughout most of my years in prison, and I weighed little more than a hundred pounds. The dysentery caused me considerable discomfort. Food and water would pass immediately through me, and sharp pains in my stomach made sleeping difficult. I was chronically fatigued and generally weak from my inability to retain nourishment.

Bud, whose injuries were nearly as debilitating as mine, helped me enormously by building my confidence in my eventual recovery. He joked often about our condition, and got me to laugh about it as well. When other POWs teased us as they observed us hobbling along to the showers, no one laughed harder than Bud.

Bud had an indomitable will to survive with his reputation intact, and he strengthened my will to live. The only sustenance I had in those early days I took from the example of his abiding moral and physical courage. Bud was taken to a prison, "the Zoo," where the conditions and the cruelty of camp authorities made the Plantation seem like a resort. He would suffer terribly there, confronting the full force of man's inhumanity to man. But he was a tough, self-assured, and amazingly determined man, and he bore all his trials with an unshakable faith that he was a better man than his enemies. I was distraught when he left, but better prepared to endure my fate thanks to the months of his unflagging encouragement. I bid good-bye to him warmly, trying not to betray the sadness I felt to see him go. I would remain in solitary confinement for over two years.

It's an awful thing, solitary. It crushes your spirit and weakens your resistance more effectively than any other form of mistreatment. Having no one else to rely on, to share confidences with, to seek counsel from, you begin to doubt your judgment and your courage. But you eventually adjust to solitary, as you can to almost any hardship, by devising various methods to keep your mind off your troubles and greedily grasping any opportunity for human contact.

The first few weeks are the hardest. The onset of despair is immediate, and it is a formidable foe. You have to fight it with any means necessary, all the while trying to bridle the methods you devise to combat loneliness and prevent them from robbing your senses.

I tried to memorize the names of POWs, the names and personal details of guards and interrogators, and the details of my environment. I devised other memory games to keep my faculties sound. For days I tried to remember the names of all the pilots in my squadron and our sister squadron. I also prayed more often and more fervently than I ever had as a free man.

Many prisoners spent their hours exercising their minds by concentrating on an academic discipline or hobby they were proficient in. I knew men who mentally designed buildings and airplanes. I knew others who spent days and weeks working out complicated math formulas. I reconstructed from memory books and movies I had once enjoyed. I tried to compose books and plays of my own, often acting out sequences in the quiet solitude of my cell. Anyone who had observed my amateur theatrics might have challenged the exercise's beneficial effect on my mental stability.

I had to carefully guard against my fantasies becoming so consuming that they took me permanently to a place in my mind from which I might fail to return. On several occasions I became terribly annoyed when a guard entered my cell to take me to the bath or to bring me my food and disrupted some flight of fantasy where the imagined comforts were so attractive that I could not easily bear to be deprived of them. Sadly, I knew of a few men in prison who had grown so content in their imaginary worlds that they preferred solitary confinement and turned down the offer of a roommate. Eventually, they stopped communicating with the rest of us.

For long stretches of every day, I would watch the activities in camp through a crack in my door, grateful to witness any unusual or amusing moment that broke the usual monotony of prison administration. As I began to settle into my routine, I came to appreciate the POW adage "The days and hours are very long, but the weeks and months pass quickly."

Solitary also put me in a pretty surly mood, and I would resist depression by hollering insults at my guards, resorting to the belligerence that I had relied on earlier in my life when obliged to suffer one indignity or another. Resisting, being uncooperative and a general pain in the ass, proved, as it had in the past, to be a morale booster for me.

Hypochondria is a malady that commonly afflicts prisoners held in solitary confinement. A man becomes extremely conscious of his physical condition and can worry excessively over every ailment that plagues him. After Bud and I were separated, I struggled to resist concern bordering on paranoia that my injuries and poor health would eventually prove mortal.

I received nothing in the way of medical treatment. Three or four times a year, Zorba, the prison medic, would drop by for a brief visit. After a quick visual appraisal of my condition he would leave me with the exhortation to eat more and exercise. That I often could not keep down the little food allowed me after the guards had taken their share did not strike Zorba as paradoxical. Nor did Zorba bother to explain how I might manage to exercise given my disabling injuries and the narrow confines of my cell. I was routinely refused permission to spend a few minutes a day out of doors where I might have had the space necessary to concoct some half-assed exercise regimen.

I did try, despite my challenging circumstances and uncooperative guards, to build up my strength. In the summer of 1968, I attempted to do push-ups, but lacked the strength to raise myself once from my cell floor. I was able to perform a single standing push-up off the wall, but the experience was so painful that it only served to exacerbate my concern about my condition.

By late summer in 1969, my dysentery had eased. The strength I gained from holding down my food enabled me to begin exercising my leg. Whenever possible, I limped around my cell on my stiff leg, and I was greatly cheered when I noticed the limb slowly becoming stronger.

My arms were another matter. Over a period of two years, I began to regain some use of them, but even then exercise occasionally resulted in my arms' total immobility for a period that could last up to a month. After I returned to the States, an orthopedic surgeon informed me that because the fracture in my left arm had not been set, using my arm as much as I had during my imprisonment had worn a new socket in my left shoulder.

In the last two years of my captivity, prisoners were quartered together in large cells. Because of the improvement in our food and living conditions, I was strong enough to perform a rigorous daily exercise routine. Lopsided push-ups and a form of running in place that resembled hopping more than it did running gave my daily workout a comical aspect. But in addition to endlessly amusing my roommates, the routine considerably strengthened both my mental and physical reserves.

Left alone to act as my own physician, I made diagnoses that were occasionally closer to hysterical than practical. Among its many unattractive effects, dysentery often causes rather severe hemorrhoids. When this affliction visited me, I became morose, brooding about its implications for my survival. After some time, it finally occurred to me that I had never heard of a single person whose hemorrhoids had proved fatal. When this latest infirmity disappeared after a couple of months, I made a mental note to stop acting like an old man who stayed in bed all day fussing about his angina.

There is little doubt that solitary confinement causes some mental deterioration in even the most resilient personalities. When in 1970 my period of solitary confinement was finally ended, I was overwhelmed by the compulsion to talk nonstop, face-to-face with my obliging new cellmate. I ran my mouth ceaselessly for four days. My cellmate, John Finely, who had once been held in solitary himself and understood my exuberant reaction to his company, listened intently, frequently nodding his head in assent to my rhetorical points even though he could not possibly have taken in more than a fraction of my rambling dialogue.

I have observed this phenomenon in many other men when they were released from solitary. One of the more amusing spectacles in prison is the sight of two men, both just released from solitary, talking their heads off simultaneously, neither one listening to the other, both absolutely enraptured by the sound of their voices. Most "solos" settled down after spending a few days with a roommate and recovered the strength and confidence of men who were sound in both mind and body.

We had a saying in prison: "Steady strain." The point of the remark was to remind us to keep a close watch on our emotions, not to let them rise and fall with circumstances that were out of our control. We tried hard to avoid seizing on any small change in our treatment as an indication of an approaching change in our fortunes.

We called some POWs "gastro politicians," because their spirits soared every time they found a carrot in their soup. "Look at this. They're fattening us up," they would declare. "We must be going home." And when no omen appeared in the next day's meal, the gastro politician's irrational exuberance of the previous day would disappear, and he would sink into an equally irrational despondency, lamenting, "We're never getting out of here."

Most of the prisoners considered it unhealthy to allow themselves to interpret our circumstances like tea leaf readers divining some secret purpose in the most unremarkable event. Prison was enough of a psychological strain without riding an emotional roller coaster of our own creation. Once you began investing meals or an unexpectedly civil word from a guard with greater meaning than it merited, you might begin to pay attention to the promises or threats of your captors. That was the surest way to lose your resolve or even your mind.

"Steady strain, buddy, steady strain," we cautioned each other whenever we began to take a short view of our lives. It was best to take the long view. We would get home when we got home. There wasn't anything we could do to hasten that day's arrival. Until then we had to manage our hardships as best we could, and hope that when we did get home we would have been a credit to ourselves and to the country.

When you're left alone with your thoughts for years, it's hard not to reflect on how better you could have spent your time as a free man. I had more than a normal share of regrets, but regret for choosing the career that had landed me in this place was not among them.

I regretted I hadn't read more books so I could keep my mind better occupied in solitary. I regretted much of the foolishness that had characterized my youth, seeing in it, at last, its obvious insignificance. I regretted I hadn't worked harder at the Academy, believing that had I done so, I might have been better prepared for the trial I now faced.

My regrets were never so severe that they made me despondent, but I did experience remorse to an extent I had never known in the past, an emotion that helped mature me. I gained the insight, common to many people in life-threatening circumstances, that the trivial pleasures of life and human vanity were transient and insignificant. And I resolved that when I regained my freedom, I would seize opportunities to spend what remained of my life in more important pursuits.

"All that's beautiful drifts away/Like the waters," lament Yeats's old men. Except, I discovered, love and honor. If you valued them, and held them strongly, love and honor would endure undiminished by the passing of time and the most determined assault on your dignity. And to hold on to love and honor I needed to be part of a fraternity. I was not as strong a man as I had once believed myself to be.

Of all the activities I devised to survive solitary confinement with my wits and strength intact, nothing was more beneficial than communicating with other prisoners. It was, simply, a matter of life and death.

Fortunately, the Vietnamese—although they went to extraordinary lengths to prevent it—couldn't stop all communication among prisoners. Through flashed hand signals when we were moved about, tap codes on the wall, notes hidden in washroom drains, and holding our enamel drinking cups up to the wall with our shirts wrapped around them and speaking through them, we were able to communicate with each other. The whole prison system became a complex information network, POWs busily trafficking in details about each other's circumstances and news from home that would arrive with every new addition to our ranks.

The tap code was a simple device. The signal to communicate was the old rhythm "shave and a haircut," and the response, "two bits," was given if the coast was clear. We divided the alphabet into five columns of five letters each. The letter K was dropped. A, F, L, Q, and V were the key letters. Tap once for the five letters in the A column, twice for F, three times for L, and so on. After indicating the column, pause for a beat, then tap one through five times to indicate the right letter. My name would be tapped 3-2, 1-3, 1-3, 1-1, 2-4, 3-3.

It was an easy system to teach the uninitiated, and new guys would usually be communicating like veterans within a few days. We became so proficient at it that in time we could communicate as efficiently by tapping as we could by speaking through our drinking cups. But I preferred, whenever circumstances allowed, to speak to my neighbors. The sound of the human voice, unappreciated in an open society's noisy clutter of spoken words, was an emblem of humanity to a man held at length in solitary confinement, an elegant and poignant affirmation that we possessed a divine spark that our enemies could not extinguish.

The punishment for communicating could be severe, and a few POWs, having been caught and beaten for their efforts, had their spirits broken as their bodies were battered. Terrified of a return trip to the punishment room, they would lie still in their cells when their comrades tried to tap them up on the wall. Very few would remain uncommunicative for long. To suffer all this alone was less tolerable than torture. Withdrawing in silence from the fellowship of other Americans and the doggedly preserved cohesion of an American military unit was to us the approach of death. Almost all would recover their strength in a few days and answer the summons to rejoin the living.

In October 1968, I heard the guards bring a new prisoner into the camp and lock him into the cell behind mine. Ernie Brace was a decorated former Marine who had flown over a hundred combat missions in the Korean War. He had been accused of deserting the scene of an aircraft accident, court-martialed, and discharged dishonorably from the service. Determined to restore his good name, he had volunteered as a civilian pilot to fly supply missions in Laos for the United States Agency for International Development, and, when asked, to secretly supply CIA-supported military units in the Laotian jungle.

During one such operation, Communist insurgents, the Pathet Lao, overran the small airstrip where he had just landed and captured him. His captors handed him over to soldiers in the North Vietnamese Army, who marched him to a remote outpost near Dien Bien Phu. He was imprisoned for three years in a bamboo cage with his arms and legs bound. He attempted three escapes. He was brutally tortured, held in leg stocks, and tethered to a stake by a rope around his neck. After his last failed escape attempt, the Vietnamese buried him in a pit up to his neck and left him there for a week.

In 1968, he was brought to Hanoi. Uncertain whether the United States government was aware he had been captured alive, he was greatly relieved to realize that he was now in the company of American POWs whose captivity was known to our government.

When the commotion in the cell behind me died down as the guards left Ernie alone in his new home, I tried to tap him up on the wall. In terrible shape, and fearful that the knocks he heard in the cell next door were made by Vietnamese trying to entrap him in an attempted violation of the prohibition against communicating, he made no response. For days I tried in vain to talk to him.

Finally, he tapped back, a faint but audible "two bits." I put my drinking cup to the wall and spoke directly to my new neighbor.

"Do you have a drinking cup?"

No response.

"Tap twice if you have a drinking cup and once if you don't."

No response.

"I'm talking through my cup. Do you have a drinking cup? If you have a cup, wrap your shirt around it, hold it up to the wall, and talk to me."

No response.

"You want to communicate, don't you?"

No response.

I continued at some length, vainly trying to get him to talk to me. But as he had just been given a drinking cup, his suspicion that he was being set up by the Vietnamese intensified as I urged him to make illicit use of it.

A few days later, the possibility that he could talk with another American for the first time in three years overrode his understandable caution. When I asked him if he had a cup, he tapped twice for yes.

"I'm Lieutenant Commander John McCain. I was shot down over Hanoi in 1967. Who are you?"

"My name is Ernie Brace," came the response.

"Are you Air Force? Navy? Marine?"

"My name is Ernie Brace."

"Where were you shot down?"

"My name is Ernie Brace."

To my every query, Ernie could only manage to say his name before he broke down. I could hear him crying. After his long, awful years in the jungle, the sound of an American voice, carrying with it the promise of fraternity with men who would share his struggle, had overwhelmed him.

It took some time before Ernie could keep his composure long enough to engage in informative conversation. But once he did, he became a tireless talker, hungry for all information about his new circumstances and eager to provide me with all the details of his capture and captivity.

I was somewhat surprised to learn he was a civilian. I assumed he was CIA, but refrained from asking him. As a civilian, Ernie was under no obligation to adhere to the Code of Conduct. The United States expected him not to betray any highly sensitive information, the disclosure of which would endanger the lives of other Americans. But other than that, he was not required to show any fidelity to his country and her cause beyond the demands of his own conscience.

But Ernie's conscience demanded much from him. He kept our code faithfully. When the Vietnamese offered to release him, he declined, insisting that others captured before him be released first. No one I knew in prison, Army, Navy, Marine, or Air Force officer, had greater loyalty to his country or derived more courage from his sense of honor. It was an honor to serve with him.

Incongruous though it must seem, early on, POWs could be better informed about the circumstances of other prisons and the men held there than we were about the population of our own camp. Many cells at the Plantation were uninhabited when I first came there, and we had a hard time establishing a camp-wide communications network. Some prisoners were located in other buildings or in cells some distance away and separated by empty rooms from mine. Most of our senior officers at the Plantation were kept in isolated cells. They were out of reach of our tapping, and we did not walk by their cells when we were taken to the washroom and the interrogation room.

New arrivals who had been placed in cells within my communications bloc brought us information about the men held at Hoa Lo, the Zoo, and other prisons in and around Hanoi. But we often puzzled over the identity of men held a short distance from us in different parts of the camp. A tough resister, Ted Guy, an Air Force colonel, was living in a different building. Unable to communicate with him, the men in my block assumed for several months that the senior officer nearest to us, Dick Stratton, a Navy commander, was the senior ranking officer for the whole camp. Ernie Brace informed us of our error. He had learned about Colonel Guy's presence in our ranks in a conversation with another POW.

There were about eighty Americans held at the Plantation during my first years in prison. Eventually I would come to know many of the men at the Plantation. Keeping an ever-lengthening account of the men we learned were prisoners was the solemn responsibility of every POW. We would fall asleep at night while silently chanting the names on the list. Knowing the men in my prison and being known by them was my best assurance of returning home. Communicating not only affirmed our humanity. It kept us alive.

The Plantation

The walls of the Plantation enclosed what had once been a lovely estate. Numerous trees were all that remained of the gardens, but the large mansion that had formerly housed Hanoi's mayor when Vietnam was a French colony still stood in reasonably good repair. We called it "the Big House," and we were taken there for initial interrogation. It also provided receiving rooms for American peace delegations, who arrived with great fanfare to affirm how well we were being treated despite the terrible crimes we had committed against the Vietnamese people.

Several warehouses surrounded the mansion. They were divided into cells and housed the POW population. Various other smaller buildings dotted the estate and served as quarters for the guards and other prison workers. After Bud Day and I were separated, I was kept alone in Room 13 West at the south end of the Warehouse. Directly across the courtyard from my cell was the interrogation room, where I would often reside during periods of attitude adjustment.

The cells in the Plantation were large compared to those at other prisons. Mine was approximately fifteen by fifteen feet. Each cell had a wooden board for a bed and a naked lightbulb dangling on a cord in the center of the ceiling. The light was kept on twenty-four hours a day. I got used to it after a while. It didn't bother me much in the winter, but in the summer heat, when most prisoners were suffering miserably from heat rash and boils, the extra warmth from the light made our discomfort all the harder to bear. Adding to the intensity of our discomfort was the building's tin roof, which must have increased the summer heat by ten or more degrees.

The cell windows were boarded up to prevent us from seeing out and from communicating with one another, blocking all ventilation except for some small holes near the top of wall. Every door had a peephole that turnkeys used to look in on us. Every door also had cracks in it through which we could observe our turnkeys and the daily activities of camp personnel.

The daily routine was simple and excruciatingly dull. The guards struck a gong at six in the morning, signaling the start of a new day. We rose, folded our gear, and listened from the loudspeakers in our cells to Hanoi Hannah, the "Voice of Vietnam," a half hour of witless propaganda, rebroadcast from the night before. For most POWs, Hannah was a pretty good source of entertainment.

"American GIs, don't fight in this illegal and immoral war," Hannah pleaded, before reporting the latest victories of the heroic people's liberation forces. She brought us the news from home, which was, of course, limited to updates on antiwar activities and incidents of civil strife. She often played recordings of speeches by prominent American opponents of the war. In 1972, she unwittingly informed us that an American had landed on the moon by playing a portion of a campaign speech by George McGovern chastising Nixon for putting a man on the moon but failing to end the war. The musical interlude was a mix of Vietnamese patriotic songs and a few American songs, usually some scratchy old Louis Armstrong records that some fleeing Frenchman had left behind when France relinquished its Indochinese colony.

During the Tet Offensive, in 1968, Hannah couldn't restrain her patriotic ardor as she gleefully regaled us with news of "many heroic victories" over the American imperialists and their puppet regime in the South. The guards shared her enthusiasm. On the night Tet began, they were all fired up, racing around the camp, yelling and shooting their rifles into the night air. The POWs were clueless about the cause of the commotion until Hannah brought us the news the next evening.

Hannah was especially excited about the siege of the American Marine base at Khe San, confidently predicting, night after night, its imminent surrender. Six weeks after she first alerted us to the siege, Hannah stopped updating us on the progress of the people's heroic liberation of Khe San. Evidently the Marines defending Khe San had proved heroic as well.

About an hour after Hannah's morning rebroadcast, the turnkeys opened each cell door, and, one at a time, each prisoner brought his waste bucket out, set it down, and stepped back into his cell. After all the waste buckets were placed outside and the guards had locked the prisoners back in their cells, two POWs were assigned the task of collecting the buckets, dumping their contents into a large hole in the back of the camp, washing them out, and returning them to their owners. For a brief while, the prisoners used this daily chore to pass notes on cigarette paper and other scraps of paper. The Vietnamese soon discovered our treachery and kept a closer eye on the unfortunate POWs who drew this duty.

After the buckets were returned, the guards filled our teapots. If it was a wash day, they would then take us to bathe. In winters, when water was plentiful, we would often bathe twice a week. In summer, when water was scarce, we would sometimes go weeks without bathing. After we had hung our wet clothes and washrag out to dry and returned to our cells, each prisoner was taken back out, one at a time, to pick up his breakfast, usually a piece of bread and a bowl of soup made by boiling something that vaguely resembled a pumpkin. Each prisoner was then returned to his cell and locked in before the next prisoner was allowed to collect his morning meal.

The food at the Plantation was notoriously bad, and, as the old joke goes, the portions were too small. Discipline among the Plantation's guards was poor, and we suffered from a high rate of food thievery. The pots in which our meals were prepared were never washed, and the guards who served us were only slightly cleaner. I never enjoyed a reputation for cleanliness, but my fre-

quent bouts of dysentery brought on by my filthy living conditions greatly increased my appreciation of the virtue, and I
cringed whenever I watched our food being prepared.

After we finished eating, the process was repeated in reverse as
we returned our empty bowls. There were no other activities after
breakfast until we were brought out for the afternoon meal. On
wash days we collected our dry clothes with the afternoon meal.

Shortly after lunch, around noon, they rang the gong again to
signal the afternoon nap, which lasted until two. Until the gong
sounded we weren't allowed to lie down unless we were ill. On
some afternoons they piped in additional propaganda broadcasts
over the loudspeakers, occasionally playing them all afternoon.
Other times we went for weeks without afternoon tributes to the
great patriotic struggle, although Hannah never missed an evening
or morning broadcast.

Our boredom was periodically alleviated by the provision of
reading materials. The camp literature offered little in the way of
a rewarding read. Most often, I was given a copy of the Vietnam
Courier, a propaganda rag full of decidedly tendentious news
accounts of the war and current events.

Reading the Courier, I was always amused by its descriptions
of Ho Chi Minh's many remarkable attributes, powers normally
associated with the Divinity. If a certain province reported a poor
rice harvest one year, Uncle Ho would arrive on the scene, and,
bingo, next year's harvest set a record. Got a problem with your
tractor, call Uncle Ho for an illuminating lecture on tractor maintenance. If air pirates were bombing your village, Uncle Ho
would teach the village idiot how to target a surface-to-air missile
and in no time at all he would be destroying whole squadrons. No
task was too small for Ho. He would always take a few minutes
from his busy administration of the war to cure whatever ailed
you.

Other times, I received awkwardly written books boasting of
extraordinary Vietnamese war victories, whole battalions of
American infantry annihilated by a few determined peasants,
grandmothers shooting down American aircraft. Of course, all

our literary diversions required us to endure a fulminating condemnation of American war crimes.

We were also read aloud to quite often. Works by prominent American authors who were opposed to the war and by other, less distinguished pamphleteers were haltingly, and some times unintelligibly, broadcast throughout the camp. Dr. Spock's works, sadly not his texts on child care, were a popular form of political enlightenment.

Sometimes we were made to watch movies in which Vietnamese nationalism was accorded even greater supernatural powers than it was in books and newspapers. A tank division or several American battalions were never a match for one lightly armed, gallant, kind-to-women-and-children Vietnamese fighting man. Of course, the Vietnamese took elaborate precautions when taking us to the movies, lest we hopelessly inferior Americans pull some kind of trick on our virtuous, all-knowing guards. Each prisoner watched the movies from a separate cubicle made with blankets or mosquito netting hung over a line.

Although I suppose I should have been insulted by such heavy-handed propaganda, it was so clumsy and so absurd that it seldom failed to amuse me. I came to welcome most of it as a reliably entertaining diversion, but it also exacerbated my yearning for a world in which all information was not portioned out sparingly and in disguise to advance someone's military or political objectives.

We were deprived of even the most basic comforts. It would be too time-consuming a task to list all the things I missed in prison. I missed the staples of life, of course, good and plentiful food, a comfortable bed, being out of doors. But the thing I missed most was information—free, uncensored, undistorted, abundant information.

When we were released from prison in 1973, the first thing most of us did after arriving at Clark Air Base in the Philippines was order a steak dinner or an ice cream sundae or some other food we had longed for in prison. But I was as hungry for information as I was for a decent meal, and when I placed my dinner order I asked also for newspapers and magazines. I wanted to know what was going on in the world, and I grasped anything I could find that might offer a little enlightenment.

Every night at the Plantation, except Saturday night, all the camp personnel would attend what we derisively referred to as "revival" meetings. We would lie on our hard bunks and listen to the Vietnamese fervently cheer, clap, and shout expressions of nationalism and simplistic slogans epitomizing their national ideology. Each one would take a turn reading from a tract of anti-American propaganda.

At nine o'clock every evening, the guards rang the evening gong instructing us to go to sleep, and, shivering in the cold or sweating in the stifling heat, beset by mosquitoes, and in the glare of a naked lightbulb, we tried to escape to our dreams. That was our day.

The only thing that changed my daily regimen was an interrogation. Interrogations were irregular events. Three or four weeks could pass before I was subjected to one. Other times I was interrogated twice in one day, sometimes by senior officers, sometimes by lower-ranking officers or enlisted personnel whom we called "quiz kids." The sound of jangling keys and fumbling with locks at night or at other irregular times had the effect of unexpected gunfire. I shot bolt upright the moment I heard it, gripped by terror, my heart beating so loud I thought it would be audible to the approaching guard. In the years after I came home, I never suffered from flashbacks or posttraumatic stress syndrome, as it is clinically termed. But for a long time after coming home, I would tense up whenever I heard keys rattle, and for an instant I would feel the onset of an old fear come back to haunt me.

They never interrogated or tortured us in our cells. They always took us to the interrogation rooms, spartan cells with bare walls, furnished with just a wooden table, a chair behind the table, and a stool in front of it, lower than the chair, for the prisoner to sit on.

Some interrogations were comparatively benign. Sometimes they were little more than training sessions for a new interrogator who was trying to learn English. The interrogators would demand information, or order me to confess my crimes into a tape recorder. When I refused, they would make a perfunctory threat to persuade me to reconsider. When I refused again, they just sent me back to my cell, the threatened beating forgotten.

Once I was instructed to draw a diagram of an aircraft carrier. I decided to comply with the order, but took considerable artistic license in the process. I drew a picture of a ship's deck with a large swimming pool on the fantail, the captain's quarters in a chain locker, and various other imagined embellishments.

Vietnamese propaganda about the soft, luxurious life that upper-class Westerners (a social class to which military officers were naturally thought to belong) led made the interrogators easy marks for a lot of the b.s. we devised to avoid giving them any useful information. My fantastic rendering of an American carrier didn't arouse my gullible interrogator's suspicions until I noted its keel was three hundred feet deep. Unfortunately, he knew that the shallow waters of the Tonkin Gulf couldn't accommodate a ship that drew this much water. He denounced me as a liar and ordered me punished.

After a couple of physically intense interrogations, my captors forced me to read the "news" a few times over the camp loudspeakers. On each occasion, I managed to badly fracture the syntax of the prepared text and affect a goofy, singsong delivery. The Vietnamese, observing that my prisonmates laughed whenever my voice came over the speakers, soon despaired of my qualities as a broadcaster. One of my interrogators informed me that "the other prisoners say you make fun of us," and soon my brief career as the Plantation's Walter Cronkite was over.

One spring, a young interrogator I had not seen before decided to practice his English by chatting amiably with me about Western religious customs. "What is Easter?" he asked me. I told him that it was the time of year we celebrated the death and resurrection of the Son of God. As I recounted the events of Christ's passion, His crucifixion, death, resurrection, and assumption to heaven, I saw my curious interrogator furrow his brow in disbelief.

"You say He died?"

"Yes, He died."

"Three days, He was dead?"

"Yes. Then He came alive again. People saw Him and then He went back to heaven."

Clearly puzzled, he stared wordlessly at me for a few moments, then left the room. A short time later, he returned, his friendly manner gone, an angry resolve replacing it.

"Mac Kane, the officer say you tell nothing but lies. Go back to your room," he ordered, the mystery of my faith proving incomprehensible to him.

On other occasions the interrogators were deadly serious, and if they threatened to beat you into cooperation, you were certain they would give it a hell of a try.

Often we knew how difficult things were likely to become by the identity of the interrogator. We called one interrogator "the Soft Soap Fairy," for his delicate manners and the solicitous good-cop routine he employed in well-spoken English to plead with prisoners for their cooperation. "How are you, Mac Kane," he would greet me. If another interrogator who lacked Soft Soap's gentility had recently roughed me up, he would tell me how sorry he was. "This terrible war," he would say. "I hope it's over soon."

"Me too," I would reply.

After these preliminary courtesies were concluded, Soft Soap would start questioning me with a schoolboy's curiosity about life in the States, and American movie stars.

Soft Soap was a political officer, and theoretically he had authority at least commensurate with the camp commander's. But he was never around for the less pleasant aspects of an interrogator's work. He never threatened to torture us, but would advise us that our lack of cooperation was likely to incur the camp commander's displeasure and warn us that the commander could be a harsh and unforgiving man. Whenever we personally experienced just how harsh and unforgiving, Soft Soap always claimed that he had been away from the camp at the time and unable to prevent our punishment from getting out of hand.

"I'm sorry, Mac Kane, I was not here. The camp commander sometimes cannot control himself."

"No problem."

Regrettably, I didn't always draw Soft Soap as my interrogator. In the later years of my captivity, I sometimes sat on the stool looking into the cockeyed stare of the Bug. If I refused Bug's demands or gave him any lip, he would order the guards to knock me around until I at least stopped trading insults with him. The Bug was a sadist. Or at least his hate for us was so irrational that it drove him to sadism. He was famous for accusing prisoners, when our recalcitrance had enraged him, of killing his mother. Given the wildness of his rage, I often feared that we had.

On occasions when he was particularly determined, I would find myself trussed up and left for hours in ropes, my biceps bound tightly with several loops to cut off my circulation and the end of the rope cinched behind my back, pulling my shoulders and elbows unnaturally close together. It was incredibly painful.

However, even during these difficult encounters I realized my captors were more careful not to permanently injure or disfigure me than they were with other prisoners. When they tied me in the ropes, they rolled my sleeves up so that my shirt served as padding between my arms and the ropes, a courtesy they seldom granted their other victims. The Vietnamese also never put me in ankle stocks or leg irons, a punishment they inflicted on many POWs.

With the exception of a rough time I would experience in the summer of 1968, and a few other occasions when a guard or interrogator acted impulsively out of anger, I always sensed that they refrained from doing their worst to me. The realization that my captors accorded me different treatment than the other prisoners made me bolder and at times more reckless than I should have been. It also made me feel guilty to know that my courage and loyalty had not been put to the test with the same cruelty and tenacity that marked our captors' attempts to destroy the resolve of other prisoners.

There were others who, like Bug, seemed to enjoy their work.

But many of the interrogators were bureaucrats who mistreated us simply because they had been ordered by their superiors to extract certain information from us. For them, it was a job, less dangerous than other jobs, to be sure, but not particularly pleasant. The word would come down from the ministry to get more war crimes confessions, and, dutiful to a fault, the interrogators would set about getting war crimes confessions by whatever means necessary.

We could always tell when new orders had arrived and things were about to take a turn for the worse. Prisoners would start disappearing from their cells, some for hours, others for days. When they returned to their cells they would start tapping, telling us they had been tortured, how bad it was, and what the Vietnamese were after. The rest of us sat in our cells, sometimes listening to the screams of a tortured friend fill the air, sweating out the hours until the guards came for us.

They never seemed to mind hurting us, but they usually took care not to let things get so out of hand that our lives were put in danger. We strongly believed some POWs were tortured to death, and most were seriously mistreated. But the Vietnamese prized us as bargaining chips in peace negotiations, and, with tragic exceptions, they usually did not intend to kill us when they used torture to force our cooperation.

In my case, I felt pretty certain that no matter how rough my periodic visits to the interrogation room were, my father's rank gave me value as a potential propaganda opportunity and as a proffer in peace negotiations, and thus restrained my captors from killing me.

Authority was apportioned among four categories of prison authorities. The senior officers and interrogators occupied the top of the pecking order. The camp commander, a regular army officer, was nominally in charge of the prison. But it was obvious to all prisoners that the camp political officer, drawn from the ranks of the political bureau of the army, was the man in charge. He had responsibility for all matters involving prisoner indoctrination and behavior, interrogations, confessions, and propaganda displays.

The relationship between camp commander and political officer varied somewhat from camp to camp. At the Plantation, Soft
Soap Fairy was the political officer, and he always referred to
"Slopehead," the camp commander, as the officer responsible for
torture and punishment. Slopehead did most of the dirty work,
but Soft Soap, for all his protestations of innocence, was responsible for getting the information from prisoners that Slopehead
would eventually try to beat out of us.

Next in line were the turnkeys who supervised our daily routine. They let us out of our cells to collect our meals and to bathe,
locked us back in when we had finished, monitored us constantly
to prevent communication, and, if so disposed, responded when
we called "Bao cao" to get their attention.

The turnkeys were younger than the interrogators; many of
them were still in their teens. Some of them treated us no worse
than their job description obliged, but others harbored considerable animosity toward us and seemed to relish opportunities to
degrade us. Being so young, most turnkeys, when they first took
up this line of work, were curious about the strange Americans
they guarded. But in time, increasingly irritated by our evident
disrespect for their authority, many of them grew to despise us,
and they would go out of their way to give us a hard time.

For a time, I had a turnkey who ritualistically expressed his
intense dislike of me. We called him "the Prick." He would enter
my cell and order me to bow. Our captors believed that their
advantage over us entitled them to formal displays of deference.
They expected us to bow whenever they approached us. We
believed otherwise. When the Prick ordered me to bow, I would
refuse, and he would respond to the discourtesy by smashing his
fist into the side of my head and knocking me down. On a few
occasions when I just didn't feel up to the confrontation and
bowed, he hit me anyway. These encounters were not episodic.
They occurred every morning for nearly two years.

The Prick had other, less violent means of harassing me. He
would often intentionally spill my food, trip me when I walked
to the showers, or take me to the shower on a hot summer day

and laugh when I discovered there was no water in the tank. But he seemed to regard his morning visitations as the most satisfying form of self-expression.

Occupying the last station in the camp hierarchy were the Vietnamese we called "gun guards." These were young soldiers who wandered around the camp carrying a rifle on their shoulder. Many had physical handicaps or other limitations that made them unfit for jungle fighting. Most gun guards were largely indifferent to us. Their duty was certainly preferable to fighting at the front, wherever that might be on a given day, and I'm sure they appreciated the relative security of their work. But few ever displayed a particular zeal for lording their authority over the prisoners. They just did their job, in six-hour shifts, and counted their blessings.

After one difficult interrogation, I was left in the interrogation room for the night, tied in ropes. A gun guard, whom I had noticed before but had never spoken to, was working the night shift, 10:00 p.m. to 4:00 a.m. A short time after the interrogators had left me to ponder my bad attitude for the evening, this guard entered the room and silently, without looking at or smiling at me, loosened the ropes, and then he left me alone. A few minutes before his shift ended, he returned and tightened up the ropes.

On Christmas Day, we were always treated to a better-than-usual dinner. We were also allowed to stand outside our cells for five minutes to exercise or to just look at the trees and sky. One Christmas, a few months after the gun guard had inexplicably come to my assistance during my long night in the interrogation room, I was standing in the dirt courtyard when I saw him approach me.

He walked up and stood silently next to me. Again, he didn't smile or look at me. He just stared at the ground in front of us. After a few moments had passed he rather nonchalantly used his sandaled foot to draw a cross in the dirt. We both stood wordlessly looking at the cross until, after a minute or two, he rubbed it out and walked away. I saw my good Samaritan often after the Christmas when we venerated the cross together. But he never said a word to me nor gave the slightest signal that he acknowledged my humanity.

An Air Force major lived in the cell next to me at the Plantation. Bob Craner and I were indefatigable communicators. We talked endlessly through our cups or by tap code on any subject that came to mind.

Bob was a naturally taciturn fellow. He had a roommate for a time, Guy Gruters, another Air Force officer. Had I also had a roommate, Bob might have been less inclined to talk to me as much as he did. But I was alone, and I needed to talk as much as possible with my neighbor to keep from lapsing into despair. So Bob kept up his end of our ceaseless conversation to get me through my years in solitary. We talked at great length every day about our circumstances, our families, and our lives back in the States.

He loved baseball and revered Ted Williams. Bob could recite Williams's batting average in every year he had played in the major leagues. He was never more animated than when arguing over who was the better ballplayer, Williams or Stan Musial. In high school, Bob had developed a crush on a young girl. After admiring her from afar for many months, he worked up the nerve to ask her out. When he arrived at her home to collect her for their first date, they somehow fell into a conversation about baseball, during which the young lady ventured an opinion on the Williams-Musial dispute. She thought Musial the better player. From that moment on, Bob would have nothing to do with her.

He had grown up in a family of modest means and after high school had entered the cadet program started by the Air Force, which at that time didn't have an academy of its own. He eventually earned a college degree while serving in the Air Force. He was a naturally gifted pilot, and, recognizing his talent, the Air Force had sent him to fighter weapons school at Nellis Air Force Base in Nevada, which only the best pilots were permitted to attend.

Air Force pilots were allowed to fly only one hundred combat missions in Vietnam. When Bob had completed his hundredth mission, he requested and was denied another tour by his commanding officer. He went to Saigon to argue his case with the Air Force command in Vietnam. After a long campaign, his superiors relented and granted him another tour. He was shot down on his 102nd mission.

He never complained about his misfortune nor regretted having prevailed on the Air Force to let him fly another combat tour. He joked when he told me about it, laughing when he remarked, "Well, I guess I got my wish." But I never observed a trace of bitterness or self-reproach in Bob. We both were doing what we wanted to do, what we had so long prepared to do, when our luck turned for the worse. We chose our lives and were grateful for their rewards, and we accepted the consequences without regret.

He was my dear friend, and for two years I was closer to him than I had ever been to another human being. Bob spoke for both of us when, months after we were released from prison, he described how completely we had relied on each other to preserve our humanity.

McCain and I leaned on each other a great deal. We were separated by about eighteen inches of brick, and I never saw the guy for the longest time. I used to have dreams ... we all did, of course, and they were sometimes nightmares ... and my world had shrunk to a point where the figures in my dreams were myself, the guards and a voice ... and that was McCain. I didn't know what he looked like, so I could not visualize him in my dreams, because he became the guy—the only guy—I turned to, for a period of two years.

We got to know each other more intimately, I'm sure, than I will ever know my wife. We opened up and talked about damn near everything besides our immediate problems—past life, and all the family things we never would have talked to anybody about. We derived a great deal of strength from this.

A great deal of strength indeed. And I am certain I derived

more strength from our friendship than he could possibly have derived from it. Bob Craner kept me alive. Without his strength, his wisdom, his humor, and his unselfish consideration, I doubt I would have survived solitary with my mind and my self-respect reasonably intact. I relied almost entirely on him for advice and for his unfailing ability to raise my spirits when I had lost heart.

He was a remarkably composed man with the courage to accept any fate with great dignity. There were times when I would start to lose my nerve. I would detect some sign that another camp purge was coming, and my dread of another beating would start to get the better of my self-control. Anticipating a beating could often prove more unnerving than the beating itself.

"Bob, I think it's coming again, and I don't think they'll miss us."

"If it comes, it comes," he counseled me. "If it doesn't, it doesn't, and there isn't a damn thing we can do about it."

It may strike others as odd that such fatalism could have comforted us, but it did. It was the best attitude you could hold under the circumstances. It steeled me when I was weak, and made me feel better about myself. Worrying about a beating was pointless. There wasn't much I could do to prevent it, save disgrace myself, and disgrace hurt more than the worst beating.

Whenever I was plagued by doubts about my situation or my own conduct, I turned to the voice on the other side of my wall. And it was to Bob I went for guidance one June evening in 1968, after the Vietnamese had offered me my freedom.

CHAPTER NINETEEN

The Fourth of July

For months, I had received conspicuously lenient treatment. By the time Bud and I were separated, I was able to walk for short distances, and the Vietnamese decided I was fit enough to withstand interrogations, or "quizzes," as the POWs called them. The Vietnamese had caught me communicating several times, and I was forever displaying a "bad attitude" toward my guards. During this period, I possessed the camp record for being caught the most times in the act of communicating, yet the Vietnamese often only punished my offenses with threats. Sometimes they withheld my daily cigarette ration or my bathing privileges, a punishment that served to make me even surlier toward my guards. Once in a while they would cuff me around, but not often, and they never seriously hurt me.

In my first return to the interrogation room after being left alone for many weeks, Soft Soap had asked me if I would like to go home. I had replied that I would not go home out of turn. To this, and with uncharacteristic churlishness, Soft Soap had said, "You are all war criminals and will never go home."

After I went back to my cell, I relayed Soft Soap's offer up the communication chain to Hervey Stockman, an Air Force colonel who was our senior ranking officer at the time. Offers of early release were a fairly common practice at the time, and we regarded them as nothing more than psychological torture. So neither the SRO nor I took Soft Soap's inquiry very seriously.

Sometime in the middle of June 1968, I was summoned to an

interview with the Cat. His interpreter was an English-speaking officer we called "the Rabbit," an experienced torturer who enjoyed his work. I had been brought to the large reception room in the Big House, the room they often brought visiting peace delegations to for their clumsily staged propaganda displays. The room was furnished with upholstered chairs, a sofa, and a glass coffee table supported by two decorative ceramic elephants. An inviting spread of tea, cookies, and cigarettes had been laid out on the table.

The Cat began telling me about how he had run the prison camps during the French Indochina War, and how he had given a couple of prisoners their liberty. He said he had seen the men recently, and they had thanked him for his kindness. He told me Norris Overly and the two Americans released with him had gone home with honor.

After about two hours of circuitous conversation, the Cat asked me if I wanted to go home. I was astonished by the offer and didn't immediately know how to respond. I wasn't in great shape, was still considerably underweight and miserable with dysentery and heat rash. The prospect of going home to my family was powerfully tempting. But I knew what the Code of Conduct instructed, and I held back from responding, saying I would have to think about it. He told me to go back to my cell and consider his offer carefully.

The Vietnamese usually required prisoners who were released early to make some statement that indicated their gratitude or at least their desire to be released. They viewed such expressions as assurances that the released prisoner would not denounce his captors once he was back home, and spoil whatever propaganda value his release was intended to serve. Accordingly, they would not force a prisoner to go home.

As soon as I could, I raised Bob Craner and asked for his advice. We talked the offer over for a while and speculated about what I might be asked to provide in exchange for my release. After a considerable time, Bob told me I should go home. I had hoped he would advise me not to take the offer, which would have made my decision easier. But he argued that the seriously injured should be excused from the Code's restrictions on accepting amnesty and should take release if offered. He said I should go home, as my long-term survival in prison was in doubt.

Close confidants though we had been for months, Bob and I had never really seen any more of each other than a couple of brief glimpses when the turnkeys took one or the other of us to the interrogation room or to the showers. Bob had never observed my physical condition and had only reports from other prisoners and my own occasional references to the state of my health upon which to base his judgment about my fitness for prolonged imprisonment. Yet this good man, who revered our Code of Conduct, and who braved the worst adversity with dignity, offered me a rationale to go home, out of turn, while others in at least as bad shape as I was in remained behind.

"You don't know if you can survive this," he argued. "The seriously injured can go home."

"I think I can make it," I replied. "The Vietnamese tell me I won't, but if they really thought that I'm in such bad shape they would have at least sent a doctor around to check on me."

"You can't be sure you're up to this. What do they want from you in return?"

"They didn't say."

"Well, when you go back, just play along with them. See what they want to let you go. If it's not much, take it."

"I don't think I should go down that road. I know and you know what they want, and we won't let it go any further. If I start negotiating with them, it's a slippery slope. They'll tell me they don't want anything, but they'll just wait until the day I'm supposed to go, and then tell me what they want for it. No matter what I agree to, it won't look right."

I wanted to say yes. I badly wanted to go home. I was tired and sick, and despite my bad attitude, I was often afraid. But I couldn't keep from my own counsel the knowledge of how my release would affect my father, and my fellow prisoners. I knew what the Vietnamese hoped to gain from my release.

Although I did not know it at the time, my father would short-ly assume command of the war effort as Commander in Chief, Pacific. The Vietnamese intended to hail his arrival with a propa-ganda spectacle as they released his son in a gesture of "goodwill." I was to be enticed into accepting special treatment in the hope that it would shame the new enemy commander.

Moreover, I knew that every prisoner the Vietnamese tried to break, those who had arrived before me and those who would come after me, would be taunted with the story of how an admi-ral's son had gone home early, a lucky beneficiary of America's class-conscious society. I knew that my release would add to the suffering of men who were already straining to keep faith with their country. I was injured, but I believed I could survive. I could-n't persuade myself to leave.

Bob still counseled me to take the offer if the Vietnamese were willing to let me go without getting any antiwar propaganda from me. So I spelled out the reasons why I should not do it.

"Look, just letting me go is a propaganda victory for them. I can tell they really want me to do this. I mean, they really want me to go. And if they want something that much it's got to be a bad thing. I can't give them the satisfaction, Bob.

"Second, I would be disloyal to the rest of you. I know why they're doing this—to make every guy here whose father isn't an admiral think the Code is shit. They'll tell all of you, 'We let McCain go because his father's an admiral. But your father's not and nobody gives a damn about you.' And I don't want to go home and see my father, and he wouldn't want to see me under those conditions. I've got to say no."

Bob didn't say much after that. He just wished me well, and then we dropped the matter. Several days later, I went to tell the Cat I wouldn't accept his offer.

I sat for some time in the same well-furnished room with the Cat and the Rabbit, exchanging pleasantries and helping myself to their cigarettes. Eventually, again using the Rabbit to interpret, the Cat asked me if I had considered his offer. "I have," I answered.

"What is your answer?"

"No, thank you."

"Why?"

"American prisoners cannot accept parole, or amnesty or special favors. We must be released in the order of our capture, starting with Everett Alvarez"—the first pilot captured in the North.

He then suggested that my physical condition made my long-term survival doubtful. "I think I will make it," I replied. He told me the doctors believed I would not survive without better medical care. His response amused me, and I smiled when I told him that I found that hard to believe, since I never saw a doctor except the indifferent Zorba, whose only prescribed treatment for my condition had been exercise and the consumption of my full food ration.

Cat, who evidently did not share my sense of irony, then tried to convince me that I had permission from my Commander in Chief to return home.

"President Johnson has ordered you home."

"Show me the orders."

"President Johnson orders you."

"Show me the orders, and I'll believe you."

He handed me a letter from Carol in which she expressed her regret that I had not been released earlier with Norris and the other two prisoners. It was the kind of thing you expect your wife to say. I didn't believe that Carol wanted me to dishonor myself, and the fact that the Vietnamese had kept her letter from me until now angered me, an emotion that usually serves to stiffen my resolve. I was dismissed with an order to reconsider my answer, and returned, holding my wife's letter, to my cell.

A week later, I was summoned to a third interview, much weakened by dysentery, which had worsened since our last meeting. The interview was shortened by the effect of my illness. Shortly after I arrived, I asked permission to return to my cell to relieve myself. The request greatly irritated the Cat, who accused me of being "very rude." "I'm sorry, but I have to go," I responded. He angrily terminated the interview, and I was returned to my cell.

During these sessions, the Cat had promised me that I would not be required to make any propaganda statements in return for my release. I had no doubt that he was lying. I knew that once I agreed, the Vietnamese would exert enormous pressure on me to record a statement, and I worried that my resolve would dissipate as I faced the imminent prospect of homecoming.

On the morning of the Fourth of July, Soft Soap entered my cell and mentioned that he knew I had received a generous offer to go home. "You will have a nice family reunion, Mac Kane," he suggested.

"Yes," I acknowledged, "but I can't accept it."

A few hours later, I faced a solemn Cat. That morning, the camp loudspeakers broadcast the news that three prisoners had been chosen for early release. The Cat had summoned me to offer me one last chance to accept his offer. This time I was not taken to the large reception room but to an interrogation room. There were no cookies or cigarettes offered. The Rabbit spoke first.

"Our senior officer wants to know your final answer."

"My final answer is no."

In a fit of pique, the Cat snapped the ink pen he had been holding between his hands. Ink splattered on a copy of the *International Herald Tribune* lying on the table, opened to a column by Art Buchwald. He stood up, kicked over his chair, and spoke to me in English for the first time.

"They taught you too well, Mac Kane. They taught you too well," he shouted as he abruptly left the room.

Yes, they had.

The Rabbit and I sat there for a few moments staring at each other in silence before he angrily dismissed me.

"Now it will be very bad for you, Mac Kane. Go back to your room."

I did as instructed and awaited the moment when the Rabbit's prediction would come true.

That same day my father assumed command of all U.S. forces in the Pacific. I wouldn't learn of my father's promotion for nearly a year, when two recently captured pilots were brought to the

Plantation. A few months after they arrived, one of them managed to get a one-sentence message to me:

"Your father assumed Commander in Chief in the Pacific, July 4, 1968."

CHAPTER TWENTY

Lanterns of Faith

At the end of the Korean War, America was shocked when a number of American prisoners of war chose to live in China rather than be returned to the United States. Reports about the brainwashing of POWs were publicly disclosed, along with even more disturbing accounts of some POWs who had treated their comrades inhumanely. Consequently, the military began to instruct American servicemen about what they could expect should they be captured and, more important, about what was expected of them. Toward that end, the Code of Conduct for American Prisoners of War was drafted. It reads as follows:

I
I am an American, fighting in the forces which guard my country and our way of life. I am prepared to give my life in their defense.

II
I will never surrender of my own free will. If in command, I will never surrender the members of my command while they still have the means to resist.

III
If I am captured, I will continue to resist by all means available. I will make every effort to escape and aid others to

escape. I will accept neither parole nor special favors from the enemy.

IV

If I become a prisoner of war, I will keep faith with my fellow prisoners. I will give no information or take part in any action which might be harmful to my comrades. If I am senior, I will take command. If not, I will obey the lawful orders of those appointed over me and will back them up in every way.

V

When questioned, should I become a prisoner of war, I am required to give name, rank, service number, and date of birth. I will evade answering further questions to the utmost of my ability. I will make no oral or written statements disloyal to my country and its allies or harmful to their cause.

VI

I will never forget that I am an American, fighting for freedom, responsible for my actions, and dedicated to the principles which made my country free. I will trust in God and in the United States of America.

Although the experiences of prisoners in the Korean War had necessitated this formal declaration of an American prisoner's responsibilities, the military did not anticipate how the North Vietnamese would regard POWs. Unlike the Japanese and Germans, and more insistently than the North Koreans and Chinese, the Vietnamese considered prisoner-of-war camps to be an extension of the battlefield. Ho Chi Minh had declared that the war would be won on the streets and campuses of American cities, and the Vietnamese were determined that we would serve that end. With the exception of incidents of arbitrary cruelty, many features of our treatment—forced confessions and antiwar declarations, meetings with peace delegations, early releases—were intended to help sway American public opinion against the war. Since the Vietnamese invested so much time and energy in coercing our cooperation, our fidelity to the Code was almost constantly challenged. Yet its principles remained the most important allegiance of our lives.

* * *

The days dragged on as I waited for the Cat to make good on his threat. I knew a bad time lay ahead, and that I would soon confront a greater measure of my enemy's cruelty, an experience many of my comrades had already endured but I had been spared. I had seen the Cat's fury, and it had made a deep impression on me. I tried to be fatalistic, and prepare myself to suffer the inevitable without dishonoring myself.

For almost two months nothing happened. Three prisoners had been released in early August. Their departure had been delayed for several weeks, and I assumed the Vietnamese had neglected my punishment to avoid complicating the release. Treatment for all prisoners in the camp was lax in advance of the event. I assumed that the Vietnamese were worried that if word got out that I had been tortured for refusing to leave, the prisoners who had accepted release might change their minds.

Then one evening in late August, several guards came and announced that the camp commander, the rough customer we called Slopehead, wanted to see me. They took me to a large room, a theater that had been used for Christmas services the year before.

Speaking through an interpreter, Slopehead accused me of committing "black crimes against the people" and violating all of the camp's regulations. He told me the time had come for me to show gratitude to the Vietnamese people and sorrow for my war crimes. Knowing that I was in serious trouble and that nothing I did or said would make matters any worse, I replied:

"Fuck you."

"Why do you treat your guards disrespectfully?"

"Because they treat me like an animal."

Hearing this, Slopehead gave an order, and the guards lit into me. Shouting and laughing, they bashed me around the room, slamming their fists into my face and body, kicking and stomping me when I fell. Lying on the floor, bleeding, I heard Slopehead speak to the interpreter.

"Are you ready to confess your crimes?"

"No."

With that, the guards hauled me up and set me on the stool. They cinched rope around my biceps, anchored it behind my back, and then left the room. The rope hurt and restricted my circulation, but, again, they had not tied it as tightly as they had on others, and I knew I could tolerate it. I remained there for the rest of the night.

In the morning, three guards came in, removed the rope, and took me to an interrogation room, where the deputy camp commander, a dull-witted man we called "Frankenstein" for his bulging forehead and numerous facial warts, waited for me. When I refused his order to confess, I was dragged to the room behind my cell where some time later Ernie Brace would be held.

The room was empty of any furnishings save a waste bucket. I had no bedding or personal belongings. The room didn't have a door, only a louvered window large enough to pass through. I was kept there for four days.

At two-to-three-hour intervals, the guards returned to administer beatings. The intensity of the punishment varied from visit to visit depending on the enthusiasm and energy of the guards. Still, I felt they were being careful not to kill or permanently injure me. One guard would hold me while the others pounded away. Most blows were directed at my shoulders, chest, and stomach. Occasionally, when I had fallen to the floor, they kicked me in the head. They cracked several of my ribs and broke a couple of teeth. My bad right leg was swollen and hurt the most of any of my injuries. Weakened by beatings and dysentery, and with my right leg again nearly useless, I found it almost impossible to stand.

On the third night, I lay in my own blood and waste, so tired and hurt that I could not move. The Prick came in with two other guards, lifted me to my feet, and gave me the worst beating I had yet experienced. At one point he slammed his fist into my face and knocked me across the room toward the waste bucket. I fell on the bucket, hitting it with my left arm, and breaking it again. They left me lying on the floor, moaning from the stabbing pain in my refractured arm.

Despairing of any relief from pain and further torture, and fearing the close approach of my moment of dishonor, I tried to take my life. I doubt I really intended to kill myself. But I couldn't fight anymore, and I remember deciding that the last thing I could do to make them believe I was still resisting, that I wouldn't break, was to attempt suicide. Obviously, it wasn't an ideal plan, but it struck me at the time as reasonable.

Slowly, after several unsuccessful attempts, I managed to stand. I removed my shirt, upended the waste bucket, and stepped onto it, bracing myself against the wall with my good arm. With my right arm, I pushed my shirt through one of the upper shutters and back through a bottom shutter. As I looped it around my neck, the Prick saw the shirt through the window. He pulled me off the bucket and beat me. He called for an officer, who instructed the guards to post a constant watch on me. Later I made a second, even feebler attempt, but a guard saw me fumbling with the shutter, hauled me down, and beat me again.

On the fourth day, I gave up.

"I am a black criminal," the interrogator wrote, "and I have performed the deeds of an air pirate. I almost died and the Vietnamese people saved my life. The doctors gave me an operation that I did not deserve."

I had been taken back to the theater after telling my guards I was ready to confess. For twelve hours I had written out many drafts of the confession. I used words that I hoped would discredit its authenticity, and I tried to keep it in stilted generalities and Communist jargon so that it would be apparent that I had signed it under duress.

An interrogator had edited my last draft and decided to rewrite most of it himself. He then handed it to me and told me to copy it out in my own hand. I started to print it in block letters, and he ordered me to write in script. He demanded that I add an admission that I had bombed a school. I refused, and we argued back and forth about the confession's contents for a time before I gave in to his demand. Finally, they had me sign the document.

They took me back to my room and let me sleep through the night. The next morning, they brought me back to the theater and ordered me to record my confession on tape. I refused, and was beaten until I consented.

I was returned to my cell and left alone for the next two weeks.

They were the worst two weeks of my life. I couldn't rationalize away my confession. I was ashamed. I felt faithless, and couldn't control my despair. I shook, as if my disgrace were a fever. I kept imagining that they would release my confession to embarrass my father. All my pride was lost, and I doubted I would ever stand up to any man again. Nothing could save me. No one would ever look upon me again with anything but pity or contempt.

Bob Craner tried to reassure me that I had resisted all that I was expected to resist. But I couldn't shake it off. One night I either heard or dreamed I heard myself confessing over the loudspeakers, thanking the Vietnamese for receiving medical treatment I did not deserve.

Many guys broke at one time or another. I doubt anyone ever gets over it entirely. There is never enough time and distance between the past and the present to allow one to forget his shame. I am recovered now from that period of intense despair. But I can summon up its feeling in an instant whenever I let myself remember the day. And I still wince when I recall wondering if my father had heard of my disgrace. The Vietnamese had broken the prisoner they called the "Crown Prince," and I knew they had done it to hurt the man they believed to be a king.

The following month, Averell Harriman, then serving as President Johnson's emissary to the fruitless peace negotiations in

Paris with the North Vietnamese, sent the following cable to Secretary of State Dean Rusk:

> 1. At last tea break Le Duc Tho attended, he mentioned that DRV had intended to release Admiral McCain's son as one of the three pilots freed recently, but he had refused. According to Tho, Commander McCain feared that if he was released before the war is over, President Johnson might "cause difficulties" for his father because people will wonder if McCain had been brainwashed.
>
> 2. We said that in past cases pilots had been reluctant to accept release because they did not want to feel that they were given preference over their fellow pilots. In McCain's case, perhaps it was he did not want people to think he had been released because of his father's position. Tho said that we were reversing what the pilot actually thought and that he feared difficulties would be created for his father. However, Tho added, this was only hearsay which he had picked up when he was back in Hanoi. We replied it would be difficult to understand McCain's attitude as described by Tho, and that in past cases of this kind the pilot had wanted to be loyal to his comrades. In any event, we wished the DRV would release more pilots and that way we would know what they think. We agree with Tho that ending the war is the best way of securing pilot releases, but pending that we hope DRV will release more of them.

They came back at the end of two weeks for another statement. I didn't give it to them. I had recovered enough to resist. The next year and a half would be the hardest months of my captivity.

* * *

The severe treatment of prisoners lasted until the end of 1969. During this period, we were beaten for communicating with one another, for declining to meet with visiting American "peace delegations," for refusing to make statements and broadcasts, and for mouthing off to our guards. I had a hard time suppressing the urge to verbally assault my captors as they went about the business of humiliating me. Acts of defiance felt so good that I felt they more than compensated for their repercussions, and they helped me keep at bay the unsettling feelings of guilt and self-doubt that my confession had aroused.

Whenever I emerged from the interrogation room after a few hours or a few days of punishment, I tried to make a show of my indifference to my circumstances. Whether I walked of my own accord or was dragged by guards back to my cell, I always shouted greetings to the prisoners whose cells I passed, smiled, and flashed a thumbs-up. In the years since I came home, I have occasionally been embarrassed to hear some of my fellow POWs commend me for those attempts at good cheer. They believed they were intended to boost their spirits. In truth, they were mostly intended to boost my own.

On Christmas Eve in 1968, about fifty of us were taken to the theater where a few months earlier the events leading to my humiliation had begun. There the Vietnamese intended to film a religious service that they could use to demonstrate their humane treatment of us. I was placed next to a young apprentice seaman, Doug Hegdahl, who had fallen off his ship in the Tonkin Gulf during an evening artillery barrage.

I had often watched through cracks in my door as he swept the camp courtyard. The guards assigned Doug this enviable duty because they thought he was a harmless idiot. Doug possessed neither the survival training nor the familiarity with the Code of Conduct that captured pilots had.

Yet this teenage farm boy from North Dakota had devised a ploy to convince the Vietnamese that he was dim-witted, unthreatening, and without propaganda or military value. Given what the Vietnamese perceived as his low station in the Navy, they believed breaking him wouldn't have any useful effect on the morale of the other prisoners either.

Doug convincingly played the role of an uneducated peasant

who didn't have the foggiest notion of what he was doing in this strange place. The Vietnamese left him alone and allowed him out of his cell to work at menial tasks. So engaged, Doug would serve as a conduit for communications from one part of the camp to the other, sweeping up in his pile of debris notes we had written on toilet and cigarette paper. He also seized opportunities for a little small-scale sabotage, pouring dirt into the gas tanks of trucks and making other clever minor assaults on the Vietnamese war effort.

Standing next to Doug, and realizing that the guards, knowing they were on camera, were restrained from forcing our coopera-tion, I began talking to Doug in a loud voice and recounting my recent experiences. Soft Soap Fairy motioned to me and in a stage whisper ordered, "Mac Kane, be quiet." I responded by raising my middle finger for the camera and profanely telling him and the other guards present to leave us be. Soon almost all the other pris-oners attending the service began talking and flashing hand signals to one another. Even the three-man prisoner choir joined in, smil-ing and laughing as they entered the general exchange of informa-tion. The guards hustled around vainly trying to get us to quiet down.

Trying to be heard above the commotion, a Vietnamese pastor offered a sermon in which he compared Ho Chi Minh to Jesus Christ and Lyndon Johnson to King Herod. Soon one very angry guard, forgetting that cameras were rolling, began making threat-ening gestures at me. I called him a son of a bitch and other less flattering things. He charged toward me, but other guards pulled him back. On the whole, it was a rejuvenating experience.

The service concluded, and I returned to my cell possessing a little bit more of the holiday cheer than I had expected to feel on my second Christmas in captivity. I expected to be beaten for interfering with the propaganda pageant. Two days later, I was.

The arrogance I sometimes displayed to my captors contra-dicted the humility I felt around other prisoners who were routinely and severely tortured. Dick Stratton had suffered horribly under torture. He had huge, infected scars on his arms from rope torture. His thumbnails had been torn off, and he had been burned with cigarettes. By such means, they had forced him to attend a "press conference." When they ushered him into the room, Dick affected the vacant stare of a catatonic and bowed deeply in four directions toward his surprised captors, thereby signaling to the Americans who would see the broadcast that the POWs were obviously being tortured.

* * *

In May 1969, two Air Force officers, John Dramesi and Ed Atterbury, who had been captured a few months before my shootdown, managed a daring escape from the Zoo, the prison in the southwest of the city, where conditions were awful. For nearly a year, they had planned and physically trained for the escape. On a rainy Saturday night, their faces darkened, wearing conical Vietnamese hats and carrying knives they had fashioned from bits of metal they had found, they slipped through tiles they had loosened in the roof of their cellblock and climbed over the prison wall. They made for the Red River, intending to steal a boat and be well downriver before daylight. They were recaptured at dawn the next day, before they reached the river. They were cruelly tortured for their courage. Ed Atterbury was beaten to death. But John, one of the toughest men I have ever known, survived.

I did not learn of the escape attempt until I had been moved back to Hoa Lo, where I met men who had been held at the Zoo with John and Ed. Nevertheless, those of us held at the Plantation surmised that something had happened. Our room inspections became more frequent and more thorough. Our interrogations became considerably more intense. One of the Plantation POWs had been severely tortured for information about suspected escape plans at the Plantation, his tormentors refusing to believe his protestations that there were none. These developments, together with the general worsening of our conditions, alerted us that someone had probably attempted to escape.

Incidents of surpassing courage and defiance were commonplace in those worst days of captivity, and they made my own attempts at rebellion seem minor in comparison. I derived my own resolve from the example of Bud Day, who, although seriously wounded, had valiantly attempted to evade capture, and from countless other examples of resistance that had been carried, flashed, and tapped from cell to cell, camp to camp. They were a lantern for me, a lantern of courage and faith that illuminated the way home with honor, and I struggled against panic and despair to stay in its light. I would have been lost without their example. In recurring moments of doubt and fear, I concentrated on their service, and on the service of my father, and his father, and I accepted my fate.

Of all the many legends of heroic devotion to duty I had come in this strange place to know as real, and to seek strength and solace from, none was more inspiring that the story of Lance Sijan. I never knew Lance Sijan, but I wish I had. I wish I had had one moment to tell him how much I admired him, how indebted I was to him for showing me, for showing all of us, our duty—for showing us how to be free.

He was gone before I heard of him. But Bob Craner and Guy Gruters had lived with Lance for a time, and Bob had told me his story very early in our friendship.

Air Force Captain Lance Sijan was shot down near Vinh on November 9, 1967. For a day and a half, he lay semiconscious on the ground, grievously injured, with a compound fracture of his left leg, a brain concussion, and a fractured skull. He made radio contact with rescue aircraft, but they were unable to locate him in the dense jungle. On November 11, they abandoned the search.

Crawling on the jungle floor at night, Lance fell into a sinkhole, further injuring himself. For six weeks he evaded capture. On Christmas Day, starved, racked with pain, he passed out on a dirt road, where a few hours later the North Vietnamese found him. Thus began the most inspiring POW story of the war, a story of one man's peerless fidelity to our Code of Conduct. To Lance Sijan, the Code was not an abstract ideal, but the supreme purpose of his life.

The Code is a straightforward document. Its simply worded assertions might strike cynics as posturing, a simplistic and chauvinistic relic of a time when Americans carried with them to war a conceit that they were stronger, better, and more virtuous than any enemy they would face. In truth, few prisoners could claim that they never came close to violating one or more of its principles. But the Code had its appeal, and almost all of us were mindful not to take its demands lightly.

The Code instructs every prisoner to evade capture, and when captured, to seize opportunities for escape. Most of us imprisoned in Hanoi knew that escape was almost certainly impossible. The guards never seemed to be unduly worried about preventing escape because they knew we would have to escape from a city as well as a prison. Had we been able to slip out of camp undetected, our identity would have been impossible to disguise in an isolated Asian population of a million people. Few of us ever seriously contemplated escape, and our senior officers never encouraged it. A few truly brave men tried. All were caught and tortured.

Neither did every prisoner refrain from providing information beyond the bare essentials sanctioned by the Code. Many of us were terrorized into failure at one time or another.

But Captain Sijan wasn't. He obeyed the Code to the letter.

A short time after he was captured, he overpowered an armed guard and managed to escape, taking the guard's rifle with him. Recaptured several hours later, he was tortured as punishment for his escape attempt and for military information. He refused to provide his captors anything beyond what the Code allowed. By the time he reached Hanoi, he was close to death.

Over six feet tall, he weighed less than a hundred pounds when he was placed in a cell with Bob Craner and Guy Gruters. He lived there barely a month. In and out of consciousness, often delirious, he would push on the walls of his cell and scratch on the floor searching vainly for a way out. When he was lucid and not consumed with pain, he would quiz his cellmates about the camp's security and talk with them about escaping again.

Interrogated several times, he refused to say anything. He was savagely beaten for his silence, kicked repeatedly and struck with a bamboo club. Bob and Guy heard him scream profanities at his tormentors, and then, after he had endured hours of torture, they heard him say in a weak voice: "Don't you understand? I'm not going to tell you anything. I can't talk to you. It's against the Code."

Bob and Guy tried to comfort him during his last hours. Working in shifts timed to the tolling of a nearby church bell, they cradled his head in their laps, talked quietly to him of his courage and faith, told him to hang on. Occasionally he shook off his delirium to joke with his cellmates about his circumstances.

Near the end, the guards came for him. Lance knew they were taking him away to die. As they placed him on a stretcher, he said to his friends, "It's over ... it's over." He called to his father for help as the guards carried him away.

A few days later, the Bug told Bob Craner what he already knew, that his friend was dead. And Bob, a good and wise man, resolved to share with any prisoner he could reach the legend of Lance Sijan so that all of us could draw strength from the example of a man who would not yield no matter how terrible the consequences. A few weeks later, when I was moved into the cell next to Bob's, he told me the story of Lance Sijan: a free man from a free country, who kept his dignity to the last moment of his life.

To maintain our unity, prisoners relied heavily on the senior ranking officers to promulgate policies for the camps. The primary reason the Vietnamese worked so hard to disrupt our communications was to prevent any form of military unit cohesion from strengthening our resistance. Toward that end, they segregated senior officers from the rest of the prison population, making communication with them difficult, and they kept many of the most determined and inventive communicators in solitary confinement.

Contact with senior officers is a very important element of an effective campaign of resistance, and we worked as hard to maintain communications with them as the guards worked to prevent them. If we couldn't communicate, we couldn't organize, and if we couldn't organize, the Vietnamese would pick us off one by one.

We relied on senior officers for more than affirmations or interpretations of the Code of Conduct. Frequently we needed little more than a word of encouragement from our commander to firm up our own resolve when we were preparing to endure the latest round of interrogations. Although there were periods, some quite long, when the Vietnamese succeeded in truncating our chain of command, we would eventually invent some way to restore our communication links to the SROs.

Our senior officers always stressed to us the three essential keys to resistance, which we were to keep uppermost in our mind, especially in moments when we were isolated or otherwise deprived of their guidance and the counsel of other prisoners. They were faith in God, faith in country, and faith in your fellow prisoners.

Were your faith in any of these three devotions seriously shaken, you became much more vulnerable to various pressures employed by the Vietnamese to break you. The purpose of our captors' inhumanity to us was nothing less than to force our descent into a world of total faithlessness; a world with no God, no country, no loyalty. Our faith would be replaced with simple reliance on the sufferance of our antagonists. Without faith, we would lose our dignity, and live among our enemies as animals lived among their human masters.

There were times in many a prisoner's existence when the Vietnamese came close to robbing his faith; when a prisoner felt abandoned, left to cling to faith in himself as his last strength, his last form of resistance. Certainly this had been my experience when I was broken in the fall of 1968.

Ironically for someone who had so long asserted his own individuality as his first and best defense against insults of any kind, I discovered that faith in myself proved to be the least formidable strength I possessed when confronting alone organized inhumanity on a greater scale than I had conceived possible. Faith in myself was important, and remains important to my self-esteem. But I discovered in prison that faith in myself alone, separate from other, more important allegiances, was ultimately no match for the cruelty that human beings could devise when they were entirely unencumbered by respect for the God-given dignity of man. This is the lesson I learned in prison. It is, perhaps, the most important lesson I have ever learned.

During the worst moments of captivity, keeping our faith in God, country, and one another was as difficult as it was imperative. When your faith weakened, you had to take any opportunity, seize on any sight of it, and use any temporary relief from your distress to recover it.

POWs often regard their prison experience as comparable to the trials of Job. Indeed, for my fellow prisoners who suffered more than I, the comparison is appropriate. Hungry, beaten, hurt, scared, and alone, human beings can begin to feel that they are removed from God's love, a vast distance separating them from their Creator. The anguish can lead to resentment, to the awful despair that God has forsaken you.

To guard against such despair, in our most dire moments, POWs would make supreme efforts to grasp our faith tightly, to profess it alone, in the dark, and hasten its revival. Once I was thrown into another cell after a long and difficult interrogation. I discovered scratched into one of the cell's walls the creed "I believe in God, the Father Almighty." There, standing witness to God's presence in a remote, concealed place, recalled to my faith by a stronger, better man, I felt God's love and care more vividly than I would have felt it had I been safe among a pious congregation in the most magnificent cathedral.

The Vietnamese also went to great lengths to sow doubts in our minds about our country and one another. They threatened us constantly that we would never again be free. They taunted us with insults, disparaged our loyalty to a country they claimed never asked about us or made our return the subject of negotiations. We were abandoned, they insisted, by a country busy with a war that wasn't going well and too torn apart by widespread domestic turmoil to worry about a few forgotten pilots in Hanoi.

During the long pause between bombing campaigns in the North, while the months and years dragged on, it was hard to take our interrogators' ridicule of our conviction that our loyalty to America was returned, measure for measure, by our distant compatriots. But we clung to our belief, each one encouraging the other, not with overexuberant hopes that our day of liberation was close at hand, but with a steady resolve that our honor was the extension of a great nation's honor, and that both prisoner and country would do what honor asked of us.

In prison, I fell in love with my country. I had loved her before then, but like most young people, my affection was little more than a simple appreciation for the comforts and privileges most Americans enjoyed and took for granted. It wasn't until I had lost America for a time that I realized how much I loved her.

I loved what I missed most from my life at home: my family and friends; the sights and sounds of my country; the hustle and purposefulness of Americans; their fervid independence; sports; music; information—all the attractive qualities of American life. But though I longed for the things at home I cherished the most, I still shared the ideals of America. And since those ideals were all that I possessed of my country, they became all the more important to me.

It was what freedom conferred on America that I loved the most—the distinction of being the last, best hope of humanity; the advocate for all who believed in the Rights of Man. Freedom is America's honor, and all honor comes with obligations. We have the obligation to use our freedom wisely, to select well from all the choices freedom offers. We can accept or reject the obligation, but if we are to preserve our freedom, our honor, we must choose well.

I was no longer the boy to whom liberty meant simply that I could do as I pleased, and who, in my vanity, used my freedom to polish my image as an I-don't-give-a-damn nonconformist. That's not to say that I had shed myself entirely of that attribute. I had not, and have not yet. But I no longer located my self-respect in that distinction. In prison, where my cherished independence was mocked and assaulted, I found my self-respect in a shared fidelity to my country. All honor comes with obligations. I and the men with whom I served had accepted ours, and we were grateful for the privilege.

When my interrogators played tapes to me of other POWs confessing to war crimes, expressing their gratitude for lenient treatment, or denouncing our government, I did not silently censure my comrades. I knew that they had made those statements under the most extreme duress, and I told the Vietnamese so.

"No, they are their true feelings," the interrogator would rebut, "and you should not be ashamed to state your true feelings. We will not tell anyone if you do. No one would know."

"I would know. I would know," I responded.

In these instances when the enemy entreated me to betray my country by promising to keep my disloyalty confidential, my self-regard, which had for so long been invested with an adolescent understanding of my father's and grandfather's notions of character, obliged me to resist. But there was another force now at work to brace my resolve, and to give me insight into the essence of courage in war.

Tom Kirk, a fellow prisoner whom I hold in high regard, once explained, simply and exactly, the foundation of our resistance. "You live with another guy, and you go over there and you're tortured and you're brought back in that room and he says: 'What happened?'

"'They did this.'

"'What'd you tell them?'

"'... You've got to face this guy; you're going to have to tell him the truth. I wanted to keep faith so that I knew that when I stood up at the bar with somebody after the war, that, by God, I could look him in the eye and say, 'We hacked it.'"

We were told to have faith in God, country, and one another. Most of us did. But the last of these, faith in one another, was our final defense, the ramparts our enemy could not cross. In prison, as in any of war's endeavors, your most important allegiance is to the men you serve with. We were obligated to one another, and for the duration of our war, that obligation was our first duty. The Vietnamese knew this. They went to great lengths to keep us apart, knowing we had great strength in unity.

A few men lost their religion in prison or had never been very devout. A few men were not moved by appeals to patriotism or to written codes of conduct. Almost all of us were committed to one another. I knew what the others were suffering. Sitting in my cell, I could hear their screams as their faith was put to the test. At all costs, I wanted, as Bob Craner often put it, "to hold up my end of the bargain."

My first concern was not that I might fail God and country, although I certainly hoped that I would not. I was afraid to fail my friends. I was afraid to come back from an interrogation and tell them I couldn't hold up as well as they had. However I measured my character before Vietnam no longer mattered. What mattered now was how they measured my character. My self-regard became indivisible from their regard for me. And it will remain so for the rest of my life.

Had I accepted that many of the others had surrendered their dignity voluntarily, had agreed to live with such reproachful self-knowledge, I doubt I would have resisted to the extent that I did, and thus I would probably not have recovered from the shame I felt when I was broken.

This is the truth of war, of honor and courage, that my father and grandfather had passed on to me. But before my war, its meaning was obscure to me, hidden in the peculiar language of men who had gone to war and been changed forever by the experience. So, too, had the Academy, with its inanimate and living memorials to fidelity and valor, tried to reveal this truth to me. But I had interpreted the lesson, as I had interpreted my father's lesson, within the limits of my vanity. I thought glory was the object of war, and all glory was self-glory.

No more. For I have learned the truth: there are greater pursuits than self-seeking. Glory is not a conceit. It is not a decoration for valor. It is not a prize for being the most clever, the strongest, or the boldest. Glory belongs to the act of being constant to something greater than yourself, to a cause, to your principles, to the people on whom you rely, and who rely on you in return. No misfortune, no injury, no humiliation can destroy it.

This is the faith that my commanders affirmed, that my brothers-in-arms encouraged my allegiance to. It was the faith I had unknowingly embraced at the Naval Academy. It was my father's and grandfather's faith. A filthy, crippled, broken man, all I had left of my dignity was the faith of my fathers. It was enough.

CHAPTER TWENTY ONE

Commander in Chief

As my days in captivity lengthened, the man whose example had led me to Vietnam stood at the summit of his long naval career. I have heard several accounts of how my father managed to attain command of the Pacific. The most credible is the account provided by Admiral Tom Moorer, who, as Chief of Naval Operations, was my father's boss. Although the Pacific Command is traditionally reserved for the Navy, all services vie for it, as it is one of the military's most prestigious commands. Many months before a CINCPAC retires, jockeying begins among the services to get the President to appoint one of their own to the post. The Navy usually prevails, but the competition is intense, and the outcome is seldom certain from the outset.

In 1968, when Admiral U. S. Grant Sharp was scheduled to retire as CINCPAC, Admiral Moorer not only wanted to retain the command for the Navy, but wanted my father, to whom he was very close, to get the job. My father was not considered the most likely candidate for the post by many of his contemporaries. They had been surprised when he was appointed Commander of U.S. Naval Forces in Europe. His detractors in the Navy had attributed the promotion to his political connections and his assiduous cultivation of friendships with the most senior Navy brass. They would attribute his promotion to CINCPAC to those same relationships. There is some truth to their speculation, though not enough to justify their derision of my father's success.

Both my father and my mother worked hard to build relationships with people who could help advance his career, but social networking was mainly my mother's domain. She had the charm required for success in that field. My father won the regard of his superiors, military and civilian, by proving himself useful to them. He was a competent, reliable, often innovative, and always indefatigable subordinate who could be relied upon to accept any job without complaint and to make the most of it. Additionally, he had the gift of being able to articulate his and his superiors' views with clarity and force.

My father worked awfully hard for his success, and by so doing rendered his country many years of good and faithful service. He had earned whatever help he was provided by powerful friends. In an interview for the Naval Institute's Oral History Project, Admiral Moorer's account of how my father got the Pacific Command reveals both the influence his patrons wielded on his behalf and how he came to enjoy their patronage.

Shortly before the Joint Chiefs of Staff were to meet to decide which service would assume command in the Pacific, with each service ready with its own nominee, Admiral Moorer, as luck would have it, was scheduled to attend a ceremony at the White House wel-coming the king of Nepal. That morning, General Earl Wheeler, the Chairman of the Joint Chiefs of Staff, had informed Moorer that the President was unlikely to consent to my father's appointment and that he should select another nominee for the post. Moorer, however, knew that Ellsworth Bunker, the American ambassador to Vietnam, whose wife happened to be ambassador to Nepal, would also be attending the welcoming ceremony that afternoon. Bunker and my father had worked closely together during the U.S. intervention in the Dominican Republic in 1965. Moorer knew my father had made a great impression on the ambassador, and he viewed the White House event as an opportunity to make the case for my father directly to the President and to enlist Bunker, whose judgment the President respected, in the cause.

Right after the conclusion of the ceremony, President Johnson indicated he wished to speak to Admiral Moorer. "Do you really think McCain should be CINCPAC?" the President asked. To which the admiral responded, "If I didn't think Jack McCain would be a fine CINCPAC, I would never have nominated him in the first place." Gesturing toward Bunker, Moorer suggested to the President that he solicit the ambassador's views on the appointment. As Moorer knew he would, Bunker "just went into extremes of enthusiasm about McCain." Persuaded by his trusted adviser's unqualified endorsement, Johnson immediately called a press conference and announced my father's appointment as Commander in Chief, Pacific, depriving the Joint Chiefs of the opportunity to formally consider and recommend a candidate.

"I stacked the deck and I've never regretted it," Moorer remembered. "I've had many people work with me and for me, and I've worked for many people myself, but I've never known anyone as loyal as Jack McCain was."

After his appointment as CINCPAC was announced, my father received a great many congratulatory notes. Several stand out. Among them was a letter from a chief bosun's mate who had once served under my father:

At last, a fighting admiral in a fighting command. All that you have said has come to pass. Though history and the politicians will not give you credit for it, and you cannot say, I told you so, there are many of us who can and do. In the eyes of every professional man-of-wars man, you are the greatest admiral of our time....

I am afraid I have been too personal and I mean no disrespect, but Admiral I felt I would burst if I did not let you know of my feelings.... Give 'em Sea Power, sir.

A "fighting admiral in a fighting command," my father was respected by his brother officers but loved by the bluejackets, the enlisted men who knew his respect for them was genuine and who returned his respect many times over.

He assumed command of the Pacific in the last year of the Johnson administration and held it until July 1972, the last year of Richard Nixon's first term. My wife, mother, sister, and brother attended his change-of-command ceremony, which, at his request, was held aboard the *Oriskany*, the carrier I was flying off the day I was shot down.

Henry Kissinger once told me that whenever he suspected President Nixon's resolve to make difficult decisions about the war was wavering, he arranged for my father to brief the President. My father's no-nonsense determination, Dr. Kissinger claims, was infectious and served as a tonic for the President's flagging spirits.

My father wasn't much of a believer in fighting wars by half measures. He regarded self-restraint as an admirable human quality, but when fighting wars he believed in taking all necessary measures to bring the conflict to a swift and successful conclusion. The Vietnam War was fought neither swiftly nor successfully, and I know this frustrated him greatly. In a speech he gave after he retired, he argued that "two deplorable decisions" had doomed the United States to failure in Vietnam: "The first was the public decision to forbid U.S. troops to enter North Vietnam and beat the enemy on his home ground.... The second was ... to forbid the [strategic] bombing of Hanoi and Haiphong until the last two weeks of the conflict.... These two decisions combined to allow Hanoi to adopt whatever strategy they wished, knowing that there would be virtually no reprisal, no counter-attack."

For the rest of his life, he believed that had he been allowed to wage total war against the enemy, fully employing strategic airpower, mining Vietnamese ports early on, and launching large-scale offensives in the North, he could have brought the war to a successful conclusion "in months, if not weeks." He was exaggerating, I'm sure, to make a point. Given the resilience of the enemy, and their fierce willingness to pay a very high price and resolve to prevail over time, I doubt the war could have been wrapped up as quickly as my father envisioned even had we escalated our campaign to the extent he deemed necessary. But, given the dismal consequences of our haphazard, uncertain prosecution of the war, with its utterly illogical restraints on the use of

American power, his frustration was understandable and appropriate.

Like other senior commanders, he believed the United States had squandered its best opportunity to win the war in the aftermath of the Tet Offensive, "when we had destroyed the back of the Viet Cong.... And when we had finally drawn North Vietnamese troops out into the open."

He recalled with resentment Washington's refusal to accede to the military's plans for a major offensive to be launched from the old imperial capital, Hue. The plan called for an amphibious assault on Hue to spearhead a drive around the flanks of the North Vietnamese Army and across the country to the border, cutting the enemy's supply lines from the North. "Permission for this operation was refused," he lamented, "because Washington was afraid that the Red Chinese might then enter the war. It was a ridiculous conclusion based on no evidence. Just fear and anxiety."

Even before he assumed command in the Pacific, when he was still the Navy chief in Europe, he had prepared and delivered a briefing to the Joint Chiefs of Staff on the feasibility and necessity of mining the port of Haiphong. Like any other capable military strategist, he knew that the support the North Vietnamese and the Vietcong received from the Soviet Union and China was critical to their ability to simply outlast us. They hoped to suffer whatever losses were inflicted on them by their vastly more powerful adversary until they had exhausted America's patience and will to see the war through to a successful conclusion. Without the massive support of their allies they would fail.

What my father didn't share with his civilian commanders and many of his fellow military commanders was an overly acute fear that doing something about Chinese and Soviet support would involve us in a wider, perhaps global war. He doubted either country would be provoked to the point of war if we rightly decided to disrupt their efforts to aid our enemy, efforts that, after all, resulted in the deaths of many thousands of Americans. Indeed, he interpreted Soviet and Chinese actions as a far more reckless provocation of a great power than any response on our part was likely to be.

Like the men who flew missions to the North, he knew the enemy's resolve was greatly strengthened by the material assistance their allies provided them, and he wanted to do something about it. As a submarine commander he had executed his country's policy of total war, a policy that attacked the sources of the enemy's material support just as vigorously as it attacked the enemy's armed forces. He had sunk a great many merchant ships on his patrols in the Pacific. He couldn't believe that the United States would simply leave unchallenged this clear threat to the war effort that he was now commanding.

Most of the arms and supplies used by North Vietnam's armies entered the country through the port of Haiphong, with lesser amounts entering through the smaller ports of Cam Pha and Hong Gai. Thanks to the strategic foresight of Admiral Moorer, the Navy was well prepared to conduct mining operations in the enemy's ports, and my father and other senior commanders repeatedly urged their civilian commanders to order the action. Washington invariably rejected their appeals on the grounds that the mining would probably result in damage to Soviet and Chinese merchant ships, and thus would seriously escalate the war by involving those countries further in the hostilities, and possibly even provoke a global war.

As early as 1966, military commanders began urging Washington to approve a mining operation, but they could not overcome Defense Secretary McNamara's and President Johnson's apprehension that the action entailed too great a risk of a wider war.

When the North Vietnamese launched a major offensive in December 1971, at a time when U.S. forces in Vietnam had been reduced to 69,000 men, President Nixon finally directed my father to mine Haiphong and other northern ports immediately. The Nixon administration had dispensed with much of the micromanaging of the war that had so ill served the Johnson administration, particularly the absurd target restrictions imposed on

American bomber pilots. Relations between military commanders and their civilian superiors improved when President Nixon and Defense Secretary Melvin Laird entered office. The new administration was clearly more interested in and supportive of the views of the generals and admirals who were prosecuting the war. My father had a good relationship with both Nixon and Laird, as well as with the President's National Security Adviser, Henry Kissinger.

President Nixon had continued and even accelerated the drawdown of American forces in country begun by his predecessor, while seeking a negotiated end to the war. But he resolved to apply greater military pressure on the enemy while negotiations and "Vietnamization," the name given to the strategy of preparing South Vietnam to ultimately fight the war on its own while simultaneously drawing down American forces, were under way. In the interim, Nixon intended to escalate hostilities, both to hasten his diplomacy's successful conclusion and to strengthen the South Vietnamese regime.

In May 1970, with my father and General Abrams strongly urging it, the administration had authorized an incursion into Cambodia by U.S. and South Vietnamese forces. The enemy had used the sanctuary of the neighboring country to establish formidable military positions, especially along the border, from which they threatened much of the South, including Saigon. The incursion was of brief duration, and it was based on sound military reasoning. Nevertheless, given the considerable growth in domestic opposition to the war at the time, the decision provoked a firestorm of criticism. Neither the President nor his advisers nor his senior commanders wavered in their support for the action.

When North Vietnam launched its offensive in late 1971, Washington was very receptive to the requests of my father and his fellow commanders to respond to the North's aggression decisively. The administration authorized the immediate use of B-52 bombers, for the first time, to strike North Vietnamese targets.

The following May, the administration ordered my father to commence mining operations in North Vietnamese harbors. The

President announced to the nation his conclusion that "Hanoi must be denied the weapons and supplies it needs to continue the aggression."

Most of the mining was conducted by carrier-based A-6 Intruders. The operation was a resounding success. Casualties were minimal. Twenty-seven foreign merchant ships remained trapped behind the blockade for the nine months the mining campaign was in effect. Almost all other ships were prevented from entering North Vietnamese ports. The flow of foreign arms and supplies to the North was abruptly and completely halted.

Neither did the war's escalation, so long anticipated as the unavoidable result of mining the harbors, occur. The administration's opening to China and its policy of détente with the Soviets were by this time well established and contributed significantly to the response of the Soviets and the Chinese to the mining of their client's harbors. Their reaction to what was once feared as a casus belli was remarkably muted.

The reaction in both the higher and lower reaches of the United States military was relief. The men charged with fighting the war believed that for the first time a rational policy to undercut the enemy's critical lifeline was in effect. Thus, they and their civilian bosses reasoned, the war's end would be hastened.

The reaction among the Americans held as prisoners in Hanoi, who learned of the actions from new arrivals to our ranks, was unanimous approval.

Despite their approval of the administration's more aggressive approach to the war, General Abrams and the other commanders in the field, including my father and most of the military establishment, doubted the efficacy of the administration's overall strategy to Vietnamize the war while seeking a negotiated conclusion in Paris. Abrams had profound misgivings that the South Vietnamese could develop the military capability the administration assumed possible. My father concurred, and strongly supported his subordinate's concerns.

Admiral Vasey, whom my father appointed as head of strategic plans and policies for the Pacific Command, told me that my

father "fired some tough messages to Washington." His most frequent back-channel correspondents were the Chairman of the
Joint Chiefs and the Secretary of Defense. Henry Kissinger and
Secretary of State William Rogers were also recipients of my
father's appeals to rethink their strategy. However, his arguments, while fairly considered, were not successful in persuading
them of the necessity of the reevaluation he and Abrams believed
was necessary. The drawdown of American forces continued,
while the progress of the peace talks in Paris waxed and waned,
and South Vietnam reluctantly and without adequate resolve or
preparation approached nearer the day when it would stand
alone. The American public grew ever more impatient for the war
to end. The administration, even after the President was reelected
in a landslide, did not possess enough political strength to oppose
the people's will. Washington did what it could to ensure "peace
with honor," but the country's priority was to get out of
Vietnam, and get out we would.

By the time the end did come, with the signing in Paris of the
peace accords, my father had retired from active duty. No longer
restrained by his role as a subordinate to civilian superiors, he dismissed the agreement. "In our anxiety to get out of the war, we
signed a very bad deal." This he offered even though the "very bad
deal" would bring his son home. He was an honest man, with an
exacting sense of duty.

Long after the war, I once rashly remarked that the entire senior command of the armed forces had a duty, which they shirked,
to resign in protest over Washington's management of the war,
knowing it as they did to be grievously flawed. Obviously, my
father was implicitly included in my indictment. It was a callous
remark that I probably should have refrained from offering, but I
felt strongly about the obligation of military leaders to place the
country's welfare before their own careers. So did the men whom
I criticized. They were honorable people, including, certainly, my
father. Their opposition to the war's course, which in many of
their cases they pressed in the strongest possible terms to the
politicians who designed it, almost surely led many of them to

consider resigning. But their country was at war. And I am sure that their sense of duty to help see the thing through to the end, a value first embraced in a great war thirty years before, far more than any career consideration, prevailed over a conscientious contemplation of a principled resignation.

Having once served as the Navy's liaison officer to Congress and enjoying several close friendships with members of Congress, my father was quite familiar with the character of politicians. But he was puzzled and troubled by widespread and mounting congressional opposition to the war. Likewise, he was astonished at the breadth of opposition among the American people. He was, of course, respectful of the subordinate relationship of the military to the people of a democracy and their elected representatives. But it is fair to say that he believed something had gone badly wrong in a country that did not, by his lights, stand behind the men it had sent into harm's way to fight for it.

As CINCPAC, my father was expected to testify periodically before the committees of the House and Senate that authorized and appropriated the Defense Department's budget. The Pacific Command's vast expanse, including all of the Pacific and Indian oceans, from the West Coast of the United States to the Persian Gulf, encompassed a number of highly charged security situations in addition to the ongoing hostilities in Vietnam. Although our forces in Vietnam were progressively reduced during my father's watch, tensions on the Korean peninsula and in the Taiwan Strait were always a danger, and there was fear that the Soviets might generate a major crisis in the region while we were preoccupied with the war. It was the Pacific Command's responsibility to safeguard the shipping lanes and air traffic of half the world.

Accordingly, it was necessary for the United States, as the only military guarantor of regional stability, to maintain a large and expensive presence in Asia while executing the endgame of an unpopular war in Indochina. And my father was not one to subordinate his responsibilities to the prevailing political sentiments of the time, which assumed that our presence in the Pacific should be accorded lesser significance once the unfortunate war in

Vietnam was finally ended. Even if the region's other tinderboxes were to become unexpectedly tranquil, my father's long-standing apprehension of the emerging Soviet naval threat was enough to persuade him that Pacific Command should retain its priority for American military planners. Thus, he could not countenance on his watch force reductions that he believed would jeopardize our supremacy in the area whether we were engaged in open hostilities or not.

In his opening statement to a Senate committee in 1971, my father gave his projection of the necessary force requirements for the Pacific, after first assessing the state of the war and the various security threats in the region confronting the United States. Many of the senators in attendance were familiar with my father and his views. Some of them he considered friends. They listened respectfully to my father's presentation, even if one or another of them had doubts about the size of the force level my father was advocating.

One senator, an outspoken opponent of the war, was not an intimate of my father's, nor, apparently, was he familiar with my father's ethics. When his turn came to question my father, he immediately took issue with his central argument, that we needed to increase our presence in the Pacific, and he did so in the one manner that anyone familiar with my father's reputation for probity knew better than to pursue. In effect, he accused him of lying.

He callously implied that my father had intentionally exaggerated his threat assessments to justify force levels that were excessively large and unnecessary. To this senator, my father was an archetype, the old military hawk used to getting his way from unquestioning legislators who had always left military decisions to the military. But times had changed. The World War II–vintage military brass were no longer accorded automatic respect by younger members of Congress, who, though they may have lacked much if any military experience themselves, prided themselves on their modern sensibility and ability to see through an old hawk's con. To this particular senator, men like my father had gotten us into an unwinnable, unpopular, and probably immoral war. They were not to be trusted.

This was not, of course, the first time my father had testified before a congressional committee. Nor was it the first time my father had encountered a quarrelsome legislator. He had forged personal relationships with a good many politicians and over the years had had any number of spirited debates with them on all manner of military subjects. It was, however, the first time any member of Congress had challenged his honesty, and that was an injury he would accept from no one.

Once the insult was offered, my father forgot all thought of the purpose of his testimony. Neither did he particularly give a damn about disputing the senator's view of our force requirements. All that mattered to him was that he respond to the attack on his good name, which he did instantly and forcefully.

According to Admiral Vasey, who had accompanied my father to the hearing room and was seated right behind the witness table, the moment the senator finished making the offensive remark, my father jumped to his feet. Red-faced, and jabbing his finger in the direction of his accuser, he proceeded to deliver a heated and sarcastic lecture on strategy and the responsibilities of the Commander in Chief, Pacific. "I don't remember his specific words," Admiral Vasey recounted in a letter to me, "but he made it crystal-clear that he was an officer of the highest integrity, as was his father before him, and he strongly objected to any insinuation that reflected on the moral character of himself or his testimony, or of the United States military."

When it appeared that my father was not about to let up on the offending senator, Admiral Vasey discreetly grasped the bottom of my father's coat and pulled him down into his seat, "but not before observing the sly smiles on the faces of other committee members."

Such outbursts were rare in those days in the ostentatiously formal precincts of Capitol Hill. They are even rarer today. There were few things in his life my father valued more dearly than his career. But his good name was one of them. He would have sacrificed anything to defend it, as the errant senator found out that day.

Of course, my father was at the end of his career, and already wore four stars. He had achieved his life's ambition, and there was nothing an antagonistic member of Congress could do about it. My father did have hopes of extending his tour as CINCPAC, and that, of course, could have been put at risk by his publicly upbraiding a sitting member of Congress. I am confident, however, that my father did not give a damn about the risks involved in what some might have viewed as his astonishingly rash behavior. I doubt he believed any job was worth having if it required him to suffer such an insult in silence.

My father prided himself on being a strategic thinker. Obviously, the war consumed most of his time, but, as he had for most of his career, he focused much of his attention on the future threats to American naval supremacy in the Pacific. He had long been concerned about the growing strength of the Soviet Navy, and he believed one of his most important duties as CINCPAC was to ensure that the United States was prepared to contain the emerging Soviet naval threat. Toward that end, my father worked not just to maintain the Navy's military advantage in the Pacific, but to strengthen the United States' relationships with the countries in the region.

Needless to say, American diplomats in Asia were not always delighted to share their responsibilities with a naval officer, especially one as outspoken and often unpredictable as my father. But my father enjoyed warm, personal relationships with many Asian leaders and could speak to them more forthrightly and often to better effect than could a good many American ambassadors in Asia. Many Asian heads of state had come to power as military leaders. Many were not philosophically well disposed toward the virtues of democracy. They were often more comfortable in the company of a senior American military official who wished to talk with them only about questions of regional security and military power, and in a language familiar to them, than they were in the company of our diplomats.

My father's reputation as a frank, gruff, and engaging American military representative was widespread throughout Asia. Most, if not all, of the Asian heads of state whose countries were either allies of the United States or officially nonaligned with either superpower considered him a personal friend. He was accorded extraordinary courtesies whenever he paid official visits to their countries.

A few years ago, I met with Lee Kuan Yew, who as Singapore's "senior minister" has governed the city-state for decades and is considered by many to be the elder statesman of Asia. My visit was an official one, but Lee began our conversation by reminding me that he had been a friend of my father's. He went on to talk at great length about my father, in a tone suffused with fond regard for his memory. He paid polite but rather less close attention to the official subjects I had come to discuss. Throughout our discussion, he kept returning to my father, and repeating how highly he had valued my father's friendship and counsel. That was fine with me.

On another official visit, this time to Taiwan, I was invited to be the guest of honor at a luncheon banquet hosted by most of the Taiwan military command. The affair lasted over two hours, and considerable quantities of a Chinese rice wine that tastes more like whiskey than wine were consumed by the twenty or more aging generals in attendance. Every ten minutes or so, one or another of the generals rose to his feet and reverently offered a toast to the memory of my father, "the great American admiral, John McCain."

Joe Vasey accompanied my father on his official visits to Asian capitals. He tells a humorous story about a trip they made to Indonesia during which they paid a call on President Suharto, who, until very recently, was one of Southeast Asia's most durable dictators. The story illustrates my father's diplomatic style and the respect accorded him by Asian leaders.

My father and Suharto enjoyed each other's company, and the meeting lasted much longer than planned. Near the end of their conversation, my father surprised his host and the American diplomats who accompanied him to the meeting by commenting on Indonesia's recent purchase of Soviet ships. "Why in the hell did you accept motor torpedo boats and submarines from the Soviets? Our intelligence reports indicate they are a bunch of junk." Before Suharto could respond, my father asked his permission to visit one of the subs. After briefly consulting with an aide, Suharto agreed, and the next day my father and Admiral Vasey were flown to a naval base at the other end of Java.

When they arrived, they instantly confirmed the opinion of naval intelligence that the submarines in question were junk. They were freshly painted and immaculate, and the officers and crew were well turned out. But the two veterans of the American submarine service knew an antiquated ship when they saw one. It was clear to both of them that the sub had never been submerged or even under way since it had arrived some months earlier. Nevertheless, my father wanted to make a complete inspection. He asked the Indonesian admirals accompanying them to permit them to continue their inspection belowdecks, which, after a brief delay to prepare the crew, they were allowed to do.

When he reached the forward torpedo room, my father asked his host to fire a water slug, a standard test routinely performed by all navies. The outer door of the tube is opened, and after the tube fills with water a blast of air blows the water back out. The Indonesians agreed, assuring my father that the test was performed weekly on all their submarines. However, it seemed to take an inordinate amount of time for the demonstration to be performed, and it was obvious the Indonesians were uncertain how to proceed. When at length they attempted to fire the slug, the procedure was done in reverse. My father and Vasey were standing just a few feet behind the tube when high-pressure air blew open the tube's heavy bronze inner door. The door narrowly missed Admiral Vasey, he recalled, and the "great whoosh of high pressure air and oily vapor immediately engulfed the entire torpedo room in a dark cloud as our Indonesian friends scrambled up the vertical ladder to safety." As they gasped for air, Vasey guided my father to the ladder and out of harm's way.

Although much amused by the mishap, my father never remarked on it in subsequent meetings with his hosts.

Few, if any, American diplomatic or military officials could have expected such elaborate courtesies from the government of a country that was not an ally of the United States. But because of the respect Asian leaders had for my father he could use his influence to obtain important diplomatic and intelligence opportunities for the United States, always thinking ahead to future challenges to our security. He would even do his own intelligence work when the opportunity arose, as was the case on this occasion.

Admiral Vasey put the incident in a strategic perspective, observing that Washington was preoccupied with Vietnam and less concerned with Soviet overtures to Indonesia that were intended to promote political entente between the two nations. But Indonesia's proximity to vital sea-lanes concerned my father very much. He feared that Indonesia's drift into the Soviet sphere of influence would "drastically change the strategic face of Southeast Asia." According to Vasey, after my father's visit, "no further Russian military assistance was provided."

In time, I think the State Department came to value my father's somewhat unorthodox diplomacy, recognizing the opportunities his familiar relations with Asian rulers provided to U.S. statecraft. He was the first CINCPAC to be a regular participant in the annual conference of American ambassadors in Asia. Admiral Vasey observed that the ambassadors initially viewed my father "with great apprehension, but once they knew him and understood his style, they looked forward to his visits. His close rapport with and the confidence in him by Asian leaders always resulted in handsome dividends, insights and information." I know that President Nixon and Dr. Kissinger valued his influence in the region, for in later years they told me so.

He flew to Vietnam about once a month to confer with General Creighton Abrams and assess the war's progress. He held Abrams in very high regard, and I believe Abrams reciprocated his admiration. Their appointments were announced by the President in the same press conference. But where my father's appointment had come as something of a surprise to official Washington, Abrams's appointment had been expected. He had been his predecessor's second in command, in which capacity he had acquitted himself well. My father outranked him, and Abrams was expected to report through my father to the Joint Chiefs. But as a practical matter, his opinion was expected to hold greater sway with Washington than my father's, at least to the extent that any military commander's could influence an administration that was so directly involved in both strategic and tactical decision making. And my father was a firm believer in giving his commanders in the field the full support they sought from CINCPAC, a policy he insisted on to his staff at Camp Smith, CINCPAC headquarters.

Disagreements and hard feelings within the Military Assistance Command in Vietnam, MACV, about Washington's management of the war abated somewhat with the inauguration of the Nixon administration, but that is not to say that they disappeared altogether. No military operation, before or since, experienced the extraordinarily close involvement of political decision makers in day-to-day military decisions. But then no war since the Civil War was as politically controversial as Vietnam. MACV relied on my father to pass on its views and concerns to Washington, and he did not let MACV down. After every visit to the field, he dutifully passed up the line, unvarnished and with his full concurrence, whatever was bothering General Abrams and the other commanders of MACV.

Understandably, my father's appointment initially occasioned some apprehension in the field. He was, after all, an admiral. Vietnam was essentially a ground war, and most of its commanders were generals. It was, I'm sure, MACV's hope that my father would confine his visits to a few routine briefings and not attempt to impose a sailor's views on the infantry's war. But although he ably supported his commanders, he was not content to supervise the war from a distance. The war was his responsibility, and he never ducked his responsibilities. He quickly proved himself an astute commander and an important resource for MACV. He won the respect of Abrams and the other senior officers in Vietnam, who came to welcome his frequent visits as opportunities not just to vent their frustrations with Washington but to take advantage of the old man's counsel.

My mother accompanied him on all his trips to Vietnam. Frequently, my mother's sister, Rowena, joined them. My father's contemporaries often kidded him for having two wives, a reference to the fact that my mother and aunt were identical twins and to their constant presence at his side. He delighted in amplifying the joke himself. Whenever anyone asked him how he managed to tell his wife and sister-in-law apart, he would gruffly respond, "That's their problem."

In truth, my father was delighted and flattered by the attention his wife and sister-in-law received. He was, in his way, as devoted to his wife and sister-in-law as they were to him. He enjoyed being constantly attended by two beautiful women, and what contentment he knew in his life, which was less, I think, than other men knew, he usually found in their company. My mother always traveled with my father. Had the Navy allowed it, I am sure she would have accompanied him on sea duty, and found in the alternately exciting and dull world of men at sea some useful and interesting way to occupy her time.

My father seldom went to Vietnam simply to receive official briefings. On most of his visits, after conferring with Abrams and senior officers, he would go into the field to talk with the younger officers and enlisted men who were doing the fighting. While he was in the field, my mother and Aunt Rowena remained in Saigon, shopping, sightseeing, visiting, and waiting for his return.

My father did not affect a regard for the opinion of his soldiers in a transparent attempt to boost their morale. He genuinely believed that their views about how the war was going were just as important as the views of their commanders in Saigon. Like his father before him, he believed that the men who executed combat orders were the best judges of their soundness. He wanted to know what they thought about operations that had been completed and about those that were imminent or in the planning stages. He wanted to know how news from home was affecting their morale. He wanted to know if they thought we would win the war. He based his own opinions on the war's conduct in large part on what he learned from the colonels, captains, lieutenants, sergeants, and privates who were conducting it.

A participant in one of my father's field briefings described the experience in a letter to me. In the summer of 1968, my father and General Abrams unexpectedly arrived at a battalion base camp in the Mekong Delta. There they received an improvised briefing on the battalion's operations from the battalion commander. My correspondent, Randy Carpenter, was then a twenty-two-year-old draftee who had through attrition been made a platoon leader. He had been asked to present my father with a captured AK-47 rifle. He recounted what happened after the brief ceremony concluded.

> Your father, smoking a very large cigar, in a rough voice politely thanked everyone and asked if he and General Abrams could talk to me in private. He excused the three of us and we went to a small isolated area. Your father asked all of the questions. He wanted to know how much and what kind of action my platoon had seen. He asked general questions about the morale of my men and my morale. What kind of news we were getting from the states and how we were getting it? Had I been inside Cambodia on any operations? Did we have any men missing in action? Would I or my men have any problem expanding the operation into neighboring countries? What would the men's reaction be if we were asked to go into North Vietnam?... The meeting lasted about fifteen minutes and at the end I was ordered not to discuss any of what we talked about with anyone.

He was the commander my grandfather surely had hoped he would become: forceful, determined, clear thinking, and respectful of his men. Had my grandfather held the post, I believe he would have commanded in the same way. I like to believe my father recognized this, and that the recognition strengthened his confidence, and brought him a good measure of satisfaction.

Late in the war, my father would give the order that sent B-52s to rain destruction upon the city where I was held a prisoner. That was his duty, and he did not shrink from it.

While I was imprisoned, he never spoke about me at length to anyone other than my wife and mother. When friends offered their sympathy, he would thank them politely and change the subject.

He received hundreds of letters from members of Congress, dignitaries, fellow officers, enlisted men, family friends, and acquaintances offering their sympathy and prayers for my return. He politely and briefly replied to each one.

His responses were almost always written in the same style. The first paragraph of each began with an expression of his appreciation for the correspondent's sympathy, and closed, almost unvaryingly, with the line "God has a way of solving problems and we have great faith in the future." The next paragraph would address another subject, often extending an invitation to visit my parents in London.

Copies of his letters are kept with my father's official papers. There are only three I have reviewed that differ substantially from the others. The first is a letter my father wrote to the wife of Colonel John Flynn. John was the most senior American officer in captivity. He had been shot down the day after I was captured and taken to the same hospital where I was held. We never saw each other in the hospital, although one day Cat, in his usual bragging mood, had shown me his identity card. For the first three years of his captivity, John, like the other higher-ranking officers, was kept segregated from the rest of us and out of our communication chain.

My father wrote empathetically to Mrs. Flynn, commiserating with her that they must resign themselves to trusting in God and the courage of their loved ones as the only assurance that they would come home. "There is little anyone can say and even less they can do when personal tragedy strikes," he wrote. "Our hearts are with you."

The second letter was a reply to the friend with whom I had completed the escape and evasion course in Germany. He had written my parents to share his observations of me, assuring them that I had been well prepared for my present adverse circumstances and possessed the ability to "come away from this situation in good condition, and to be an example to others." My father wrote back that he and my mother had "derived much reassurance from the account of your experiences [with John]."

The last letter was a reply to Admiral B. M. "Smoke" Strean, who was the Deputy Chief of Navy Personnel and had approved my transfer to the *Oriskany* after the *Forrestal* fire. Admiral Strean had "hesitated to write because I feel I had a part in this—in helping him get what he wanted—and thus a feeling of some blame in the outcome." Strean assured my father that his normal practice was to go slowly when considering requests for "unscheduled assignments which carry some hazard.... [But] your son badly wanted this assignment."

My father quickly wrote back to reassure his apologetic friend: "I deeply appreciate your letter. You are a great man in every respect. You should have no regrets. I have no regrets. John wanted to go back and I know he would not have been happy otherwise. I am proud of him."

Few close observers of my father ever detected that my captivity caused him great suffering. He never let his concern affect his attention to duty or restrain him from prosecuting the war to the greatest extent his civilian commanders allowed.

However, his closest aides knew he kept a personal file containing all reported information about the POWs, the location and conditions of the camps, and every scrap of intelligence about me that could be obtained. Included in my father's file were copies of the letters I had written to Carol, as well as some copies of letters that other prisoners had written to their wives.

During my first months of captivity I was allowed to write several letters to Carol, a privilege I attributed to the publicity surrounding my capture. Eventually, the Vietnamese withdrew the privilege and restricted me to one or two letters a year. Not until late in 1969 would prisoners be allowed to write home on a monthly basis.

Carol wrote me every month. The Vietnamese withheld all but a few of her letters from me. She also sent me many packages, few of which I received, and none of which contained all the items she had sent. With the exception of 1971 and 1972, I would usually receive a package at or sometime after Christmas.

It was always clear that the guards had taken most of the contents as their share before passing a package on to me. Sometimes I received candy, instant soup, socks, and underwear. Once I received pipe tobacco but not the pipe that had been included with it. One package contained only a single pair of skivvies and a bottle of vitamins. The Vietnamese had neglected to remove the shipping receipt that indicated the package had originally contained five pounds of material.

That I received so few of Carol's letters and packages is probably attributable to Carol's refusal to send them through the offices of the antiwar organization COLIAFAM, the Committee of Liaison with Families of Servicemen Detained in North Vietnam. COLIAFAM had arranged with the Vietnamese government to be exclusively authorized to process letters and packages to the POWs. Many families, including mine, refused to sanction this abridgment of a prisoner's right under the Geneva Convention to receive mail without interference from his captors or any agency working on his behalf.

One Christmas, Carol received a letter from COLIAFAM denouncing the resumption of the bombing campaign in the North and demanding an immediate and total withdrawal of American forces from Vietnam. A postscript contained a none too veiled threat, warning her that letters that were not delivered by COLIAFAM "will not be accepted and ... may jeopardize [the prisoner's] mail rights."

When I was a prisoner of war I resented the antiwar activists who had visited Hanoi and, wittingly or unwittingly, made our life in prison more miserable than it already was. Today I no longer bear any ill will for most of these people. I have made far too many mistakes in my own life to forever disparage people, most of whom were very young at the time, who long ago, and in the name of peace, made a bad mistake. I have not yet, however, managed to relinquish my resentment of COLIAFAM.

To exploit the anguish of families for the purpose of propagandizing and giving aid and comfort to the enemy is an offense so grievous that it merits denunciation even today, many years after the fact. Had COLIAFAM not intervened, the Vietnamese, for their own sake, would have eventually allowed us to send and receive mail without insisting that it serve the antiwar cause at home. Although I would have dearly loved to receive more mail, I was proud of Carol for refusing to cooperate in a plan to dishonor me. It took courage and wisdom on her part not to be enticed by COLIAFAM's "humanitarian gesture" into aiding my enemies.

My father never wrote me a letter during the war. He knew that the Vietnamese would have regarded a missive from him as a propaganda bonanza. He did try once to secretly pass a message to me.

Prisoners were required to write letters home on a preprinted six-line form. We were instructed to write only on the lines provided, to write legibly, and to restrict our message to comments about our health and family. Many POWs, however, managed to exceed our captors' instructions and pass encoded messages in their letters home.

For example, after my years in solitary ended, my first cellmate, John Finley, wrote a letter to his wife that asked her to say "hi to cousin King Mc, Abel and his brother." His wife was puzzled by the request, as she knew no one by the name of Mc or Abel. Naval intelligence analyzed the letter, interpreted "Abel and his brother" as an allusion to Cain, and thus concluded that the writer was making a reference to McCain.

Two months later, John wrote another letter to his wife in which he very subtly distinguished certain letters. When the letters were read together they spelled mccain my mate.

I, too, tried to pass hidden messages in my letters. Lacking

John Finley's ingenuity, I was considerably less subtle in the means I used. Vietnamese writing makes frequent use of accent marks. I borrowed the fashion for my letters to Carol, placing marks above certain letters to spell out my secret message.

My technique was quite obvious, and Carol noticed it immediately. In the first letter in which I attempted covert communication, the marked letters spelled out lcol guy, a reference to Ted Guy, who was then my senior at the Plantation. In another I passed on that cranermate [Craner and Gruters] well. In another, I informed her that I get no mail i am ok.

After reading these letters, Carol, properly, sent them on to naval intelligence, where my lack of sophistication in encryption aroused considerable concern. An intelligence officer wrote my father's aide to apprise him of my efforts, and of their concern that my messages were so indiscreet that it was "hard to see how they passed even basic censorship."

The officer asked my father's permission to use one of Carol's letters to me to transmit a carefully hidden caution. My father agreed and ordered the message to read, junior urges caution please stop this.

I would have been surprised to receive the message, for I thought I was a fairly clever communicator, or, more honestly, I trusted in the dull wits of the Vietnamese censors to compensate for my indiscretion. As it turned out, my trust was well placed. I never received my father's warning, because the Vietnamese withheld Carol's letters from me. So I kept on sending messages in my letters. The Vietnamese never caught me.

Had I received the old man's message, I might have been a little put out, but I think I also would have appreciated the indication of his concern. I would have taken some comfort in the knowledge that he was, as best he could, watching out for me.

The Navy did manage to get one message through to me. Some weeks after my transfer to Hoa Lo in late 1969, the Vietnamese gave me a package from Carol that they had been holding for a while. It had survived inspection with a few of its original contents intact: a few cans of a vitamin-rich baby formula, a bottle of vitamins, several handkerchiefs, and one tin of candy.

Carol hoped the baby formula would compensate for the nutrition-free diet the Vietnamese provided us. It was intended to be mixed with milk. Lacking any, I had to mix it with water. The result was so unpalatable that despite my chronic hunger, I simply couldn't stomach the stuff, and I threw the rest away.

The candy was another matter. The can contained about twenty pieces of chocolate with vanilla centers. They were such a prized treat that I decided to ration them, savoring one piece each day. On the fourth or fifth day, as I was rejoicing in the pleasure of eating my daily ration, chewing it slowly and deliberately, I felt a foreign particle in the center of the chocolate. I spit it on the ground and finished eating.

A few moments later, thinking it strange that the manufacturers of the candy would have tolerated such poor quality control, I picked the object up to inspect it. It was a tiny plastic capsule. Excitedly, I moved into the shadows in a corner of my cell, where I tried to open the capsule. Although a naked lightbulb lit my cell twenty-four hours a day, it was of such low wattage that it only dimly illuminated a small area. Almost no natural light infiltrated my cell, and I was free to work on the capsule unseen even in daylight hours.

The capsule was fitted very tightly, and I had a difficult time prying it open. I spent a long time working at it unsuccessfully. Finally I found a sliver of bamboo and used it to push the capsule apart. Inside was a small, folded, incredibly thin piece of plastic. I unfolded it and read the message that the Navy had written on it.

The message read something like:

> i hope you are well. your family is fine. the liner of this can works like invisible ink. place it over your letters. press a hard object on it. it will write secret message.

I was elated and very encouraged. The Navy was trying to communicate with me, a clear sign that our country had not forgotten about us. I extracted the white paper liner from the can, inspected it to see if I could detect the invisible residue that coated it, and impatiently waited for my first opportunity to put the thing to good use.

Unfortunately, the Vietnamese chose this particular time to change their normal practice of supervising the prisoners' letter writing. Over the last year, they had allowed me to write home once every few months. They would give me the form, and I would write my few lines, which they then took away and inspected. If it met with their approval, they would return with it and tell me to copy it word for word on a second form. Up until this time, I had always been left alone in my cell to transcribe the letter onto the second form.

The next time they gave me leave to write home, I hurriedly scribbled a few lines on the first form and anxiously awaited the guards' return with the second. To my great disappointment, after my letter passed inspection, the guards took me to the interrogation room to copy it while they watched. I have no idea what precipitated this change in the routine. Perhaps they had begun to suspect that I was writing in some kind of code. Or perhaps they had discovered another prisoner using a device to pass hidden messages in his letters home. I never learned what had aroused their suspicions. But whatever it was, it effectively prevented me from ever using the device the Navy had hoped would enable me to pass messages by less obvious means than I had been employing.

After this latest letter, the Vietnamese curtailed my letter-writing privilege for a long time. When many months later they restored the privilege, they never again allowed me to write a single word outside the presence of guards. I was never able to use the liner.

Despite my disappointment, the experience, on the whole, was an uplifting one. The attempt to facilitate communication with naval intelligence was welcome evidence of the Navy's concern and its desire to gain a fuller understanding of our situation, information I assumed it would use to our benefit. I was cheered and gratified by the effort even though it was unsuccessful.

My father did not meet with any of the prisoners who had
been released early. But his file contained all their debriefing
reports and reports from officers who had talked with them about
me.

In a conversation that was reported to my father, a prisoner,
one of the August 1968 releases whom I had been invited to join,
informed his debriefing officer that according to camp rumor I
had refused release.

Doug Hegdahl and two other prisoners were released in
August 1969. An intelligence officer who interviewed Hegdahl
asked them for information about me, and cabled my father the
following report:

YOUR SON WAS SERIOUSLY WOUNDED WHEN SHOT DOWN IN
HANOI BUT HAS MADE FINE RECOVERY AND NOW, ACCORD-
ING THIS GROUP, LOOKS "QUITE WELL." HE HAS BEEN EVERY-
THING YOU WANT YOUR SON TO BE AND HAS STOOD UP
MANFULLY AGAINST ALL EFFORTS TO PERSUADE HIM TO
UTTER TRAITOROUS STATEMENTS.

In a subsequent report from Hegdahl, my father was informed
about my efforts to disrupt the Christmas service in 1968.
Hegdahl also remarked that "John is known in the camp as a daredevil. He frequently gets caught attempting to communicate with
other PWs." Hegdahl thoughtfully concluded his report with the
observation that the other prisoners respected me for refusing to
cooperate with the North Vietnamese.

As grateful as the old man must have been to receive this
information, the men providing it had been released nearly a year
after I had been broken and made my confession. The knowledge
of this diminished considerably the satisfaction I otherwise would
have derived from knowing my father had, at last, received a
report that his son had good grease.

Hegdahl and the others knew I had been offered release, and
they were also certainly aware of the events that occurred after
my refusal. I had told Hegdahl at the Christmas service that I had

been beaten for turning down the Vietnamese offer. And had the Vietnamese played over the camp loudspeakers a tape of my confession, as I believed happened, they would have heard it. But they made no mention of this in their report, or, if they had, the reporting officer failed to pass it on to my father.

They need not have bothered. A month before my father was apprised of their debriefing, he had received a report that a heavily edited propaganda broadcast, purported to have been made by me, had been analyzed, and the voice compared to my taped interview with the French journalist. The two voices were judged to be the same. In the anguished days right after my confession, I had dreaded just such a discovery by my father.

After I came home, he never mentioned to me that he had learned about my confession, and, although I told him about it, I never discussed it at length. I only recently learned that the tape I dreamed I heard playing over the loudspeaker in my cell had been real; it had been broadcast outside the prison and had come to the attention of my father.

If I had known at the time my father had heard about my confession, I would have been distressed beyond imagination, and might not have recovered from the experience as quickly as I did. But in the years that have passed since the event, my regard for my father and for myself has matured. I understand better the nature of strong character.

My father was a strong enough man not to judge too harshly the character of a son who had reached his limits and found that they were well short of the standards of the idealized heroes who had inspired us as boys. And I am strong enough now to know that my father had sufficient faith in me to assume I had done the best I could, and that learning I had been broken would only have aroused in him an increased concern for my welfare.

On the one occasion when I briefly recounted the experience for him, he listened impassively until I finished, put his hand on my shoulder, and said, "You did the best you could, John. That's all that's expected of any of us."

My mother knew that my father suffered from the burden of

commanding a war in a country where his son was imprisoned. She believes the strain aged him considerably. She told me later of how she would hear him in his study, praying aloud on his knees, beseeching God to "show Johnny mercy." He continued to politely rebuff all attempts by friends to discuss with him what he considered to be his personal misfortune. To the world, he was, as ever, a competent, tireless naval officer, strictly devoted to his duty. Whatever private anguish he suffered, he suffered in silence.

I received a letter once from a retired Army colonel who had been a Cobra helicopter platoon commander in Vietnam. He recounted for me a New Year's Day he had spent unhappily at Quang Tri, having flown a fire team north to guard against violations of the holiday cease-fire. As he ate his lunch and waited miserably for nightfall, a Navy helicopter unexpectedly landed near his Cobra. An officer stepped out of the helicopter, walked to the end of the strip, and remained there for a while.

"One of his pilots came over to us to look at our ships and visit, and one of my warrants remarked, 'Who's that?'—referring to the officer about fifty yards from us. The Navy pilot said, 'That's Admiral McCain. He has a son up north and this is as close as he can get to him.'"

Every year he was CINCPAC, my father spent the Christmas holidays with troops near the DMZ. The letter quoted above represents dozens of reports I have received over the years that mentioned my father's custom of withdrawing from his company at the end of the meal, walking north, and standing alone for a long time, looking toward the place where he had lost his son.

My father served two tours as CINCPAC. During his second tour, he suffered a mild stroke. Admiral John Hyland, who commanded the Pacific Fleet at the time, and with whom my father had a somewhat difficult relationship, remembered being told by my father's executive assistant that the old man would "never be able to come back. He's finished." But my father had other plans. According to Hyland, "Things just continued to run.... We'd all go down ... to see him every day or so and talk with him and so on. But, not very long after that, he came back to duty, and he was fine."

As the end of his second tour approached, my father lobbied Washington to extend his tenure for another year so that he could continue in command until the war ended. His request was turned down. President Nixon flew to Honolulu to attend the ceremony that officially ended my father's command in the Pacific. Two months later, after forty-one years on active duty, he retired from the Navy.

Despite his apparent recovery, he was never again a well man after his stroke. He lived for nearly nine years after he retired. But, in truth, he had, like his father before him, sacrificed his life to hold a command in his country's war.

CHAPTER TWENTY TWO

The Washrag

Our treatment reached its nadir after the Atterbury and Dramesi escape attempt. Reprisals were ordered at every camp. Many prisoners were tortured to reveal other escape plans. Beatings were inflicted for even minor infractions of prison rules. The food was worse. Security was tightened and our cells were frequently and thoroughly inspected. Many of us suffered from boils—in the sweltering heat, our lymph glands clogged up and baseball-sized boils developed under our arms. All we had to treat them with was small vials of iodine. The guards took them away from us because Ed and John had used iodine to darken their faces the night of their escape.

During that spring and summer, I was caught communicating several times. Sometimes I earned a beating for my efforts, but other times I was just made to sit on a stool in the corner for a day or two like a disobedient schoolboy. Once I was ordered to stand facing the wall for two days and two nights. On the second day, exhausted, I sat down. A guard discovered me, mistook my weariness for insolence, and, in a rage, beat and jumped on my bad leg. The resulting pain and swelling in my leg forced me to use a crutch again. Surprisingly, camp officials chastised the guard for physically abusing me without their approval.

During another of my punishments, a severe one, I again complained that I was being treated like an animal. My guards were then ordered to feed me like an animal. Every day for a week, they brought me a bowl of soup with a piece of bread thrown in it and ordered me to eat it with my hands.

The summer of 1969 was a long, difficult time. But as autumn arrived, our treatment began to improve. By the end of the year, the routine beatings had all but stopped. Prisoners were still physically mistreated as punishment for communicating or other violations of camp regulations. But beatings to extract propaganda information all but ceased. We occasionally received extra rations of food. For a brief period, the guards came to my cell every night and removed the boards blocking the transom over my cell to let in the evening breeze. At times, some of the guards were almost pleasant in their dealings with us. We had hard times ahead of us, but from October of that year until our release, our circumstances were never as dire as they had been in those long early years of captivity.

This welcome change in our treatment coincided with the death of Ho Chi Minh, leading many POWs to think that old Uncle Ho must have had a less than avuncular affection for the air pirates occupying his prisons. A funereal dirge was broadcast over loudspeakers everywhere in Hanoi on the morning of September 4, and the black-and-red mourning patches worn by the guards that day aroused our suspicion that old Ho had passed on to his eternal reward.

I don't know for certain whether the terrible summer of 1969 was partly a consequence of Ho's animosity to us, and the change in our fortunes explained by the fact that death had finally silenced his exhortations to the people to treat us like criminals. What we learned from new shootdowns late in the war was that word of our treatment had finally reached the rest of the world, and the discovery that there was a darker side to the plucky North Vietnamese nationalists had begun to cloud Hanoi's international horizons.

In August 1969, the Vietnamese released, to an American antiwar delegation, Doug Hegdahl, Wes Rumble, and Robert Frishman. Defense Secretary Melvin Laird had showed photographs of Hegdahl and Frishman to members of the Vietnamese delegation in Paris and demanded their release. All of them were in bad shape. Frishman had no elbow, just a limp, rubbery arm. Rumble had a broken back. Hegdahl had lost seventy-five pounds. Dick Stratton and our senior ranking officer, Ted Guy, had ordered him to accept the release. He had memorized the names of most of the POWs held in the North.

In a change from Johnson administration policy, the Nixon administration allowed the three returned POWs to publicly reveal details of torture and deprivation. The ensuing public fury, led by the newly organized National League of Families of POWs and MIAs in Southeast Asia, of which my brother, Joe, was an active member, began to turn world opinion against Hanoi. And the Vietnamese, ever mindful of their reliance on international goodwill, decided to suspend their campaign to beat and starve us into submission.

The first indication that the Vietnamese had revised their "humane and lenient" policy was evident in changes in the way we were exploited for propaganda purposes. We were no longer threatened or tortured to make us confess war crimes or renounce our country. The Vietnamese were now extremely anxious to convince the world that we were well treated.

POWs were filmed playing cards and other games, reading their mail, attending religious services, and opening packages from home. Fewer and fewer prisoners were kept in solitary confinement, although I remained alone for several more months. The Vietnamese more often dispensed with physical intimidation to extract statements from us and instead appealed to our thoughts about our families, or tried to plant doubts about the progress of the war or our government's good faith to win our cooperation.

Their present public relations dilemma was much on our captors' minds. "The whole world supports us" was Hanoi's proudest boast, parroted by politburo member and lowly prison guard alike. They were clearly exasperated by this setback in their design to win the war on America's campuses and streets, and at odds over what to do about it.

Soft Soap burst into my cell once, highly agitated, and complained, "Even the Russians criticize us. You tell lies about us. You say we pull out your fingernails and make you live in rooms with no ventilation." That Soft Soap made this complaint while I languished in the suffocating environment of my unventilated cell made the experience only slightly less surreal than listening to the loudspeaker in my cell inform me that the American government was lying about Vietnam's mistreatment of prisoners.

There were, at this time, various personnel shake-ups among camp authorities that were evidently related to our change in treatment. My turnkey, the Prick, who had started every day by attempting to humiliate me, disappeared from the prison's guard roster. I derived considerable satisfaction from imagining him humping it down the Ho Chi Minh Trail cursing his bad luck and carrying an impossibly heavy burden, or sweating out a night fire-fight with a company of better-armed Marines.

The Cat may have suffered the most from the bad turn in Vietnam's public relations. He was relieved as commander of all the camps and thereafter seemed to function as the senior officer of one part of the Hanoi Hilton. He was still accorded the deference due a senior officer, but he was no longer the highest authority.

From this period on, he seemed almost solicitous of the prisoners' well-being. He often appeared nervous and distressed. He was observed complaining that prisoners should not be badly mistreated, and, reportedly, he would grow quite agitated upon discovering that a guard had discharged too enthusiastically the responsibilities of his office.

Later on, I learned from another POW that the Cat had been obliged to denounce himself in front of the party for mistreating prisoners in violation of Vietnam's policy of "humane and lenient" treatment for all prisoners.

On a bitter cold Christmas night in 1969, after I had been transferred from the Plantation back to Hoa Lo, the prison where I had spent my first days of captivity, I received an unexpected visitor. Moments after the last Christmas song had played over the camp loudspeakers, my cell door burst open, and to my complete surprise, the Cat entered my room, dressed in suit and tie, and began to chat with me about home and Christmas. Unlike our previous encounters, he had no need of an interpreter. He spoke English well enough. He offered me cigarettes, which I smoked one after the other. He talked about his experiences in the war, and in the French Indochina War before it. He talked about his family, showing me a diamond tie pin his father had given him. He asked about my family, and expressed his regret that I could not be with them this holiday.

At one point he told me about a particularly beautiful part of Vietnam, near the Chinese border, Ha Long Bay, famous for the thousands of volcanic islands that rise dramatically from its waters. He mentioned that Ho Chi Minh loved the place, and had occasionally enjoyed resting in an old French villa on one of the bay's islands. Not long ago I visited Ha Long Bay, and I can attest to Ho's good taste in vacation spots.

As he got up to leave, he reminded me that had I accepted release the year before, I would be enjoying a far more pleasant holiday this evening.

Without rancor, he remarked, "You should have accepted our generous offer. You would be with your family tonight."

"You will never understand why I could not," I responded.

"I understand more than you think," he shot back as he left my cell.

I didn't know what to make of this unusual encounter at first, fearing that it was the precursor to another attempt to release me. After a while, however, it occurred to me that the Cat was simply in an expansive holiday mood, and being a man who evidently possessed some Western tastes, he had wanted to affect the image of a courtly enemy enjoying a brief Christmas truce with a fellow officer. I didn't mind. I enjoyed the cigarettes.

Despite our improved fortunes in the fall and winter of 1969, we continued to suffer moments of despair, occasioned by grim misfortune, and sometimes by less serious experiences.

Keeping a sense of humor was indispensable to surviving a long imprisonment without losing our minds, and most of us looked hard to find some humor in our experiences. Many greeted the most difficult moments with a dark gallows humor, and we were always grateful for occasions to laugh about the embarrassments and absurdities of daily prison life. When we are asked today about our years in prison, many of us are apt to include in our account, "We had a lot of fun, too."

As implausible as that glib response is—and surely it is exaggerated—we did manage to have some fun despite our dreary, often depressing existence. And the prisoners whose company we valued the most were those who could make the rest of us laugh at our circumstances and ourselves.

Bob Craner had a ready wit, and he favored a droll, ironic brand of humor that never failed to cheer me up when I was down. When the death of seventy-nine-year-old Ho Chi Minh and the appointment of his seventy-six-year-old successor was announced, Bob commented, "Ah, the Young Turks are taking over." Our daily dose of propaganda often included tributes to the skilled marksmen who defended North Vietnam from American bombers. Hannah's frequent reports of downed American aircraft invariably claimed that the plane had been destroyed "with the very first round." Bob often responded to Hannah's familiar boast by speculating that the Vietnamese must have a warehouse somewhere where thousands of crates of shells were stored, each one labeled "Very First Round."

Although we were neighbors during the worst years of my imprisonment, we managed to make light of our conditions whenever we could, and to laugh about the peculiar predicaments we frequently found ourselves in as we tried to make the most of our dismal existence.

Queenie was a pretty, slender young girl with lovely long hair. She worked as a secretary at the camp and occasionally helped out in the kitchen. We would see her when the guards brought us out to collect our bowls of soup, and Bob Craner and I would look through cracks in our cell doors to see her float around the camp, giggling and tossing her ponytail. All the guards mooned over her, but child though she was of a classless society, she only had eyes for the camp officers.

There were only two other women in the camp, a kitchen worker we called "Shovel" for her unusually flat profile, and the cook, "Mammy Yokum," a wizened old crone who chewed betel nut and screamed bloody murder at any guard who had the temerity to enter her kitchen unbidden.

Inevitably, we began to have fantasies about Queenie, which she kindled with shy smiles when she caught either of us gazing at her. Bob and I would joke about plans for the day we won the war, when we would forsake family and country to live quietly with Queenie in Thailand. But our love was unrequited.

One terrible day, my ardor got the better of me. A guard had taken me, hobbling on my crutches, to the stall where we were allowed to bathe and wash our clothes by taking water from a tank, a cup at a time, and pouring it on ourselves and our belongings. The stalls the prisoners used were directly across the open courtyard from a washroom the Vietnamese used. They had old, splintered wooden doors. When we were inside, the guard would place a steel bar in brackets across the door to prevent our escape, then wander away to chat with his friends.

The door had cracks in it, which I would look through to observe the daily activities in camp. On this day, I was thrilled to discover that Queenie had decided to take a turn at the washroom; I saw her carrying a load of her clothes in that direction. I suspended my bath to watch her while she washed her clothes, holding each article up to closely inspect her progress. As I maneuvered for a better view, I lost my balance and fell against the door. The guard had decided he didn't need to lock me in, as I was unlikely to get very far on crutches, and had set the bar next to the door. The door flew open, and I fell, naked and noisily, onto the bricks in front of the washroom.

Because of my bum leg, I couldn't stand up, and I thrashed around on the ground frantically trying to scramble back into the stall. Startled, Queenie briefly appraised my humiliating situation, then demurely covered her eyes. My guard, hearing the commotion, rushed back, saw what had happened, cuffed me around a bit, and threw me back in the stall, where I finished cleaning up in abject misery. From that moment on, whenever Queenie saw me she would shoot me a look of utter disdain. I suffered her contempt in agony. My kind friend Bob Craner commiserated with me, but did not bother to restrain his laughter over my misfortune, and by so doing turned my embarrassment into a welcome source of amusement for both of us.

I was, and remain, deeply indebted to Bob for his warm fellowship and for the humor he used so effectively to brighten our small, hostile world. So it was with deep guilt, second only to the guilt I felt over my confession, that I discovered I had done Bob a grave injustice. That the experience concluded humorously is a testament to the kind of guy Bob was, and how important his friendship was to me.

The Vietnamese allowed us certain amenities. We all received one short-sleeved shirt, one long-sleeved shirt, one pair of pants, and one pair of rubber sandals fabricated from old tires. We each had a drinking cup, a teapot, a toothbrush, toothpaste, and a bar of soap stamped "37%" (37 percent of what we never learned). We received a daily ration of three cigarettes (often withdrawn as punishment). But our most prized possession was a small, coarse square of cotton rag that served as both washcloth and towel.

I appreciate how difficult it must be for the reader to understand the inflated value of such an unremarkable article. But to a man who is deprived of almost all material possessions, who lies day after day in a dirty, oppressively hot cell, glazed in sweat and grime, a washcloth, no matter how undistinguished, is an inestimable comfort.

On wash day, when we were brought out to collect our first meal of the day, we would each hang our wet clothes and our washrag to dry on a wire strung in the courtyard. We would retrieve the articles as we brought back the afternoon meal.

On one such day in the fall of 1968, between our two meals, the guards hauled me out of my cell and took me to a punishment room for ten days of attitude adjustment. This was during a time when my attitude was frequently adjusted. As I was being transported, I noticed my belongings drying nicely in the sun and immediately began to long for the comfort of my cherished washrag.

Ten days later, my attitude well adjusted, I returned to my cell, and to my intense sorrow found that my washrag was no longer on the wire. Nor was it anywhere else to be found. I was beside myself, and, I am ashamed to admit, I began to feel resentful of the good fortune of my fellow POWs, who were not suffering the deprivation I was then experiencing. Some POWs in the camp had roommates, each with his own washrag—two and three washrags to the cell! Surely, I rationalized, three men could make do with two washrags.

When next I saw a rag hanging on the line, I took it, and joyfully used it for days, although I had to suppress incipient feelings of remorse to sustain my joy.

Some months later, on my way back to my cell, I spied my old washrag drying on the line. I recognized it as my long-lost rag by a distinctive hole in its center. With a sigh of relief, I retrieved it and hung the stolen rag in its place.

That evening Bob Craner tapped me up on the wall. He was enraged.

"Dammit, the worst thing ever has happened to me," he exclaimed. "A couple of months ago some rotten bastard stole my washrag, and I went for weeks without one. One day when I was sweeping leaves in the courtyard, I found an old rag in the dirt. I spent a long time cleaning it up. I never hung the thing on the wire because I was afraid some jerk would steal this one too. But today was such a nice, sunny day, I couldn't resist, and I hung it out to dry. And can you believe it, some son of a bitch stole it. Dammit. I can't believe it. Again I have no washrag."

I said nothing as he poured out his troubles. When he finished, I sank to the floor, feeling as remorseful as I ever have, but I was not brave enough to confess my crime.

Every day, I heard Bob yell, "*Bao cao, bao cao*"—the phrase we used to summon the guards—"Washrag, washrag, give me a washrag, goddammit." They ignored him.

On Christmas Day, after a good meal and a few minutes spent

outside, Christmas carols played from the camp loudspeakers. They were a welcome relief to the atonal patriotic hymns the Vietnamese favored most other days, trying to crush our resolve with "Springtime in the Liberated Zone" and "I Asked My Mother How Many Air Pirates She Shot Down Today."

That evening, listening to "I'll Be Home for Christmas" on a full stomach, longing for home, and feeling the spirit of Christmas, I resolved to confess my crime to Bob. I tapped him up on the wall, reminded him that Christmas was a time for forgiveness, and explained what I had done. When I finished, he made no response. He just thumped on the wall, which was our sign for approaching danger and the signal to cease communicating.

Later in the evening, he called me.

"Listen. In the Old West the worst thing you could do to a man was steal his horse. In prison the worst thing you can do to a man is steal his washrag. And you stole my washrag, you son of a bitch." Although he intended his complaint to be humorous, I still felt terribly guilty.

Bob remained without the comfort of a washrag for quite a while after my confession, and he would often decry the injustice of it to me. "I get so sick of drying my hair with my pants," he would lament as pangs of guilt stabbed at my conscience. I felt bad about the injury I had done Bob throughout the remainder of our captivity, finally relieving my guilt on our first Christmas as free men by sending Bob a carton of five hundred washrags as a Christmas present.

Hanoi Hilton

By next Christmas, in 1969, Bob and I were no longer neighbors. On December 9, another prisoner and I were moved to Hoa Lo, where most of our most senior officers were held. Loaded into the back of a truck, we were blindfolded during the short ride to the Hilton. Unaware of who my traveling companion was, I placed my hand on his leg and tapped: "I am John McCain. Who are you?" He tapped back a reply: "I am Ernie Brace."

Ernie and I were taken to a section of the prison the POWs called "Little Vegas," where each building was named after a different casino. We were locked in "the Golden Nugget." We were given cells near each other, with only one other cell between us, and we were able to communicate with each other with little difficulty. Our cells faced the bath area, and by the end of my first day in Vegas I was able to contact many of the men in the camp.

I occupied three different rooms in Little Vegas that year. All of them offered excellent opportunities for communication, and I formed many close friendships with men whom I greatly admired. Treatment continued to improve, although we were periodically subjected to physical abuse for communicating.

I remained alone in the Golden Nugget until March, when my period of solitary confinement was finally ended with the arrival of John Finley, whom I was relieved to welcome as my new roommate.

That first Christmas in the Golden Nugget, while I was puzzling over my surprise social visit from the Cat, my wife was hovering between life and death in the emergency room of a Philadelphia hospital.

Carol had taken the kids to her parents' house for the holidays. After dinner on Christmas Eve, she drove to our friends the Bookbinders' to exchange gifts. It had begun to snow by the time she started back to her parents, and the roads were icy. She skidded off the road and smashed into a telephone pole, and was thrown from the car. The police found her some time later in shock, both legs fractured in several places, her arm and pelvis broken, and bleeding internally.

Several days passed before she was out of immediate danger. It would be six months and several operations before she was released from the hospital. Over the next two years, she would undergo many more operations to repair her injured legs. By the time the doctors were finished she would be four inches shorter than she was before the accident. After a year of intensive physical therapy she was able to walk with the aid of crutches.

Carol has a determined spirit. Had she less courage and resolve, I doubt she would have walked again. Her injuries had been so serious that at first the doctors had considered amputating her legs, but she had refused them permission. With her husband in prison on the other side of the world and three small children to raise alone, she now faced a long, painful struggle to recover from her nearly fatal injuries, resisting the prospect of having to live the remainder of her life in a wheelchair. I've known people with better odds who gave in to despair and self-pity. Not Carol. She suffered her hardships with courage and grace. She persevered, brave and hopeful, confident that our luck would turn and all our lives would somehow work out all right.

When the doctors told her they would attempt to notify me about her accident, she told them not to; she didn't wish to add to my burdens. She would see her way through her misfortune without even the small comfort she might have derived from a few words of concern from me. I've never known a braver soul.

My family was often on my mind. I spent a part of each long

day wondering and worrying about them. I didn't worry about their material well-being. I knew they were receiving my pay. But I worried, as all POWs worry, about the psychological burden my long absence imposed on my wife and children.

My children were so young when I had left for war. Sidney had not yet reached her first birthday. I feared my absence, and the uncertainty about my ever coming home, would rob them of part of the joy of living that children from happy homes naturally possess. I had to fight back depression sometimes, thinking that they might have become sullen, insecure kids.

Not too long after my capture, Sidney's memories of me had faded. To her I had become an object of curiosity, a man in a photograph whom her mother and brothers talked about a lot. She did not remember me so much as anticipate me, praying at night and on holidays with the rest of the family for the long-awaited reunion with a father she did not really know. In the years I was away, Carol allowed the children to accumulate a menagerie of pets—dogs, cats, fish, and birds. In 1973, when my release from prison had been announced and Carol informed the kids that I would be home soon, Sidney was confused.

"Where will he sleep?" she asked.

"With me," Carol answered.

"And what will we feed him?"

In prison, I pictured my family as they had been when I last saw them: my wife healthy and happy; my sons, not much older than toddlers, rambunctious and curious; my daughter a content-ed, beautiful infant; all of them safe and sound and carefree. So few of Carol's letters ever reached me that I had little detailed knowledge of how they were all getting along. I didn't know how Carol was managing to raise the kids alone or how the children's personalities were developing. The boys were now old enough to take an interest in sports, but I couldn't think of them as budding athletes. I had a hard time even picturing them at their current age. Sidney was no longer a baby, but I couldn't imagine what she looked like. When I closed my eyes, I just saw the small faces I had bid good-bye to, and I worried that the calamity that had befallen us might have touched them with a sadness they were too young to sustain.

I derived much comfort, however, from knowing that the Navy takes care of its own. Growing up in the Navy, I had known many families that had met with misfortune, the man of the house having gone off to war and not returned. And I had seen the Navy envelop them in a supportive embrace, looking after their material needs, the men from other Navy families helping to fill the void in fatherless households. I knew that the Navy was now looking after my family, and would, to the best of its ability, see to their needs and happiness, trying to keep the disruption caused by our misfortune from devastating their lives.

Our neighbors in Orange Park, many of whom, but not all, were Navy families, were extraordinarily kind and generous to my family while I was in Vietnam. They were the mainstay of my family's support, and I owe them a debt I can never adequately repay. They helped with the maintenance of our home, took my kids to sporting events, offered whatever counsel and support were needed, and generally helped my family hold together, body and soul, until I could get back to them. During Carol's long convalescence and therapy they were nothing less than an extended family to my family, and their love and concern was as much a mark of their good character as it was a blessing to the people they helped.

Today, at odd times, I find myself becoming quite sentimental about America. In the distant past, that was not how my patriotism typically found expression. I attribute much of my emotion to the good people of Orange Park, Florida. I no longer think of the country's character in abstract terms. Now, when I think about Americans, and how fortunate I am to be included in their number, I see the faces of our neighbors in Orange Park, and give thanks that by a lucky accident of birth, I was born an American.

The Cat came to see me one day and asked that I meet with a visiting "Spanish" delegation. I told him that it would not be worth his while, because I wouldn't make any antiwar or pro-Vietnam statements or say anything positive about the way prisoners were being treated. To my surprise, he said I would not be asked to make such statements.

I consulted Commander Bill Lawrence, the SRO of the Golden Nugget and "the Thunderbird," another nearby building. He told me to go ahead. That night I was taken to a hotel to meet the delegation, which turned out to be one man, Dr. Fernando Barral, a Cuban propagandist masquerading as a psychiatrist and moonlighting as a journalist. He interviewed me for half an hour, asking rather innocuous questions about my life, the schools I had attended, and my family. When he asked me if I hoped to go home soon, I replied, "No. I think the war will last a long time, but the U.S. will eventually win."

He then asked me if I felt remorse for bombing the Vietnamese. "No, I do not." The interview was published in a Cuban publication, Gramma, and later broadcast over the Voice of Vietnam. In it my interviewer observed that I had the attributes of a psychopath, as I showed no remorse for my crimes against the peace-loving Vietnamese people. Near the end of the interview, Barral offered his professional opinion of my personality:

He showed himself to be intellectually alert during the interview. From a morale point of view he is not in traumatic shock. He is neither dejected nor depressed. He was able to be sarcastic, and even humorous, indicative of psychic equilibrium. From the moral and ideological point of view he showed us he is an insensitive individual without human depth, who does not show the slightest concern, who does not appear to have thought about the criminal acts he committed against a population from the almost absolute impunity of his airplane, and that nevertheless those people saved his life, fed him, and looked after his health, and he is now healthy and strong. I believe that he bombed densely populated places for sport. I noted that he was hardened, that he spoke of banal things as if he were at a cocktail party.

During the interview he quietly drank three cups of coffee and smoked one of the cigarettes the Vietnamese had placed on the central table.

After I returned to my cell, I reported the interview to Bill Lawrence and to Commander Jeremiah Denton, the SRO of Little Vegas. Bill thought I had handled the situation appropriately, but something about it must have troubled Jerry. He made no comment immediately, but a little while later, he issued a new policy, that prisoners were to refuse all requests to meet with "visitors." Given that our enemies made some use of every such exchange, Jerry's order was certainly a sound one, even though it deprived me of further opportunities to demonstrate my "psychic equilibrium" to disapproving fraternal socialists, not to mention the extra cigarettes and coffee.

About a month later, both John Finley and I declined to meet with another peace delegation. That afternoon I was taken to a courtyard of the prison and ordered to sit on a stool for three days and nights. I was not beaten, although Bug checked in periodically to threaten me. After my punishment had ended, I was taken to the Cat's office, where I was puzzled to hear him apologize for my three days on the stool. He claimed he had been absent from the camp when the punishment was ordered. "Sometimes," he allowed, "my officers do the wrong thing."

In April, John and I were moved to a cell in Thunderbird, and were delighted to receive news that the POWs in Little Vegas would be allowed out of their cells for a period each day to play pool and Ping-Pong on tables set up in an empty cell. Our new recreation period, besides being a welcome distraction from prison drudgery, provided an excellent opportunity to improve communications between different parts of the camp.

I was designated as the Thunderbird "mailman," responsible for carrying notes to and from Stardust, where Jerry Denton was held. Air Force Major Sam Johnson, a great friend and an imaginative and always cheerful resister, was the mailman for Stardust. We hid encoded notes behind a wooden light switch in our new recreation room and thus managed to disseminate Jerry Denton's policies to all the parts of the camp under his command.

In June, I was involuntarily relieved of my duties as mailman. I was caught trying to communicate with Dick Stratton, who was held at that time in a cell in "the Riviera," next door to the pool room. I declined when ordered to confess my crime, and spent a night sitting on the stool.

The next day, I was taken to "Calcutta," a filthy punishment room, six feet by three feet, with only a tiny louvered window for ventilation. I would be confined there for three months.

Prior to my arrival, Bill Lawrence had been languishing in Calcutta for weeks. He had been shot down four months before me, taken to Hoa Lo, and locked in a torture room, known only by its number, Room 18. There he suffered five days of beatings and rope torture. From his cell he could hear the screams of his backseater, Lieutenant j.g. Jim Bailey, who was being tortured in a nearby room.

Bill Lawrence was a natural leader. He had already had a remarkable Navy career. He had been brigade commander at the Naval Academy, a four-letter man, and president of the Class of 1951. After graduation, he was asked to remain at the Academy to rewrite the honor code. He was sent to test pilot school, where he graduated first in his class, and went on to fly the new F-4 Phantom. He had been one of the first members of his class, if not the first, to be selected early for lieutenant commander.

While commanding a squadron in Vietnam, Bill received word that Admiral Tom Moorer, the Chief of Naval Operations, wanted him to serve as his aide, the most prestigious assignment that a young officer could be offered. Bill asked that he be allowed to remain in Vietnam to finish his squadron command tour.

When I was moved to Little Vegas, many of our most senior officers were kept isolated from the rest of us. Bill was my immediate superior. He was a model commander, steady as a rock, always in control of his emotions, never excited, never despairing or self-consumed. Several guys in Vegas had been Bill's classmates. Because he had been promoted early, he outranked them. Thus,

Bill had to provide leadership not only to junior guys like me, but to his peers. He had to tell his classmates what to do. That is a challenging assignment, but I never heard a single man reject, dispute, or resent Bill's commands. He was universally respected.

I used to tap him up on the wall for guidance all the time. I shared with Bill every question or concern I had. He had a way about him, very calm and reassuring, that put you at ease and inspired confidence in his judgment.

Some guys, burdened with despair, needed to be fired up. Bill would do it, convincing them that they were more than a match for their antagonists. Rambunctious and impatient, I needed a commander with quiet resolve who could help rein in my impulsiveness.

"Take it easy, John. Do the best you can, John. Resist as much as you can. Don't let them break you completely," Bill would caution me, gently warning me not to be so reckless that I plunged headlong into trouble. He was a remarkable commander.

Calcutta had space enough for only one prisoner. My dread of being confined in squalid, isolated Calcutta was alleviated a bit by the knowledge that my bad luck would liberate Bill. When I returned from Calcutta, considerably the worse for wear, Bill cheerfully thanked me for going to so much trouble to get him out.

I was a fairly skillful communicator, adept at tapping and better than average at recognizing and seizing unexpected opportunities for passing messages. I was not, I'm sorry to say, a very cautious one, and I often had reason to regret it. As was the case at the Plantation, the guards frequently apprehended me in the act.

Most of the punishments I received from 1969 on, some tolerable, others less so, were a result of my repeated indiscretions. Calcutta was one of the less tolerable punishments. I had been roughed up a few times, but not severely. Nor was the prospect of a few months' solitary confinement particularly terrifying to me. I certainly didn't welcome it, but I had survived worse before.

What made Calcutta so miserable was its location, at least fifty feet from the next occupied cell. It was impossible to communicate with anyone. Communicating was the indispensable key to resistance. Without that, it was hard to derive strength from others. Absent the counsel of fellow prisoners, I would begin to doubt my own judgment, whether I was resisting effectively and appropriately. If I was in communication only for a brief moment once a day, I would be okay. When I was deprived of any contact with my comrades, I was in serious trouble.

Calcutta was the first time since I had been released from the hospital that I was unable to communicate with anyone for an extended period of time. My isolation was awful, worse than the beatings I had been sentenced to for communicating. Compounding my misery was the cell's poor ventilation, and I suffered severe heat prostration in the extreme warmth of a Vietnamese summer, one of the effects of which was a constant buzzing in my ears that nearly drove me crazy. I was seldom allowed to bathe or shave. The quality of my food rations worsened. I became ill with dysentery again, and started to lose weight.

During my confinement in Calcutta, I was periodically taken to an interrogation room for quizzes. Unlike the bad old days, quizzes were now comparatively benign events. We were seldom beaten for information. My Calcutta quizzes were usually pro forma attempts to persuade me to meet with delegations. Mindful of Jerry Denton's order, I refused them.

On one occasion, an interrogator we called "Staff Officer" told me, "Everybody wants to see Mac Kane. They all ask about Mac Kane. You can see anybody you want."

"Well, I hate to disappoint them," I replied, "but I have to."

I had become very accustomed to close contact with my fellow prisoners since I had been released from solitary confinement. My state of mind had become so dependent on communicating with them that I worried my spell in isolation would fill me with such despair that I might break again. Blessedly, my fears were unfounded.

I had been greatly strengthened by the company of the good men of Little Vegas, and my resolve was firmer than it had ever been. I was sustained by the knowledge that the others knew where I was and were concerned about me. I knew they were demanding my release. And, most important, I knew they would be proud of me when I returned if I successfully resisted this latest tribulation. This was especially comforting to me because I suffered still from the knowledge that I had usually been better treated by the Vietnamese than had most of my comrades.

I was finally released from Calcutta in September and moved with John Finley to a cell in the Riviera, two doors down from Air Force Colonel Larry Guarino, with whom we immediately established good communications. I also managed to cut a small hole in the louvers above our cell door. Standing on my upended waste bucket, I could talk to a great many prisoners from different parts of the camp who were, by this time, allowed outside for a few moments to exercise. In retaliation for my various offenses, I was denied this privilege and allowed outside only once a week to bathe.

In what had now become a routine occurrence, I was again caught communicating, and once more confined for a period in an interrogation room. There I encountered the only two prisoners of my acquaintance who had lost their faith completely. They had not only stopped resisting but apparently crossed a line no other prisoner I knew had even approached. They were collaborators, actively aiding the enemy.

I do not know what caused these men to forsake their country and their fellow prisoners. Maybe they had despaired of ever being released, fearing the war wouldn't end before they were old men. They might have eventually fallen for routine Vietnamese denouncements of the "criminal American government," and grown to resent their civilian commanders for leaving them in this godforsaken place. Maybe they bought the whole nine yards of Vietnamese propaganda, that the war was unjust, their leaders warmongers, and their country a craven, imperial force for evil. Or maybe they were that rarest breed of American prisoners in Vietnam, POWs who, in exchange for certain comforts and privileges, had surrendered their dignity voluntarily and agreed to be the camp rats.

Whatever the cause, it cannot excuse their shameful conduct. I cannot say I ever observed any trace of shame in them as they whiled away the months and years in their unique circumstances. Indeed, during the time I closely observed them, they seemed to thrive, apparently undisturbed by the contempt of the rest of us.

When I encountered them, they had been kept away from the other POWs for some time. The interrogation room I had been taken to was located close to their cells. To pass the time until I was returned to the Thunderbird, I would stand on my waste bucket and look out through the louvered window at the top of my cell door. From my vantage point I could watch the two spend what in Hoa Lo amounted to fairly pleasant days.

The guards would bring them eggs, bananas, and other delicacies to eat. They were on quite friendly terms with the guards, who spoke to them politely and seemed almost solicitous about their comfort. They spent most of every day in a small courtyard back of the washroom where bamboo mats had been erected to screen them from observation by the rest of us. But from my elevated position standing on top of my bucket, I could see over the mats, and I watched them as they sunned themselves, read their mail, and talked to each other, apparently entirely at ease.

I had a nearly devout belief in the restorative power of communicating, as my recurring detentions for violating the camp rule indicate. I assumed, wrongly in this instance, that any American who was in regular communication with his superiors and other prisoners would, by and large, adhere to the Code of Conduct. Even when broken, a man could recover his dignity if he was able to contact his friends for support. Certainly that had been my experience when, my defenses shattered, I had relied on Bob Craner to bring me back from the dead.

But my two new neighbors waged the first assault on my until-then unassailable regard for communications as the force that bound us together and gave us the courage and strength to resist.

One morning as I set my bowl outside my cell after finishing breakfast, the guard walked away from me for some reason without locking me back in and was briefly out of sight. For a moment, I was at liberty. I decided to make good use of the unexpected privilege to establish contact with the two men, who were in their usual place of recreation.

I hustled over to the courtyard and pulled down the bamboo mat. "Hey, guys, my name's McCain. Who are you?"

I did not intend to chastise them for their disloyalty or even encourage them to start acting like officers and recover their dignity. I only hoped that I could briefly establish contact, and by taking that risk motivate them to try to keep in communication with me, reasoning that a few days' contact with another prisoner might bring them back to their senses. I was wrong.

Startled by my greeting, they looked at me for a second as I grinned back at them, and then, to my intense disappointment, they began shouting "Bao cao" to summon the guard. I was stunned, and the few blows I received for my audacity from the annoyed turnkey were insignificant compared to the melancholy I felt after discovering that there were at least two men who were indifferent to my evangelical zeal for communicating.

The two men who had betrayed my concern by ratting me out to the guard remained segregated from the rest of us for the duration of the war. They never attempted, as far as I know, to atone for their disloyalty and regain their self-respect. When we were all released, the two were brought up on charges. The charges were dropped, but they were dismissed from the service. Their superiors, like the rest of the country, wanted to put the war and all its bitter memories behind them. I wasn't disappointed in the decision. The two have to live with the memory of their treachery. I suspect that is punishment enough.

Not long after that discouraging experience, in early December, I was moved to another cell next door to my dear friend Bob Craner. A couple of weeks later, I was allowed outside half of each day. Prison life was improving, and it was about to get a whole lot better.

CHAPTER TWENTY FOUR

Camp Unity

Christmas, 1970. The most welcome event of my imprisonment. I was transferred with a great many other prisoners to large rooms in an area we called "Camp Unity." Camp Unity had seven cellblocks with, initially, thirty to forty prisoners held in each. Ultimately, after captured B-52 pilots and crewmen began to arrive and more prisoners from other camps were brought in, our total number would reach over 350.

In the center of each room was a concrete pedestal on which we all slept. A few of the badly injured POWs and our senior ranking officers were kept in different cells. The Vietnamese refused to recognize rank and never allowed our seniors to speak for us. This angered us greatly and worked to the disadvantage of our captors. Had they worked through our SROs, they would have found it a little easier to deal with us.

At Camp Unity I was reunited with many old friends, including Bob Craner and my first roommate, Bud Day. I was moved there when many of the toughest men in prison were moved into the camp. Jerry Denton, Jim Stockdale, Robbie Risner, Dick Stratton, George Coker, Jack Fellowes, John Dramesi, Bill Lawrence, Jim Kasler, Larry Guarino, Sam Johnson, Howie Dunn, George McKnight, Jerry Coffee, and Howie Rutledge, all legendary resisters, were relocated in Unity's cellblocks. We were overjoyed to be in one another's company, and a festival atmosphere prevailed.

If you have never been deprived of liberty in solitude, you cannot know what ineffable joy you experience in the open company of other human beings, free to talk and joke without fear. The strength you acquire in fraternity with others who share your fate is immeasurable.

That first night, when so many of us were unexpectedly allowed one another's company, not a single man slept. We talked all night, and well into the next day. We talked about everything. What might this change in our fortunes mean? Were we going home soon? Had the Vietnamese some public relations reason for putting us together? Had they been embarrassed by some new disclosure of their abusive treatment of us? We talked about what we had endured at the hands of the enemy; about the escapes some men had attempted and the consequences they suffered as a result. We talked about news from home. We talked about our families, and the lives we hoped to return to soon.

No other experience in my life could ever replicate my first night in Camp Unity, and the feeling of relief that overcame me to be living among my friends. I have lived many happy years since, and am a blessed and contented man. But I will never experience again the supreme happiness I felt my fourth Christmas in Hanoi.

POWs who had been lately held at camps outside Hanoi had learned of a recent, nearly successful American rescue attempt at a camp twenty miles outside Hanoi called Son Tay. The attempt had scared the hell out of the Vietnamese, and they had begun to bring prisoners from all outlying camps into prisons in Hanoi. Many of the Son Tay prisoners had been moved into Camp Unity a couple of weeks before the rest of us were.

In Camp Unity our SROs ordered us to form into a cohesive military unit—the Fourth Allied POW Wing. The wing's motto was "Return with Honor." Colonel Flynn would soon end his long years of isolation when he was moved into a room with the other Air Force colonels and assumed command of the wing.

Each room served as a squadron, with the senior ranking officer in each room in command. Each squadron was broken into flights of about six men, each with a flight commander. We were organized to continue resisting. It was a lot easier to defy your enemy when you are surrounded by fellow resisters.

Among my closest friends was Orson Swindle, one of the Son Tay prisoners, a tough, good-natured Marine pilot from Georgia. In our first months in Unity, he lived in the room next to mine, and we first met by tapping through the wall that separated our rooms. Orson had been shot down near the DMZ on November 11, 1966. He had been beaten and rope-tortured repeatedly during the thirty-nine days it took his captors to reach Hanoi. From the beginning of his captivity, Orson had impressed the Vietnamese as a hard man to crack.

In August 1967, Orson was held at "the Desert Inn" with three other determined resisters, George McKnight, Wes Schierman, and Ron Storz. One night an enraged Vietnamese officer accompanied by several guards burst into their cell accusing the Americans of various infractions of camp regulations. They locked Ron Storz in leg stocks, roped his arms behind him, and stuffed a towel down his throat. When George McKnight screamed at them to stop, they did the same to him.

Orson and Wes were also put in the stocks and rope-tortured, but not gagged. When the guards began savagely beating McKnight and Storz, the two ungagged men screamed, "Torture!" The guards turned to Orson and Wes and began beating them, trying to force gags into their mouths. Twisting their heads to avoid the gags, the two kept shouting, "Torture, torture," until all the prisoners in Little Vegas began screaming with them.

The beatings continued mercilessly until the men were an unrecognizable bloody mess. McKnight had nearly suffocated to death before his gag was removed. Eventually the four were led through a crowd of cursing, spitting, striking Vietnamese to separate stalls in the washroom. There they were beaten all night long.

The next morning, shortly after several American planes had flown over the city, the guards rushed at Orson, kicking him repeatedly in retaliation for the appearance of American airpower. The four spent the rest of the day in separate interrogation rooms, enduring long hours of continued torture until they were all forced to make a confession.

Later that day, Orson, George, and Wes were transferred to a prison they called "Dirty Bird," for its exceptionally filthy conditions, and kept, shackled, in solitary confinement. The prison was nothing more than a single building. The Vietnamese had decided to convert it into a jail because of its advantageous location. It was adjacent to an important target for American bombers, and the Vietnamese hoped that the presence of American prisoners in the vicinity would dissuade American military commanders from ordering any air strikes on it. The target was a thermal power plant—the target I had attempted to bomb in my last moment of freedom. Orson would joke later that "as scared as I was when they bombed the power plant, I would have really been scared had I known John was on the way, knowing he'd hit everything around the target except the power plant itself."

McKnight, along with another inmate, George Coker, eventually managed to free themselves from their leg irons and make a daring escape from Dirty Bird. They were recaptured the next day.

Ron Storz had not been taken with his cellmates to Dirty Bird. After they tortured him to the point of submission, the Vietnamese intended to use Ron to inform on his SRO, Jim Stockdale. Attempting to kill himself, Ron used an ink pen to cut his wrists and chest. He was eventually taken to a place its inhabitants called "Alcatraz," located behind the defense ministry a short distance from Hoa Lo. He was one of eleven men kept there, among them several high-ranking Americans including Jim Stockdale and Jerry Denton, and McKnight and Coker, who had been taken there after their failed escape.

The Alcatraz Eleven had distinguished themselves as die-hard resisters. Their new prison, situated across the courtyard from an open cesspool, reflected their distinction as special cases. The cells were tomblike, windowless, and measuring four feet across. They were locked in leg irons at night.

Ten of the men kept there, most of them for over two years, would remember the place as the worst of many difficult experiences. The eleventh, Ron Storz, would never leave Alcatraz. He had been physically and mentally abused for so long that he had lost either the will or the ability to eat, and had slowly wasted away. The Vietnamese kept Ron behind when they released the others from Alcatraz, claiming he was too sick to move. He died there, alone.

Orson had been spared the deprivations of Alcatraz. He had been taken from Dirty Bird to Little Vegas shortly after we bombed the power plant. In November 1968, he was transferred to the prison at Son Tay, where his captors ordered him to write approvingly to prominent American politicians who opposed the war. He refused.

His steadfastness earned Orson a trip to the punishment room, where he was seated on a low stool and locked in leg irons. The guards were ordered to prevent him from sleeping. Whenever he nodded off, a guard slapped him awake. After several days and nights, Orson began to suffer from hallucinations. Still he would not write. During one particularly vivid hallucination, Orson became violent. After subduing him, the guards relented and let him sleep. He was given food and allowed to rest for three days.

On the third day, he was again ordered to write. Refusing, he was subjected to further mistreatment. Chained to his stool and denied sleep for another ten days and nights, he finally relented.

After Orson's ordeal, another prisoner who had refused to write was given the same punishment. He broke after a day. The guards told him, "You're not like Swindle."

Although I did not meet Orson Swindle until I was moved into Unity, I, like most other prisoners, had heard of him. His reputation for being as stouthearted as they come was a camp legend by the time I met him.

As a resistance leader, Jim Stockdale had few peers. He was a constant inspiration to the men under his command. Many of his captors hated him for his fierce and unyielding spirit. The Rabbit hated him the most. One day, the Rabbit ordered Jim cleaned up so that he could be filmed for a propaganda movie in which he would play a visiting American businessman. He was given a razor to shave. Jim used it to hack off his hair, severely cutting his scalp in the process and spoiling his appearance, in the hope that this would render him unsuitable for his enemies' purpose. But the Rabbit was not so easily dissuaded. He left to find a hat to place on Jim's bleeding head. In the intervening moments, Jim picked up a wooden stool and repeatedly bashed his face with it. Disfigured, Jim succeeded in frustrating the Rabbit's plans for him that evening.

On a later occasion, after being whipped and tied in ropes at the hands of the demented Bug, Jim was forced to confess that he had defied camp regulations. But Bug was not through with him. He informed Jim that he would be back tomorrow to torture him for more information. Jim feared he would be forced to give up the names of the men he had been communicating with. In an effort to impress his enemies with his determination not to betray his comrades, he broke a window and slashed his wrist with a shard of glass. For his extraordinary heroism, Jim Stockdale received the Medal of Honor when he returned home, a decoration he had earned a dozen times over.

Robbie Risner was another of my Camp Unity cellmates whose reputation preceded him. Air Force Lieutenant Colonel Robinson Risner commanded a squadron in Vietnam. He had also been a much-decorated pilot in the Korean War. Early in 1965, *Time* magazine had featured the air ace on its cover, praising Robbie as one of America's greatest combat pilots.

Several months later, on September 16, 1965, Robbie was shot down ninety miles south of Hanoi. When he arrived at Hoa Lo two days later, he was taken to an interrogation room. There the Rabbit, seated at a table with a copy of the aforementioned issue of *Time* in full view, greeted him: "Ah, Colonel Risner, we've been waiting for you."

I can only imagine the sinking feeling Robbie must have had as he discovered the Vietnamese were regular readers of American periodicals. Nevertheless, from the first moment of his imprisonment to the last, Robbie Risner was an exemplary senior officer, an inveterate communicator, an inspiration to the men he commanded, and a source of considerable annoyance to his captors. Among the longest-held prisoners, he suffered the appalling mistreatment regularly inflicted on POWs during the brutal early years of imprisonment. Throughout his trials, he gave the Vietnamese good cause to appreciate the physical courage and strength of character that had landed him on the cover of *Time*.

In my first cellblock in Unity, Building Number 7, I lived with many of the more senior prisoners. Air Force Colonel Vernon Ligon was the senior ranking officer. Robbie Risner, Jim Stockdale, and Jerry Denton were his deputies. Near the end of 1971, I would be moved into another cellblock, Number 2, with Orson. Bud Day, the ranking officer in Number 3, assumed command of our squadron.

Until we were all moved into Unity, I had not had the pleasure of Bud's company since we had parted at the Plantation three years earlier. Bud had been held at Hoa Lo while I was living in Little Vegas, but out of reach of my communication chain. For most of the years preceding our reunion, Bud had suffered awful conditions and monstrous cruelty at the Zoo, where mass torture was a routine practice. For a time, the camp personnel at the Zoo included an English-speaking Cuban, called "Fidel" by the POWs, who delighted in breaking Americans, even when the task required him to torture his victim to death.

Bud was the third-ranking officer at the Zoo, after Larry Guarino and Navy Commander Wendell Rivers. When Larry and Wendy were moved to Vegas, Bud became the SRO. To the poor souls who shared the misfortune of being imprisoned in the Zoo, Bud was as great an inspiration as he had been to me during our few months together.

I doubt I will ever meet a tougher man than Bud Day. After the Dramesi-Atterbury escape, treatment worsened in all the camps, but it reached an astonishing level of depravity in the camp they had escaped from—the Zoo. Men were taken in large groups to various torture rooms where they were beaten, roped, stomped on, and struck with bamboo clubs. Their wrists and ankles were shackled in irons. Few were gagged. The Vietnamese wanted the others to hear the screams of the tortured. This new terror campaign was intended to destroy any semblance of prisoner resistance. It lasted for months.

The Vietnamese introduced a new torment to their punishment regime—flogging with fan belts. Prisoners were stripped and forced to lie facedown on the floor. Guards would take turns whipping them with fan belts, which unlike ropes and cords would only raise welts on the sufferer's back and not tear his flesh. They would not relent until their victim had mumbled his assent to whatever statement their torturers demanded he make. The senior officers were spared this treatment for some time. The Vietnamese wanted them to witness the suffering of their subordinates before turning the full brunt of their malevolence on them.

Guarino was the first senior to be taken. He was rope-tortured, sleep-deprived, clubbed, and whipped for weeks, until at long last he broke and gave the Vietnamese an acceptable confession.

Bud was next. His arms were still useless from the rope torture he had experienced after his capture. This time they would flog him nearly to death before he relented. They made him confess to knowledge of elaborate escape planning in the camp, planning that John or Ed would have been grateful for had it truly existed. The Vietnamese wanted names. Bud would only give them his. They flogged him some more until to his great sorrow he gave them two more names. When they stopped, he took it back, claiming that the men he named were innocent, as indeed they were.

They resumed the torture, demanding that Bud inform on another prisoner, Wendy Rivers. Bud refused, and was whipped again. After six weeks his ordeal finally ended.

Nothing that happened to me during my time in prison approximated the suffering that these men, who had steeled themselves with an unyielding devotion to duty, survived. That they had survived was itself an act of heroism. I had experienced a few rough moments, and, out of spite for my enemies as much as from my sense of duty, I had tried to fight back. But these men, and the many other prisoners whose heroism made them legends, humbled me, as they humble me today whenever I recall what they did for their country and for those of us who were once privileged to witness their courage.

CHAPTER TWENTY FIVE

Skid Row

In February 1971, we began a dispute with the Vietnamese over their refusal to allow us to conduct religious services in a manner we thought fitting. The Church Riot began when the camp edict against POWs gathering in groups larger than six and against one man addressing large groups was used to forbid us to hold services. Our SRO ordered us to challenge the prohibition. On Sunday, February 7, we held a church service. We had informed our warden, Bug, of our intentions. George Coker began the service, and Rutledge gave the opening prayer. Robbie Risner read the closing prayer. A four-man choir sang hymns.

Soon Bug arrived and yelled at us to stop. He ordered the choir to cease singing. He was ignored, and the service continued. In a rage, Bug had the guards haul Risner, Coker, and Rutledge out into the courtyard. As they were led out, Bud Day started singing "The Star-Spangled Banner," and soon every man in every cell-block joined in. When we finished the anthem, we started on a succession of patriotic tunes. The whole prison reverberated with our singing, and the wild applause that erupted at the end of every number. It was a glorious moment.

Finally, the Vietnamese managed to disrupt our fun when they marched in en masse, arrayed in full riot gear, and broke up the party.

Risner, Rutledge, and Coker were taken to a punishment cell in the part of the Hilton we called "Heartbreak Hotel." Our SRO, Vernon Ligon, warned Bug that we would hold church services next Sunday, and every Sunday after that.

Bud Day, Jim Kasler, and I were among a number of POWs ordered out of the room to be interrogated and harangued by camp authorities for our criminal behavior. We were taken out separately, and the expression on the guards' faces as they escorted us at bayonet point indicated the seriousness of the situation.

A number of senior Vietnamese officers from various camps were standing together in the courtyard, officers who had been responsible for the brutality we had endured in the bad old days. But they were no longer permitted to use torture as a first resort to coerce our submission, and they appeared anxious and uncertain about how to cope with our new assertiveness.

When we were returned to our room, Bud, Bill Lawrence, and I discussed our captors' predicament, and how at odds they all seemed. We were emboldened by their confusion. The guards placed ladders against our building and stood on the rungs to peer into our window and scribble notes about our behavior. Their notes were used by the camp officers to determine which POWs should be moved to other cells and camps. The quality of the food declined from bad to awful. Jerry Denton ordered us to begin a hunger strike until our grievances were settled and Risner, Rutledge, and Coker were returned to us.

One evening, a few nights after the riot, one of the two collaborators at Hoa Lo who had ratted on me for trying to talk to them read a poem over the camp loudspeakers that he had written about the riot. The poem was titled "Cowards Sing at Night." It scorned us for raising our voices in protest to sing the national anthem.

By this time, the poem's author did not have any friends in camp besides the Vietnamese and his fellow collaborator. Most of us pitied him more than we hated him. That night, however, after he finished his poetry reading, there were any number of prisoners who would have killed him had they had the opportunity to do so.

At week's end, Soft Soap Fairy announced that it had always been the policy of camp authorities to permit religious expression.

Therefore, we would be allowed to hold brief religious services as long as we didn't abuse their tolerance to further our "black schemes."

As part of Vietnamese efforts to convince the world that we were being well treated, they had recently stopped using letter-writing privileges as a tool to force our cooperation and begun encouraging us to write home often. It occurred to me that this change in prison policy offered an excellent opportunity to take advantage of our enemy's eagerness to improve their public image. I thought it fitting to use a privilege that had often been denied us to suit Hanoi's war ends as a means to suit our own.

I proposed to our senior officers that we begin a letter-writing moratorium until our treatment and conditions were improved. If men were physically abused for refusing to write home, I suggested we write honestly about our mistreatment. I was confident the Vietnamese would never let such letters reach our worried families.

After some discussion our senior officers agreed, but, wisely, made the no-letter policy voluntary. Some men had not communicated with their families for years and were understandably anxious to let their families know they were all right. By summer, however, nearly everyone was refusing to write home.

On the evening of March 17, less than three months after we had begun living in large groups, Bud Day, Orson Swindle, and I were taken from our rooms. Along with twenty-four others, several men from each room in Camp Unity, we were blindfolded, loaded into trucks, and driven to a punishment camp ten miles outside Hanoi, a place we called "Skid Row."

During the trip, some of the prisoners tried to fix the location of our destination. It was a common practice for POWs to keep a mental record of directions and distance when we were being relocated. One man was designated to control the vectors by memorizing each turn of the truck in sequence while another silently counted the time that elapsed between turns.

The exercise required extraordinary concentration, but usually yielded a remarkably accurate estimate of our location. It was not something that I was very good at it, however, and so I never seriously attempted to join in the exercise. Wherever we were heading, we would still be prisoners of war in North Vietnam when we arrived there. While I was as curious as the next guy about our destination, I knew that those basic facts of our existence would not be affected by a change of scenery. So that night I bounced along in the back of the truck, blindfolded and tied in ropes, silently cursing my bad luck, while my friends concentrated on their labors.

We had been singled out for our bad attitude, which I somewhat regretted, for it had cost me the open society of Camp Unity. But punishment wasn't the only purpose of our exile from Camp Unity. The Vietnamese had decided to round up all the troublemakers whose influence with the other prisoners made it difficult to maintain order and discipline in the new living arrangements at Hoa Lo. Thus, though we were not happy about our relocation, we all took a certain pride in our distinction as the camp's hard cases. The POWs who remained at Camp Unity called us the "Hell's Angels."

We were kept in solitary confinement in small cells, six by four feet, each with a narrow wooden bunk. The cells had no ventilation and were without lights or bathing facilities. The camp had a stinking well with human waste floating in its dank water. My morale sank.

Bud Day remained our SRO. He was kept in one of the cells in the back of the building, while I occupied one in the front. Miserable, we took to insulting and arguing with our guards. Bud ordered us to knock it off, believing that beatings were unlikely to improve our wretched circumstances. His order was occasionally disobeyed, as our anger undermined our discipline. Frustrated, Bud kept insisting that while we should not accept mistreatment without complaint, we should also refrain from unnecessarily provoking the guards.

Bud himself had been beaten and threatened with a fan belt a few weeks after our arrival at Skid Row, and had for a few days been locked on his bunk in stocks. He wanted to spare the rest of us such abuse if it could be avoided without compromising our principles. Overall, when we left the guards alone, they left us alone, satisfied that leaving us to suffer in such squalor was adequate punishment for our crimes. But Bud had a hard time keeping control over several of us. I regret that I occasionally added to my dear friend's burden. My temper, worsened by my return to solitary confinement in this dismal camp, occasionally got the better of me.

A small space separated the cells in the front of the building from a brick wall. The upper part of each cell door was barred, but otherwise uncovered. Wooden shutters that could have been used to cover the bars were kept open for those of us in the front, while the windows in the back cell were usually kept closed. The Vietnamese routinely tried to undermine our solidarity by according some prisoners a privilege of open shutters while denying it to others. I was pleased to receive this particular privilege, as it mitigated the effect solitary confinement had on my morale.

During our first days in Skid Row, we communicated freely with each other through our barred windows, talking constantly and loudly, our voices bouncing off the wall in front of us. Initially the guards didn't seem to mind our ceaseless chattering. Occasionally they warned us not to talk so loudly, but they made no other objection to our conversations.

After a week or so, senior prison authorities must have reminded our guards that Skid Row was meant to be a punishment camp for recalcitrant prisoners and instructed them not to show any leniency to us. One morning, as soon as we resumed our conversations of the previous day, the guards appeared, shouting, "No talking. No talking."

"Bullshit," I yelled back. "I'm going to talk." Too accustomed now to unconstrained conversation, and still angry over our expulsion from Unity, I was in no mood to be silenced.

"No talking, Mac Kane!"

"Bullshit. I'm going to talk. You bastards kept me in solitary for years. You're not going to shut me up now."

One of the guards, intending to terminate any further protest on my part, slammed and locked the wooden shutter over the bars of my door, leaving me fuming in my darkened cell.

Refusing to back down, my anger now completely beyond control, I screamed at the guards, "Bao cao, bao cao. Open it up. Bao cao, bao cao. Open it up, you bastards, open it up." The guards scurried off to find an officer. When they located one, they led him back to my cell and opened up the shutter, finding me red-faced and glaring at them through the bars.

"What's wrong with you, Mac Kane?" the officer inquired.

"I'm not putting up with this shit anymore. That's what's wrong with me," I answered. "I want to talk, and you're not going to shut me up."

The officer left without responding to my declaration, the guards hurrying after him. Ten minutes later, the guards returned and instructed me to roll up my sleeping mat and other belongings. I did as instructed. They escorted me from my cell and chucked me into the cell next door, which was occupied by Navy Lieutenant Pete Schoeffel.

This new arrangement suited me fine, and I quickly cooled off. But I doubt Pete welcomed the idea of sharing quarters as much as I did. The cells were hardly suited to cohabitation, measuring little larger than a cardboard box. Two men could barely stand shoulder to shoulder. Nevertheless, Pete took it all in good humor, graciously giving me leave to sleep in his bunk because of my bad leg, while he found what little comfort he could on the concrete floor.

In August, monsoon rains threatened to flood the Red River and Skid Row, and we were transferred back to Hoa Lo. For a brief moment we held out hope that we were being returned to Camp Unity.

Our hope was crushed when were marched into Heartbreak Hotel, where we were kept four and five to a room. The rooms were small and the conditions miserable. Many of the men became ill; a few were suffering from hepatitis. Tempers were frayed, and morale sank even lower. A couple of months later we were taken back to Skid Row, which, given the awful conditions at Heartbreak, was almost a relief. While conditions remained miserable, the Vietnamese lightened up on the discipline, and we were allowed to talk among ourselves without fear of further punishment.

We were released from Skid Row in three groups. Bud, Orson, and I, our bad attitudes uncorrected by our time in exile, were in the last group to leave. In November 1971, we were finally reunited with our friends at Camp Unity and put into a cellblock together, our morale restored.

CHAPTER TWENTY SIX

Pledge of Allegiance

During the last fourteen months at Camp Unity, I served as entertainment officer, appointed to the post by Bud Day. In this capacity I was ably assisted by a number of my roommates, most notably Orson Swindle and Air Force Captains Jim Sehorn and Warren Lilly. We enjoyed the work.

Bud designated me room chaplain, an office I took quite seriously even though I lacked any formal training for it. Orson and I also served as the communication officers for the room, charged with maintaining regular contact with the other rooms in Unity. We both had plenty of experience for the work, and despite my reputation for recklessness, I prided myself on the job we did.

We never let a holiday or a birthday pass without arranging a small, crude, but welcome celebration. Gifts fashioned out of odd scraps of material and our few meager possessions were bestowed on every prisoner celebrating a birthday. A skit, always ribald and ridiculous, was performed to commemorate the occasion by embarrassing the celebrant. Marine Corps, Navy, and Air Force anniversaries were also formally observed.

Both an avid reader and a movie fan, I took great pride in narrating movies and books from memory. With a captive audience, I would draw out the telling of a novel, embellishing here and there to add length and excitement, for hours before I lost the audience's interest. Among the texts both the audience and I enjoyed most were works of Kipling, Maugham, and Hemingway.

Our most popular entertainments, however, were our productions of Sunday, Wednesday, and Saturday Nights at the Movies. I told over a hundred movies in prison, some of them many times over. I tried to recall every movie I had ever seen from *Stalag 17* to *One-Eyed Jacks* (a camp favorite). Often running short of popular fare, I would make up movies I had never seen. Pilots shot down during air raids in 1972 were a valuable resource for me. They had seen movies that I had not. Desperate for new material, I would pester them almost as soon as they arrived and before they had adjusted to their new circumstances. "What movies have you seen lately? Tell me about them." On first acquaintance, they probably thought prison life had seriously affected my mind. But they would give me a few details, and from that I would concoct another movie for Saturday night. Movies had become a lot more risqué in the five years I had been away. I narrated a few of these as well, and my audience was all the more attentive.

My performance was usually well received, although on occasion some of the men's interest flagged when watching a repeat performance for the fourth or fifth time. However, I always enjoyed the undivided attention of one inveterate movie fan.

Air Force Major Konrad Trautman, a reserved, precise son of German immigrants, never missed a performance. He would take his seat early and wait patiently for the movie to begin. With a pipe filled with cigarette tobacco clenched tightly between his teeth, he sat impassively, never making a sound. He listened intently to every word I uttered. No matter how many times he had seen a movie or how crude the production, Konrad never betrayed the least hint of disappointment. Fans like that are hard to come by for even the most celebrated actor, and I always took great encouragement from Konrad's evident appreciation of my qualities as a thespian.

During the Christmas season we performed a different skit and sang carols in our crudely decorated room every night for the five nights before Christmas. A longer production was saved for Christmas night. Orson Swindle and I, with a few other guys, staged a mangled production of Dickens's *A Christmas Carol*. We livened up the venerable tale with parody, most of it vulgar, to the great amusement of our howling audience. Jack Fellowes played Tiny Tim, attired in nothing but a makeshift diaper. Another, not known for his particularly feminine appearance, was chosen to play Bob Cratchit's wife.

A week before, Bud had asked Bug for an English-language Bible. Bug initially dismissed the request with a lie, claiming that there were no Bibles in North Vietnam. A few days later, perhaps remembering that his interference with the practice of our religion had resulted in the Church Riot earlier that year, Bug announced that a Bible, "the only one in Hanoi," had been located. One prisoner was to be designated to copy passages from it for a few minutes.

As room chaplain, I was given the assignment. I collected the Bible from where it had been left by a guard, on a table in the courtyard just outside our cell door. Hastily, I leafed through its tattered pages until I found an account of the Nativity. I quickly copied the passage, and finished just moments before a guard arrived to retrieve the Bible.

On Christmas night we held our simple, moving service. We began with the Lord's Prayer, after which a choir sang carols, directed by the former conductor of the Air Force Academy Choir, Captain Quincy Collins. I thought they were quite good, excellent, in fact. Although I confess that the regularity with which they practiced in the weeks prior to Christmas occasionally grated on my nerves.

But that night, the hymns were rendered with more feeling and were more inspirational than the offerings of the world's most celebrated choirs. We all joined in the singing, nervous and furtive at first, fearing the guards would disrupt the service if we sang too loudly. With each hymn, however, we grew bolder, and our voices rose with emotion.

Between each hymn, I read a portion of the story of Christ's birth from the pages I had copied.

"'And the Angel said unto them, Fear not: for, behold, I bring you good tidings of great joy, which shall be to all people. For unto you is born this day, in the city of David, a Savior, which is Christ the Lord.'"

The night air was cold, and we shivered from its effect and from the fever that still plagued some of us. The sickest among us, unable to stand, sat on the raised concrete sleeping platform in the middle of the room, blankets around their shaking shoulders. Many others, stooped by years of torture, or crippled from injuries sustained during their shootdown, stood, some on makeshift crutches, as the service proceeded.

The lightbulbs hanging from the ceiling illuminated our gaunt, unshaven, dirty, and generally wretched congregation. But for a moment we all had the absolutely exquisite feeling that our burdens had been lifted. Some of us had attended Christmas services in prison before. But they had been Vietnamese productions, spiritless, ludicrous stage shows. This was our service, the only one we had ever been allowed to hold. It was more sacred to me than any service I had attended in the past, or any service I have attended since.

We gave prayers of thanks for the Christ child, for our families and homes, for our country. We half expected the guards to barge in and force us to conclude the service. Every now and then we glanced up at the windows to see if they were watching us as they had during the Church Riot. But when I looked up at the bars that evening, I wished they had been looking in. I wanted them to see us—faithful, joyful, and triumphant.

The last hymn sung was "Silent Night." Many of us wept.

We held a Christmas dinner after the service. We had arranged our room to resemble a "dining-in," a much-loved military ritual, in which officers, attired in their best uniforms, sit at table according to rank, to dine and drink in elaborate formality. Lacking most of the necessary accouterments, we nevertheless made quite an evening of it. The senior officers sat at the head of the table, while numerous speeches and toasts to family, service, and country were honored. All of us were proud to have the opportunity to dine again, even in our less than elegant surroundings, like officers and gentlemen.

After dinner we exchanged gifts. One man had used his cotton washcloth and a needle and thread he had scrounged somewhere to fashion a hat for Bud. Other men exchanged dog tags. Most of us exchanged chits for Christmas gifts we wished each other to have. We all gave one man who had been losing at poker lately an IOU for another $250 in imaginary chips.

Back from Skid Row that Christmas, we were overjoyed to entertain ourselves again in the company of men who had managed through all those years to retain their humanity though our enemies had tried to turn us into animals. From then on, with brief exceptions, our existence in Hanoi was as tolerable as could be expected when you are deprived of your liberty.

The Vietnamese had given us several decks of cards, and we played a lot of bridge and poker. My luck at the table usually ran bad, to the endless amusement of Orson, who liked to taunt me for what he considered my unskilled approach to the games. Almost every Sunday afternoon, we held a bridge tournament that included six tables of players.

We had more profitable uses for our time as well, which made our days pass just as quickly as did our reproductions of various popular entertainments. An education officer was designated and classes were taught in almost every imaginable subject, all the POWs called on to share their particular field of learning. Language classes were popular and to this day I can read more than a few words in several languages. The guards frequently confiscated our notes, however, an impediment that greatly complicated our grasp of foreign languages. Other subjects ranged from quantum physics to meat-cutting.

Lectures were held on the four nights when we were not required to stage a movie reproduction. Orson and I taught classes in literature and history, and I took as much pride in my history lectures as I did in my movie performances, calling our tutorial "The History of the World from the Beginning."

Our classes and amateur theatrics made time, the one thing we had in abundance, pass relatively pleasantly and helped temper the small conflicts that inevitably arise when men are confined together in close quarters. No matter how irritated we occasionally felt over slight grievances with one another, nothing could ever seriously detract from the pleasure we took from our own company in the last full year of our captivity.

Our situation improved even more in April 1972, when President Nixon resumed the bombing of North Vietnam and, on my father's orders, the first bombs since March 1968 began falling on Hanoi. Operation Linebacker, as the campaign was called, brought B-52s, with their huge payload of bombs, into the war, although they were not used in attacks on Hanoi.

The misery we had endured prior to 1972 was made all the worse by our fear that the United States was unprepared to do what was necessary to bring the war to a reasonably swift conclusion. We could never see over the horizon to the day when the war would end. Whether you supported the war or opposed it— and I met few POWs who argued the latter position—no one believed the war should be prosecuted in the manner in which the Johnson administration had fought it.

No one who goes to war believes once he is there that it is worth the terrible cost of war to fight it by half measures. War is too horrible a thing to drag out unnecessarily. It was a shameful waste to ask men to suffer and die, to persevere through awful afflictions and heartache, for a cause that half the country didn't believe in and our leaders weren't committed to winning. They committed us to it, badly misjudged the enemy's resolve, and left us to manage the thing on our own without authority to fight it to the extent necessary to finish it.

It's not hard to understand now that, given the prevailing political judgments of the time, the Vietnam War was better left unfought. No other national endeavor requires as much unshakable resolve as war. If the government and the nation lack that resolve, it is criminal to expect men in the field to carry it alone. We were accountable to the country, and no one was accountable to us. But we found our honor in our answer, if not our summons.

Every POW knew that the harder the war was fought the

sooner we would go home. Long aware of the on-and-off peace negotiations in Paris, we were elated when the Nixon administration proved it was intent on forcing the negotiations to a conclusion that would restore our freedom.

As the bombing campaign intensified, our morale soared with every sortie. It was after one raid, and our raucous celebration of its effect, that the guards dragged Mike Christian from our room.

Mike was a Navy bombardier-navigator who had been shot down in 1967, about six months before I arrived. He had grown up near Selma, Alabama. His family was poor. He had not worn shoes until he was thirteen years old. Character was their wealth. They were good, righteous people, and they raised Mike to be hardworking and loyal. He was seventeen when he enlisted in the Navy. As a young sailor, he showed promise as a leader and impressed his superiors enough to be offered a commission.

What packages we were allowed to receive from our families often contained handkerchiefs, scarves, and other clothing items. For some time, Mike had been taking little scraps of red and white cloth, and with a needle he had fashioned from a piece of bamboo he laboriously sewed an American flag onto the inside of his blue prisoner's shirt. Every afternoon, before we ate our soup, we would hang Mike's flag on the wall of our cell and together recite the Pledge of Allegiance. No other event of the day had as much meaning to us.

The guards discovered Mike's flag one afternoon during a routine inspection and confiscated it. They returned that evening and took Mike outside. For our benefit as much as Mike's, they beat him severely, just outside our cell, puncturing his eardrum and breaking several of his ribs. When they had finished, they dragged him bleeding and nearly senseless back into our cell, and we helped him crawl to his place on the sleeping platform. After things quieted down, we all lay down to go to sleep. Before drifting off, I happened to look toward a corner of the room, where one of the four naked lightbulbs that were always illuminated in our cell cast a dim light on Mike Christian. He had crawled there quietly when he thought the rest of us were sleeping. With his eyes nearly swollen shut from the beating, he had quietly picked up his needle and thread and begun sewing a new flag.

I witnessed many acts of heroism in prison, but none braver than that. As I watched him, I felt a surge of pride at serving with him, and an equal measure of humility for lacking that extra ration of courage that distinguished Mike Christian from other men.

CHAPTER TWENTY SEVEN

Release

The bombing of North Vietnam was halted in October when peace talks resumed in Paris. By December, it was clear that the talks had stalled because of North Vietnamese intransigence. On December 18, at around nine o'clock in the evening, it was renewed with a vengeance as Operation Linebacker II commenced and the unmistakable destructive power of B-52s rained down on Hanoi.

Despite our proximity to the targets, we were jubilant. We hollered in near euphoria as the ground beneath us shook with the force of the blasts, exulting in our guards' fear as they scurried for shelter. We clapped each other on the back and joked about packing our bags for home. We shouted "Thank you!" at the night sky.

No prisoner betrayed the slightest concern that we were in any danger. I didn't hear anyone say, "We might be hit." We just cheered the assault on and watched the show. Once in a while a guard came by and yelled at us to shut up, to which we responded by cheering even louder.

When a Vietnamese SAM hit a B-52, as, regrettably, happened on several occasions, the explosion and burning fuel would illuminate the whole sky, from horizon to horizon, a bright pink-and-orange glow. In this unnatural light, we could see the Vietnamese gasping at the strange sight and tearing around the camp in a panic.

Some of the gun guards had responded to the shriek of the air raid sirens by manning their defense stations slowly, joking and laughing with each other, apparently indifferent to the coming assault. They probably believed it to be only a drill. Now they were racing around trying to figure out how to defend themselves from this unexpected, massive bombardment. Terrified, some of them fired their rifles into the sky at targets that were miles above them.

For many of our guards this was their first taste of modern warfare, and their confidence in the superiority of their defenses was visibly shaken. Many of them cowered in the shadows of our cellblocks, believing, correctly, that the B-52 pilots knew where Americans were held in Hanoi and were trying to avoid dropping their bombs near us.

It was quite a spectacular show. Antiaircraft guns booming, bombs exploding, fires raging all over the city. It is sinful to take pleasure in the suffering of others, even your enemies, and B-52s can deliver a lot of suffering. But the Vietnamese had never before experienced the full extent of American airpower. They believed that the airpower they had previously witnessed was all we were capable of delivering, and that their formidable air defenses were more than a match for it. Now they stood in awe and terror of the real thing, the full measure of conventional American power.

Before the B-52 raids, the Vietnamese had always stepped up the pressure on us whenever the United States escalated the air campaign. They knocked us around a little more often and a little more enthusiastically, just to make the point that they were still confident of victory. In the aftermath of the B-52 raids, some of the guards who had treated us the most contemptuously became almost civil when speaking to us. Some of them even began to smile at us, almost comically. It was impossible for us not to feel pride and relief as we watched people who had badly mistreated us recognize, at long last, how powerful an enemy we represented.

The first raid lasted until four-thirty in the morning. As the raids continued over the following nights, we could see that the Vietnamese air defenses were diminishing. They had few missiles left to fire, and the antiaircraft guns fell silent. Bridges were destroyed, arsenals blown up, the city's defense infrastructure devastated. They were being beaten, and they knew it.

The day after the first bombing raid, one of the officers burst into our room and screamed hysterically, "We are not afraid! We are not afraid!" He added that the Vietnamese were certain to win the war, thereby convincing us that, for the moment at least, he thought they were losing. After the last raid, an officer entered our cell smiling broadly as he informed us that they had destroyed all the B-52s. I was standing with Bud Day and Jack Fellowes when we received this distressing news. Bud looked at the officer for a moment, then laughed and said, "Bullshit."

In the bad old days, Bud would have been dragged out of there and tied in ropes for such defiance. Now all the officer was disposed to do was argue with Bud. "Look, no more bombs. We destroyed all your bombers."

I've often thought that the more perceptive Vietnamese must have realized, as we did, that the raids would shorten the war, and though they were distressed by the ferocity of the attacks, they might have regarded them as a harbinger of peace.

During one raid that did not involve B-52s, a bomb fell so close to us that shrapnel sprayed the camp courtyard. Our momentary apprehension that the pilot's targeting was not so accurate that our safety was guaranteed did not dampen our high spirits. We took what shelter we could, of course, just in case. But we greeted the low distant grumble of every approaching sortie like a long-lost friend.

We knew that the peace talks were entering their last phase. With the encouragement of the B-52s, we were confident they would be concluded in short order. We all believed, for the first time, that this would be our last Christmas in prison, and we were drunk with the thought of going home.

The B-52s terrorized Hanoi for eleven nights. Wave after wave they came. During the days, while the strategic bombers were refueled and rearmed, other aircraft took up the assault. The Vietnamese got the point. The Paris peace talks resumed on

January 8, 1973, and were swiftly concluded. The accords were signed on the 27th, but we were not informed of the event until the next day, when we were ordered to form in the courtyard for an important announcement.

As a Vietnamese officer read the full text of the peace agreement, including the part that provided for the release of prisoners of war, we stood silently at attention. Our senior officers, knowing that this moment was imminent, had warned us not to demonstrate our emotions when the agreement was announced. They suspected that the Vietnamese intended to record the event for its propaganda value and broadcast pictures of jubilant POWs celebrating peace to a worldwide audience.

They were right. Film crews were on hand for the ceremony, with their cameras rolling. Not a single POW betrayed the slightest emotion as the accords were read and we were informed we would all be released in two months. When the ceremony concluded we broke ranks and walked quietly back to our cells, seemingly indifferent to the news we had just received. Back in our cells, we waited for the disappointed film crew and the other assembled Vietnamese to disperse before we began to embrace one another and express our unrestrained joy.

By this time I had been transferred back to the Plantation, where I remained until my release. The guards left us alone for the remaining weeks, and we walked about the courtyard freely, played volleyball, and talked with whomever we pleased. We were not yet at liberty, but we were beginning to remember what it felt like to be free.

Henry Kissinger arrived in Hanoi to sign the final agreement. Near the end of his visit, the Vietnamese offered to release me to him. He refused the offer. When I met Dr. Kissinger back in the States some weeks later and he informed me of the Vietnamese offer and his response, I thanked him for saving my honor.

The prisoners were released in four increments in the order in which we had been captured. On March 15, the Rabbit called my name off the roster of POWs to be released that day. A few days earlier we had received, for the first time, Red Cross packages.

The night before, we were given a large dinner, complete with wine, our first substantial meal in a long time.

On the day before my release, I had been ordered to see the camp commander and a high-ranking political officer who spoke English. The political officer told me that he had recently seen the doctor who had operated on my leg, and that he had expressed his concern about my condition.

"Would you like to write a note to your doctor or see him to tell him how you are, and to thank him for your operation?"

Noticing a tape recorder sitting on the table, I answered in the negative.

"Why not?"

"Well, I haven't seen the asshole in five years and I wonder why he should have his curiosity aroused at this point. I know he's been very busy."

Dressed in cheap civilian clothes, we boarded buses for Gia Lam airport on the outskirts of Hanoi. As I stepped off the bus at the edge of the airport tarmac, I saw a big, green, beautiful American C-141 transport plane waiting to take us to Clark Air Force Base in the Philippines. I nearly cried at the sight of it. At the airport, lined up in formation according to our shootdown date, we maintained our military bearing as a noisy crowd of Vietnamese gawked at us. I could hear cameras whirring and shutters clicking. Vietnamese and American officers were seated at a table, each holding a list of prisoners. When it was time for a prisoner to step forward, representatives of both militaries called off his name. An officer from his service then escorted each prisoner across the tarmac and up the ramp into the plane. When my name was called, I stepped forward. The American officers seated at the table outranked me, so I saluted them.

Just prior to my departure, the Vietnamese had supplied me with another pair of crutches, even though I had been getting along fine without any. I decided to leave them behind. I wanted to take my leave of Vietnam without any assistance from my hosts.

Three days before my release, the *Los Angeles Times* had run a huge banner headline proclaiming: hanoi to release admiral's son. My father had been invited to join his successor as CINCPAC, Admiral Noel Gaylor, at the welcoming ceremony at Clark. He asked if the parents of other POWs had been invited. Told they had not, my father declined the offer.

CHAPTER TWENTY EIGHT

Free Men

We cheered loudly when the pilot announced that we were "feet wet," which meant that we were now flying over the Tonkin Gulf and in international airspace. A holiday atmosphere prevailed for the rest of the flight. We were served sandwiches and soft drinks, which we hungrily consumed. We clowned around with each other and with the military escorts and nurses who accompanied us and seemed as happy to see us as we were to see them. Our animated conversations rose above the droning of the aircraft's engines.

Although I am sure I celebrated my liberation with as much exuberance as the next man, I recall feeling that the short flight to Clark lacked the magnitude of drama I had expected it to have. I had envisioned the moment for many years. The event itself seemed somewhat anticlimactic. I enjoyed it, but before we arrived at our destination I was thinking ahead to the next flight, the flight home. The flight to Clark resides in my memory as an exceptionally pleasant ride to the airport.

I felt a little different when we left Clark for home and I bade farewell to men with whom I had formed such strong bonds of affection and respect. We sent one another off with best wishes and promises to reunite soon. But the sudden separation hurt a little, and on the flight home a strange sense of loneliness nagged me even as my excitement to see my family became more intense as every passing hour brought me closer to them.

Bud Day and Bob Craner were on my flight to Clark. They

and Orson Swindle had become the closest friends I had ever had. We were brothers now, as surely as if we had been born to the same parents. Even after we resumed our crowded, busy lives as free men, we remained close. I still see Bud and Orson often, and I am most at ease in their company. Bob Craner died of a heart attack in 1981, too young and too good to have left this earth so long before the rest of us. I have never stopped missing him.

In an interview he gave not long after our homecoming, Bob explained, as well as anyone could explain, how regret mixed with happiness on the day when our dreams came true. "It was with just a little melancholia that I finally said good-bye to John McCain," he remembered. "Even at Clark, we were still a group ... and the outsiders were trying to butt in, but we weren't having too much of that.... On the night before I was to get on an airplane at eight o'clock the following morning, I could sense that here was the end. Now this group is going to be busted wide open and spread all over the United States. It may be a long time, years, before we rejoin, and when we do, it won't be the same."

I flew to freedom in the company of many men who had suffered valiantly for their country's cause. Many of them had known greater terror than I had; resisted torture longer than I had held out, faced down more daunting challenges than I had confronted, and sacrificed more than had been asked of me. They are the part of my time in Vietnam I won't forget.

Bob was right—it was an end, and it would never again be quite the same. But the years that followed have had meaning and value, and I am happy to live in the present.

Prior to the pilot's announcement that we had left Vietnamese airspace, most of us were restrained, having not quite shaken off the solemn formality with which our departure ceremony was conducted.

Of course, we expected it would take much longer to shake off entirely the effects of our experiences in prison. Many of us were returning with injuries, and at best it would take some time for our physical rehabilitation to make satisfactory progress. I worried that my injuries might never heal properly, having been left untreated for so many years, and that I might never be allowed to fly again or perhaps even remain in the Navy. I faced a difficult period of rehabilitation, and I was for a long time uncertain that I would ever recover enough to regain flight status. Although I never regained full mobility in my arms and leg, I did recover, thanks to my patient family and a remarkably determined physical therapist, and I eventually flew again.

Neither did we expect to soon forget the long years of anguish we had suffered under our captors' "humane and lenient" treatment. A few men never recovered. They were the last, tragic casualties in a long, bitter war. But most of us healed from our wounds, the physical and spiritual ones, and have lived happy and productive lives since.

We were all astonished at the reception we received first at Clark and later when we stopped at Hickham Air Force Base in Hawaii en route to our homes. Thousands of people turned out, many of them wearing bracelets that bore our names, to cheer us as we disembarked the plane. During our captivity, the Vietnamese had inundated us with information about how unpopular the war and the men who fought it had become with the American public. We were stunned and relieved to discover that most Americans were as happy to see us as we were to see them. A lot of us were overcome by our reception, and the affection we were shown helped us to begin putting the war behind us.

I once heard the Vietnam War described as "America's fall from grace." Disagreements about the purpose and conduct of the war as well as its distinction of being the first lost war in American history left some Americans bereft of confidence in American exceptionalism—the belief that our history is unique and exalted and a blessing to all humanity. Not all Americans lost this faith. Not all Americans who once believed it to be lost believe it still. But many did, and many still do.

Surely, for a time, our loss in Vietnam afflicted America with a kind of identity crisis. For a while we made our way in the world less sure of ourselves than we had been before Vietnam. That was a pity, and I am relieved today that America's period of self-doubt has ended. America has a long, accomplished, and honorable history. We should never have let this one mistake, terrible though it was, color our perceptions forever of our country's purpose. We were a good country before Vietnam, and we are a good country after Vietnam. In all of history, you cannot find a better one.

* * *

I have often maintained that I left Vietnam behind me when I arrived at Clark. That is an exaggeration. But I did not want my experiences in Vietnam to be the leitmotif of the rest of my life. I am a public figure now, and my public profile is inextricably linked to my POW experiences. Whenever I am introduced at an appearance, the speaker always refers to my war record first. Obviously, such recognition has benefited my political career, and I am grateful for that. Many men who came home from Vietnam, physically and spiritually damaged, to what appeared to be a country that did not understand or appreciate their sacrifice carried the war as a great weight upon their subsequent search for happiness. But I have tried hard to make what use I can of Vietnam and not let the memories of war encumber the rest of my life's progress.

In the many years since I came home, I have managed to prevent the bad memories of war from intruding on my present happiness. I was thirty-six years old when I regained my freedom. When I was shot down, I had been prepared by training, as much as anyone can be prepared, for the experiences that lay ahead. I wasn't a nineteen- or twenty-year-old kid who had been drafted into a strange and terrible experience and then returned unceremoniously to an unappreciative country.

Neither have I been content to accept that my time in Vietnam would stand as the ultimate experience of my life. Surely it was a formative experience, but I knew that life promised other adventures, and, impatient by nature, I hurried toward them.

Vietnam changed me, in significant ways, for the better. It is a surpassing irony that war, for all its horror, provides the combatant with every conceivable human experience. Experiences that usually take a lifetime to know are all felt, and felt intensely, in one brief passage of life. Anyone who loses a loved one knows what great sorrow feels like. And anyone who gives life to a child knows what great joy feels like. The veteran knows what great loss and great joy feel like when they occur in the same moment, the same experience.

Such an experience is transforming. And we can be much the better for it. Some few who came home from war struggled to recover the balance that the war had upset. But for most veterans, who came home whole in spirit if not body, the hard uses of life will seldom threaten their equanimity.

Surviving my imprisonment strengthened my self-confidence, and my refusal of early release taught me to trust my own judgment. I am grateful to Vietnam for those discoveries, as they have made a great difference in my life. I gained a seriousness of purpose that observers of my early life had found difficult to detect. I had made more than my share of mistakes in my life. In the years ahead, I would make many more. But I would no longer err out of self-doubt or to alter a fate I felt had been imposed on me. I know my life is blessed, and always has been.

Vietnam did not answer all of life's questions, but I believe it answered many of the most important ones. In my youth I had doubted time's great haste. But in Vietnam I had come to understand how brief a moment a life is. That discovery did not, however, make me overly fearful of time's brisk passing. For I had also learned that you can fill the moment with purpose and experiences that will make your life greater than the sum of its days. I had learned to acknowledge my failings and to recognize opportunities for redemption. I had failed when I signed my confession, and that failure disturbed my peace of mind. I felt it blemished my record permanently, and even today I find it hard to suppress feelings of remorse. In truth, I don't even bother to try to suppress them anymore. My remorse shows me the limits of my zealously guarded autonomy.

My country had failed in Vietnam as well, but I took no comfort from its company. There is much to regret about America's failure in Vietnam. The reasons are etched in black marble on the Washington Mall. But we had believed the cause that America had asked us to serve in Vietnam was a worthy one, and millions who defended it had done so honorably.

Both my confession and my resistance helped me achieve a balance in my life, a balance between my own individualism and more important things. Like my father and grandfather, and the Naval Academy, the men I had been honored to serve with called me to the cause, and I had tried to keep faith with them.

I discovered I was dependent on others to a greater extent than I had ever realized, but that neither they nor the cause we served made any claims on my identity. On the contrary, they gave me a larger sense of myself than I had had before. And I am a better man for it. We had met a power that wanted to obliterate our identities, and the cause to which we rallied was our response: we are free men, bound inseparably together, and by the grace of God, and not your sufferance, we will have our freedom restored to us. Ironically, I have never felt more powerfully free, more my own man, than when I was a small part of an organized resistance to the power that imprisoned me. Nothing in life is more liberating than to fight for a cause larger than yourself, something that encompasses you but is not defined by your existence alone.

When I look back on my misspent youth, I feel a longing for what is past and cannot be restored. But though the happy pursuits and casual beauty of youth prove ephemeral, something better can endure, and endure until our last moment on earth. And that is the honor we earn and the love we give if at a moment in our youth we sacrifice with others for something greater than our self-interest. We cannot always choose the moments. Often they arrive unbidden. We can choose to let the moments pass, and avoid the difficulties they entail. But the loss we would incur by that choice is much dearer than the tribute we once paid to vanity and pleasure.

During their reunion aboard the *Proteus* in Tokyo Bay, my father and grandfather had their last conversation. Near the end of his life, my father recalled their final moment together:

"My father said to me, 'Son, there is no greater thing than to die for the principles—for the country and the principles that you believe in.' And that was one part of the conversation that came through and I have remembered down through the years."

On that fine March day, I thought about what I had done and failed to do in Vietnam, and about what my country had done and failed to do. I had seen human virtue affirmed in the conduct of men who were ennobled by their suffering. And "down through the years," I had remembered a dying man's legacy to his son, and when I needed it most, I had found my freedom abiding in it.

I held on to the memory, left the bad behind, and moved on.